Hunted Through

Paul, or Pavel, **Nazaroff** was ed...
Petersburg. His career as a geologist, mineralogist, and mining
engineer was interrupted by the Bolshevik Revolution, which
prompted him to become a counter-revolutionary agent. A
man of wide sympathies and encyclopaedic knowledge, he was
also highly skilled in the fields of ornithology, archaeology, bal-
listics, and botany, and was an accomplished linguist, hunts-
man, and taxidermist.

Malcolm Burr was a close personal friend of Nazaroff's,
whom he first encountered in Africa. A noted writer and trans-
lator from the Russian, French, Serbo-Croat, and Turkish, he
saw active service in the Eastern Mediterranean during the
First World War and was mentioned in despatches. He later
served with the Foreign Office in Yugoslavia and Turkey.

Peter Hopkirk has travelled extensively in the region where
the events in this book took place. He himself is the author of
two acclaimed books dealing with intelligence work in Central
Asia: *Setting the East Ablaze* and *The Great Game*. These, together
with *Foreign Devils on the Silk Road* and *Trespassers on the Roof of the
World*, are available in Oxford Paperbacks.

Also available in Oxford Paperbacks:

Colonel F. M. Bailey   *Mission in Tashkent*

Peter Hopkirk   *Setting the East Ablaze*
Foreign Devils on the Silk Road
Trespassers on the Roof of the World
The Great Game
Quest for Kim

Hunted Through Central Asia

PAUL NAZAROFF

Translated by Malcolm Burr

OXFORD
UNIVERSITY PRESS

OXFORD
UNIVERSITY PRESS

Great Clarendon Street, Oxford OX2 6DP

Oxford University Press is a department of the University of Oxford.
It furthers the University's objective of excellence in research, scholarship,
and education by publishing worldwide in

Oxford New York

Auckland Bangkok Buenos Aires Cape Town Chennai
Dar es Salaam Delhi Hong Kong Istanbul Karachi Kolkata
Kuala Lumpur Madrid Melbourne Mexico City Mumbai Nairobi
São Paulo Shanghai Singapore Taipei Tokyo Toronto

with an associated company in Berlin

Oxford is a registered trade mark of Oxford University Press
in the UK and in certain other countries

British Library Cataloguing in Publication Data

Data available

Library of Congress Cataloging in Publication Data
Nazaroff, P. S. (Pavel Stepanovich), b. ca. 1890.
Hunted through Central Asia / Paul Nazaroff; translated by Malcolm Burr.
Translated from Russian.
Originally published: Edinburgh; London: Wm. Blackwood & Sons, 1932.
1. Nazaroff, P. S. (Pavel Stepanovich), b. ca. 1890. 2. Soviet
Central Asia—History—Revolution, 1917-1921—Personal narratives.
3. Revolutionaries—Soviet Central Asia—Biography. I. Title.
958'.4041—dc20 DK265.8.S63.N39 1993 93-14669

ISBN 0-19-280368-9

1 3 5 7 9 10 8 6 4 2

Printed in Great Britain by
Clays Ltd., St Ives plc

CONTENTS

Dedicated to Mrs Wallace Kennedy
who did not forget me during my wanderings
and inspired me to write this book

INTRODUCTION

by Peter Hopkirk

PAUL NAZAROFF, the author of this extraordinary tale, was the ringleader of a desperate plot to overthrow Bolshevik rule in Central Asia in 1918. That much is known from British intelligence reports of the time, although in this narrative, first published in 1932, he is extremely circumspect about his precise role in the conspiracy. His reticence is understandable, for Bolshevik retribution was known to possess both a long arm and a long memory, as Trotsky himself would shortly discover.

It was the hope of Nazaroff and his fellow conspirators that British interventionist forces, then only thirty hours away by rail to the west, would come to their assistance. Consequently, until his arrest by the Bolsheviks in October 1918, he was in close touch with Colonel F. M. Bailey, a British intelligence officer sent into Russian Turkestan to try to discover the Bolsheviks' intentions towards India. However, neither Nazaroff in this book, nor Bailey in his, refer to one another. It is only in Bailey's secret report to his superiors that Nazaroff's leading role in the plot to overthrow the Tashkent commissars is revealed. He describes Nazaroff as the 'real organizer' of the counter-revolution, and also discloses that he supplied him with funds.

Although Paul Nazaroff waited for fifteen years before publishing his account of those ferocious times, he is clearly at great pains to reveal as little as possible which might be of value to the Bolshevik secret police for fear of bringing vengeance upon those he left behind him when he escaped into Chinese Central Asia and eventually to Britain. But while he plays down his leading role in the plot, he does not deny his complicity in it, or his bitter revulsion towards the Bolsheviks. As a prosperous mine-owner, and a leading member of the Russian community in Tashkent, he had everything to lose, including very probably his own life, were they to remain in power.

Not a great deal is known about Nazaroff, and perhaps that is the way he wished it to be. At one time, when I was writing *Setting the East Ablaze*, which deals with these turbulent events, I even found myself wondering whether it was his real name, reasoning that he might, quite sensibly, have changed it. But then there came into my possession Colonel Bailey's own copy of Nazaroff's book. Inside it was a letter from Nazaroff informing Bailey of his safe arrival in Kashgar, and congratulating him on his own escape from the Bolsheviks, which he had just read about in *The Times of India*. It was signed Paul Nazaroff. With Bailey, who knew him in Tashkent, there would have been no need to conceal his identity, especially as they had a shared abhorrence of the Bolsheviks.

The individual who knew Nazaroff best, however, was probably Malcolm Burr, now long dead, who translated his book from the original Russian manuscript, and contributed the brief biographical note and memoir included in this edition. There is little point therefore in repeating the facts of Nazaroff's life beyond adding that he was probably in his early forties at the time of these events, and that he was married, apparently with no children. Although he briefly mentions his wife in his narrative, he does not disclose her name, perhaps because the memory is too painful. Whether she became the victim of Bolshevik vengeance, or was merely unable ever to escape from Russia to join him, will probably never be known now that Bailey, Burr, and anyone else who might have known him are all dead.

Nazaroff's background could hardly have equipped him better for the many vicissitudes he describes in the following pages. A geologist and zoologist by training, and a fine horseman, he had spent months on end exploring the deserts and mountains of Turkestan while prospecting for minerals, precious stones, and natural-history specimens. In the course of these travels, spread over more than twenty years, he had acquired an intimate knowledge of the languages and customs of the Kirghiz nomads, as well as of the Sarts, as the Russians called the Muslim villagers. He had also made many friends among them. Moreover, he knew every inch of the harsh landscape around Tashkent and far beyond. All this was to serve him well in his hour of need. Indeed, without it, and the physical hardiness it had given him, he would almost certainly not have survived to tell this tale.

At times, while on the run from the Bolsheviks, he took refuge with the Kirghiz, lived alone in the forests, or risked hiding in towns and villages with forged credentials. Sometimes he escaped his pursuers by sheer luck or bluff. He is thus able to describe the daily lives of the ordinary Muslim peoples of Central Asia from a unique vantage point, for in all he was to spend more than a year among them. Finally, after playing a hazardous game of cat-and-mouse with the Cheka, or Bolshevik secret police, and the Chinese border guards, he crossed the Tien Shan mountains and reached the safety of Kashgar.

Today, after decades of obscurity, Central Asia has emerged from the shadows, free at last of its Marxist shackles. It is sad, perhaps, that Nazaroff did not live to see this happen after the suffering he endured at the hands of the Bolsheviks. However, the momentous changes we are witnessing in Central Asia, and its sudden opening up to the rest of the world, have awoken widespread interest in this region and its extraordinary history. The reissuing of Nazaroff's long-forgotten narrative some sixty years after it first appeared is therefore to be greatly welcomed.

What became of Paul Nazaroff afterwards I have held back for the epilogue, for I have no wish to keep the reader any longer from this remarkable man's own account of what befell him during those fateful times.

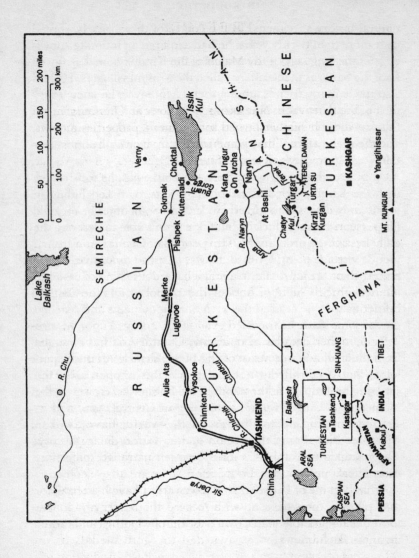

PREFACE

by Malcolm Burr

PAUL STEPANOVICH NAZAROFF was born at Orenburg in the Urals, where his father owned some mining properties and was 'head' of the town—that is, permanent mayor or burgomaster. He was of pure Russian stock of the Old Believers, whom we may most appropriately compare, perhaps, with our old English county families of the Roman Catholic faith.

He was educated at Moscow University, where he took the degree corresponding to that of Doctor of Philosophy on the basis of a thesis on Zoogeography. He then qualified as a mining engineer in the Mining Institute at St Petersburg, and became a Member of the Imperial Mineralogical Society, of the Imperial Geographical Society, and of the Society of Naturalists of Moscow.

For some years he travelled extensively, engaged upon his profession, in the Caucasus and, above all, in the Urals, then settled in Tashkend, administrative centre of the Central Asian domains of the Russian Empire, where his father owned a cotton mill. Here he had ample scope for enterprise, and devoted the better part of his life to the mineral exploration of the country, revealing a pleasant surprise in the form of great and varied wealth, unexpected after the disappointing reports of the official geologists. He opened up several mines of considerable importance of copper, silver, coal, and also deposits of oil.

A man of many hobbies, he devoted considerable attention to horticulture, on which he was a recognised authority. He introduced many of the best kinds of West European fruits and flowers into Turkestan, and was awarded the gold medals of the Ministries of Agriculture and of Finance for the introduction into the country of the ground-nut, *Arachis*, successfully demonstrating the value of its oil.

His chief recreation was shooting, his favourite game geese and boar. But he is more than a mere sportsman, he is a close observer and a scientific ornithologist. He is a fine shot with a sporting rifle. It is characteristic of him that he could not resist making a scientific study of the firearms he loves. He owned a complete collection of sporting rifles of all countries, and several times served as expert witness in criminal trials and gave evidence before the Imperial Commission upon Firearms and Ammunition.

A man of the widest sympathies and encyclopaedic knowledge, with a full share of dry humour and an absorbing love of nature, with an intense hatred of insincerity and humbug in all its forms, most tenacious of his opinions, yet ready, like a man of truly scientific instincts, to modify them in the face of evidence, Pavel Stepanovich is a delightful companion. For nearly two years we were comrades in the bush in equatorial Africa, engaged together upon congenial work in geology and zoology. Round the camp fire in the evenings we used to yarn about the subjects in which we were both interested, and I came to know the story of his wonderful odyssey from end to end. I begged him to write it, and then, on my return to the drab life of civilisation, it has been a pleasure to live for a while once more in Africa in memory, and in Turkestan in imagination, while rendering into English my friend's lucid Russian prose.

And so it is my privilege to introduce to English readers the man whom I am proud to call friend, mining engineer, geologist, mineralogist, chemist, ornithologist and skilful taxidermist, sportsman, expert on firearms and archaeologist—Pavel Stepanovich Nazároff.

MALCOLM BURR.

UNITED UNIVERSITY CLUB,
    LONDON, 1932.

CHAPTER I. AWAITING EXECUTION.

ONE evening in Tashkend, about the end of August 1918, as I was sitting in my study quietly filling cartridges for an anticipated day's snipe-shooting, there pulled up at the steps of the house a smart carriage drawn by a splendid pair of bays. Two men alighted, dressed from head to foot in soft black leather. That was the uniform of those who belonged to the reigning party, the Communists.

I recognised them. One was M., once my good friend and shooting companion, but now a member of the Bolshevik party, working on behalf of the Dictatorship of the Proletariat. The other I did not know so well; he was President of the local Committee of National Agriculture, and he too had joined the Bolsheviks for the sake of an advantageous position. Neither were Communists at heart, but at that time both held important administrative posts in the Turkestan Republic of Workers and Peasants.

I was puzzled by the visit of these two men now that the only feelings I had towards them were of supreme contempt. "Don't be surprised, Pavel Stepanovich," said one as they came into the room, "that we have come to see you. We want to take advantage of your extraordinary knowledge of Turkestan and of your great experience; you know the country better than anybody else. . . ."

"For God's sake, no compliments," I expostulated. "Get

I

on with the business ; tell me what you want and what information you expect me to give you."

" We want you to tell us something about Ust Urt. Tell us, do you consider that it is possible to get a motor across ? "

" Why are you interested in that desert ? " I asked them in surprise.

" Well," replied one of them, " you see, the Turkestan Soviet of National Agriculture is proposing to send a scientific expedition to report on that district."

" What ? " I exclaimed in astonishment. " A scientific expedition to Ust Urt ? Is this the time for scientific expeditions ? Where are you going to get the technical staff for an expedition like that ? " I asked them ironically.

" What is wrong with yourself ? "

Then at once it all became clear to me, and I understood their motive in coming to see me and their interest in Ust Urt. Communications between the Turkestan Socialistic Soviet Republic and Moscow had been cut. On the south, on the river Amu Dariá, near Chardjui, there was an Anglo-Indian contingent with some ' Whites ' ; the central Asian railway was in their hands. On the north the Cossacks of the Ataman Dutoff had cut communications with Orenburg, while in the east, in Semirechie, the peasants had risen against the Bolsheviks. In Turkestan ammunition and military supplies were nearing exhaustion, and the position of the Soviet Government in our country was becoming critical. It was surrounded by enemies on every side, so it was clear that the commissars were anxious to open communications by car through Ust Urt, a desert plateau between the Sea of Aral and the Caspian, to the Gulf of Dead Kutuk on the latter sea, where they could get boats coming from Astrakhan, which was in their hands.

It would be useless to conceal from them the possibility of communication by this route, as they were bound to find out for themselves sooner or later. I must therefore penetrate their designs and take corresponding steps, so I resolved to be cunning.

"You do not want any scientific expedition," I said to them; "you want to open communications with Moscow through Aral and the Gulf of Dead Kutuk."

They seemed a little startled, then were glad, as they could talk openly and come straight to business.

"You see," said one of them, "we naturally must examine this route, but at the same time we propose to do a little research—that corner of Turkestan is almost unknown. But tell me, can we make a motor road through Ust Urt?"

"Certainly and quite easily," said I.

"In that case, won't you take on the command of the expedition?" they asked, delighted at the good news they had from me.

"Not under any circumstances whatever," I replied decisively.

"But why?" they exclaimed in surprise. "Of course, we know your antipathy to the Bolsheviks, but we will see that none of them are with you; you can choose your own people according to your own ideas. The Soviet will give you a perfectly reliable car and everything you can want for the expedition, and plenty of money for expenses, and they will pay for your share in the undertaking. I am told that shooting is very good in Ust Urt," added one, trying to tempt me.

"I am very much obliged," I answered in a frigid tone.

"All you've got to do is to drive across Ust Urt, prove that it is possible for motors, and write a report on the road."

" This has been done years ago," I said quietly.

" What ? How ? When ? By whom ? " they exclaimed, jumping up in delight.

" If you go to the old office of the Governor-General and take out of the archives the file for 1883, you will find a complete and detailed description of the road through Ust Urt. The road was marked out by General Chernaieff when he drove through Ust Urt in a carriage to the coronation of the Emperor Alexander III. in the spring of '83. For this recklessness he was placed on the retired list by the Russian Government. The direction through Ust Urt, the road, resting-places, wells, everything there is described in detail, and you'll get all the information you want."

" How can we repay you for such valuable information ? " they asked, obviously astonished at my frankness.

" We know that you won't accept money," they went on, " nor will you take anything from the Soviet Government ; but, look here now, this carriage "—and here they pointed out of the window—" and pair of horses is always at your disposal if ever you want to go anywhere—for a day's shooting, for instance," added one, knowing my weakness.

" Please . . . really, you know . . . these horses and all this turn-out, this was all stolen, you know. The whole thing was ' socialised ' from Madam X.," I said, interrupting their expressions of gratitude.

This answer disconcerted them and, hurriedly saying good-morning, they went off.

Early next morning two men went out from my house. One was a Bokhará Jew with a grey beard in a dirty caftan, the other was even dirtier, a ' comrade ' in a black shirt and leather cap. The first was a captain in one of the regiments of the Guard, a Georgian, and he was bound for Bokhará and beyond across the desert to the headquarters of the British Indian contingent. The other was a gunner colonel who had been through the entire war on the German and Austrian fronts; he was northward bound, to Ataman Dutoff.

The stake of the Bolsheviks on Ust Urt was lost, for before the Bolshevik ' scientific expedition ' could materialise, the steamer *Skobeleff*, converted into a cruiser by the English, who were in occupation of Baku, steamed into the Gulf of Dead Kutuk, and the Orenburg Cossacks of Ataman Dutoff came down upon Ust Urt from the north. The Turkestan Republic of Workmen and Peasants remained cut off from the rest of the Bolshevik world, and was thrown upon its own resources.

A couple of months later, one fine October evening, after a good day's pheasant shooting, I was resting quietly at home in my study when a car drew up at the steps and six men dressed from head to toe in black leather, armed with rifles, jumped out. I did not wait for them to come in, but instantly bolted across the verandah into the garden. Before they had time to enter the room, I slipped across the wall into my neighbour's garden and disappeared without leaving a trace.

But two days after that, when I was looking for a better hiding-place, I walked across the open space of the native quarter of Tashkend. I saw two Russians wearing white tunics sitting on the steps of the old mosque. They were members of the all-powerful Che-Ka.

In a moment I was arrested, with four revolvers at my head. Both of these rascals had two revolvers, and were very surprised on searching me not to find any weapon.

One, a clown from the local circus, had been empowered by the Revolutionary Government of Workers and Peasants

5

to arrest, imprison and interrogate everyone whom he thought fit ; he was authorised to make domiciliary visits and to help himself to the property of the citizens just as he liked. The other, a shop assistant from the local fancy goods store who could hardly read and write, constituted himself a ' Revolutionary Examining Judge.' Such was the ' Magna Carta of Liberties ' of the citizens of the ' Most Free Soviet Republic.'

Six members of the Che-Ka interrogated me, each armed with a revolver, which he kept pointing at me when putting his questions. Every now and then all six would aim their revolvers at my head and threaten to shoot me if I did not tell the truth.

I was convinced that I should never get out of the clutches of the Che-Ka alive, but the sight of these six scoundrels sitting with their revolvers at the head of an unarmed man struck me as funny and stupid, and I could not help smiling.

" What ! You smile ? " asked the Examining Judge ; " aren't you afraid of being shot ? "

" Not at all," I answered quietly. " You have founded such a wonderful socialistic paradise and such conditions of existence that life has lost all value."

The Examining Judge was disconcerted by this unexpected answer, as he never expected that sort of testimonial to his ' constructive socialism.'

One of the incriminating documents produced against me was a letter which the Bolsheviks had seized. It had been sent to me from Ferghaná by galloper by Colonel P. G. Korniloff, brother of the well-known general. Together we had equipped and sent off a group of officers to organise a contingent of native cavalry at Ferghaná against the Bolsheviks, and in spite of all my repeated injunctions to put

6

nothing in writing, the punctilious honour of the unfortunate Korniloff compelled him to send me a detailed account of his expenses and a report of his activities, in the hope that his galloper would be able to get through the mountains and avoid the Soviet guards. In this letter, among other things, was the expression, " I have given Captain B. a loper."

The Examining Judge had not the remotest idea what was meant by a horse that was a loper, pacer or trippler, and saw in this phrase a veiled allusion to some secret or code word, and kept pressing me to reveal the hidden meaning in this mysterious phrase.

As they did not get any information out of me, they sent me down to the cellar of the Che-Ka, which had already earned itself so ill a repute.

In spite of my boiling rage and hatred of this repulsive scum of mankind, so utterly foreign to our fair land of Turkestan which they had seized and despotically ruled, I had not lost my appetite. It was already late, and I began to be seriously worried about the thought of dinner.

The window of the cellar, covered with a grid of iron bars, was high up, and just as I was staring at it pensively, wondering what and when I should get anything to eat, suddenly I heard a knock and through the grid on to the floor there fell a small parcel, followed by a second. I looked up and caught sight, through the grid, of the smiling face of a young Kirghiz boy, Karim Bai, who was employed in my stables. The ' Long Ear,' *uzun kulak*, the ' radio ' of the Kirghiz, had this time done me yeoman service. By some unaccountable means, sometimes over huge distances and with astonishing rapidity, news is spread among the Kirghiz, faster even than telegrams. The news of my arrest spread like lightning, and they sent me the parcels of food from home. If they had been sent to me through the 'red guard' instead of through the window, the sandwiches and fruit would have most certainly been eaten by them, as they do not recognise private property.

Illumination was not provided for the enemies of the Workmen's and Peasants' Government, and as soon as it was dark I had no choice but to lie down on the bare boards of the broad bench and try to sleep.

In the middle of the night I was awakened by the noise of the door being opened, by footsteps and light. Two members of the Che-Ka entered, escorted by a couple of armed soldiers of the Red Army.

" We have come to inform you," they said, " that it is resolved that you be shot."

" All right ; shoot away, then," I answered.

Once more I saw on their repulsive faces the same expression of dull incomprehension as I had previously noted on the Examining Judge.

These creatures, half-brutes, crammed with cheap Marxism, coarse ignorant materialists, could understand only mere animal fear. Death, which in their eyes was a complete annihilation of the individuality, for them was a most terrible thing. They thought that they would terrify me, and when they saw that their threats did not act, they were bewildered ; there was nothing left for them to frighten with, nothing worse to threaten. Later they had recourse to torture, for which purpose they employed Chinese and Letts, but as yet they were afraid to, as their Red soldiers and the native Sarts might object. All the same, often enough they tormented prisoners to death under the pretext of 'giving them a bath,' when they scalded them with boiling water.

8

Muttering something they went out, and I lay down and slept till the morning.

A couple of days later, at eleven o'clock at night, they took me out and upstairs into a large room. Round a table covered with a red cloth was sitting the whole Che-Ka. In triumph they handed me a sheet of paper with a long list of questions about the " plot against the Government of Workmen and Peasants." Who were in the plot ? Where did they get their funds ? Where were their arms, and how much had they ready ? What connection had they with the staff of the British-Indian contingent that was invading the peaceful land of Turkestan Socialist Republic, and so on.

" If you give detailed written replies to all these questions, we will pardon you," said the President ; " but if you refuse to answer, or if you give incorrect replies, then we will shoot you. Think well about it, and to-morrow evening give us your answer."

Running my eyes through this list of questions, I smiled, handed the paper back and said—

" Shoot away. I cannot answer you a single question, because this is all rubbish, all your fancy. There has not been any plot at all."

" Think carefully," again said the President ; " tell the truth and we will give you money and a passport, and send you secretly over the frontier abroad."

" I know where you will send me in any case, so send away," I thought to myself, and then repeated—

" There has been no plot. Some officers have got away to Ferghaná to escape from persecution by you, as you were killing everyone who fought honourably for his country. I gave them money for the journey from my own personal resources."

Not getting any further information out of me, they kept me in the cellar three days longer, and then sent me to the prison.

The prison in those days was just the same as it was in the Tsar's time. Strange to say, after the cellar of the Che-Ka I felt much better in the prison, although shut up in a solitary cell.

On the second day someone threw a local newspaper through the little observation window in the door. It contained an official notice of the Soviet authorities to the effect that the plot of ' White brigands ' to overthrow the Dictatorship of the Proletariat had been crushed, and the ringleader and chief organiser was in the hands of the Soviet Government. This notice was signed by the whole crowd of national commissars. They little suspected how entirely mistaken they were.

I spent a month in solitary confinement. Once a day they let me out for exercise in the yard under the escort of two armed soldiers. Communication with other prisoners and with my friends was impossible. My cell was ventilated only by a small window covered with iron bars, high up, almost under the ceiling. Through it I could just see a small patch of blue sky.

The beautiful Turkestan autumn had set in, dry, clear and warm, the time of the migration of vast flocks of birds from the far north. At night I often used to hear their cries as they passed; the whistling of waders, the melodious trumpeting of cranes, the deep ' honk honk ' of the geese, all came through to my ears. The birds, rejoicing in their freedom, were wending their way to warm lands far away, unhindered in the vastness of space, away to India, the land of marvels ! My spirit accompanied them to that wondrous land, then so remote from the storms and alarms of revolution. In my thoughts I bid good-bye to these old friends that I had loved so well from my boyhood, conjuring up pictures of the wonders of nature and great days of sport in Turkestan. I was never without the thought that every night might well be my last. It never entered my head that one of these days I, too, would follow by that self-same route over those mountains where the birds were flying then, away to the sunny plains of Hindustan.

Every week they took me up to be interrogated by the Che-Ka under a strong armed guard. A new 'examiner' was cross-examining me now, and, I am sorry to say, a real military jurist who had joined the service of the Bolsheviks ; but even he was so ignorant that he thought the town of Meshed was in Western China and Kashgar in Persia.

Two or three of my guard were always present at these interrogations. These were simple-minded fellows, Russian peasants out of the old armies. They told me that the Bol-sheviks tortured prisoners and tormented them with great cruelty, and so they decided to be always present at such examinations to see that nothing of that sort was done. At that time the Communists were 'democratising' every-thing and admitting soldiers and workmen to all their Soviets and institutions, and so were afraid to object to such a demand on the part of the guards. Relations between these young soldiers and Bolshevik officials and commissars were very strained.

In the prison the summons of any prisoner to the Che-Ka was followed with the greatest anxiety. Sometimes the poor devils taken simply disappeared, and sometimes they came back in a deplorable condition.

Once they kept me before the Che-Ka from the morning

until ten at night. When I returned to the prison the warder, who had formerly been a cab-driver in the town and knew me perfectly well, was delighted to see me again alive, and exclaimed—

" God be praised, Pavel Stepanovich ! You have come back safe and sound ! We were very anxious. Even in the criminal section no one went to bed, as they were so worried about you."

The prison food was horrible ; it consisted exclusively of soup and a few vegetables without any meat. Relatives and friends of the prisoners used to bring them food from the outside, and if anybody had not any friends to look after him he was doomed to hunger. Those who received food from home usually shared it with their fellow-prisoners. It was generally women who brought the food, and they used to wait at the gates of the prison, when the warders would go out to take it and leave them to wait for the dishes to be given back. This waiting was an anxious time, for often enough the warder would use the consecrated expression, " He does not want any more dinners ! " This meant, of course, that the prisoner had been shot during the night. Once my wife was waiting at the gates with my dinner just at the moment when they were taking me up to the Che-Ka. The gates were open, and I saw my wife and our faithful little fox terrier Daisy. This was the first time I had seen my wife since my arrest, so our agitation may well be imagined. Daisy was overjoyed to get a glimpse of her master again, and from that day every time my wife came with the food and waited, Daisy tried frantically to dig under the prison gates. The clever little creature knew perfectly well that I was shut up in this building and tried her very hardest to get through to me and, if she could, to set me free. She hurt her paws and damaged her claws so much on the stone paving that my wife had to tie her up when she brought my food, and poor little Daisy used to howl with grief.

At length one day the examiner told me that my interrogation was completed.

" Will you be good enough to tell me of what I am accused ? " I asked.

" Yes. As a matter of fact there are no definite charges against you, and the interrogation has not brought anything out," he answered ; " but all the same you are a known enemy of the proletariat, and therefore are deserving of the severest punishment."

The ' Sovnarkom,' or ' Council of National Commissars,' as I learnt afterwards, had devised a special court of inquiry to deal with me, the ' Revolutionary Field Tribunal,' consisting only of judges of ' proletarian origin ' and workmen Communists. There was neither procuror nor examining judge in this court, as cross-examination of the accused was considered superfluous.

" They will take you into court only for you to hear your sentence," they told me.

" A fine form of court in this most progressive socialistic state in the world," I thought to myself.

On the termination of my examination they moved me from the solitary cell to the common cell No. 22, where there were already many who had been arrested before me, among whom I found friends and comrades who had been with me in the plot against the Soviets. The identical fate awaited each of us—to be shot.

In the town among decent folk there was great anxiety about us, as they looked upon our execution as inevitable.

Not long previously ten members of the Constitutional Democrat Party had been arrested and barbarously done to death for the simple reason that they belonged to the 'bourgeois party.' They were taken out into the prison yard, undressed completely on a cold winter's night, and then the devils poured cold water over them. When frozen like statues, the drunken soldiers hacked them to pieces with their swords.

When I joined my comrades, we quickly put a completely different complexion on our position, and within a few days had established communication with our friends in the town and, what is more, with the natives, who were rising against the Bolsheviks in the district of Ferghaná, where, under the command of former officers of the Imperial Army, they were conducting an energetic campaign against detachments of the Red Army.

In the mornings and evenings they used to take us out for exercise in the inner yard. The prison, which was an old building, had two yards. The outer one opened directly upon the street, and here were the offices, officials' quarters and stores ; in the inner yard were the prisoners' cells, the kitchen and hospital.

Heavily armoured iron gates led from the street into the outer yard, and similar gates from the outer to the inner yard. These were always kept shut, and armed sentries were constantly on duty by them. They were surrounded by a massive high stone wall, and as a further precaution the whole set of buildings were encircled with barbed wire entanglements, along which patrolled ceaselessly, day and night, specially selected sentries from the Red Army.

In the first yard, up against the wall round the inner yard, was the prison shop, which communicated with the inner yard by means of a little window or hatchway. During exercise time prisoners would come up to this hatch and buy tobacco, matches, dried fruit, ' nan,' or native bread in the form of little cakes, and other sundries.

An old Sart kept this little store, and every morning he came with his porter, also a Sart, carrying on his shoulders a sack with his goods. On entry into the prison yard, the contents of the sack, of course, were subjected to a minute inspection by the prison guards.

When they moved me from the solitary cell to the common condemned cell my first anxiety was to arrange to get into the same cell a very good friend of mine, a native, by name Abdul Kaspar. He was a man who enjoyed immense influence and respect among the natives of Ferghaná. He had been arrested and imprisoned by the Bolsheviks without any cause or reason, simply as a measure of precaution, to remove and isolate a person whose prestige among the Sarts might be dangerous to the Soviet Government.

Abdul Kaspar was kept in the native section of the prison. He caught my idea at once, and petitioned the commissar of the prison to be allowed to be moved to cell No. 22.

"Why in there?" asked the commissar in surprise. "Don't you know that in there are only criminals condemned to death?"

"A good friend of mine is in there, Nazároff Bek. My people know him well, and I would like to be with him during his last days on earth. Perhaps Allah will be pleased to call me, too, before long," replied Abdul Kaspar in oriental style.

"All right. If you want to go with Nazároff to the other world, you can go along together," answered the commissar with a grin.

Three days after the transfer of Abdul Kaspar to our cell he brought from the little shop some rolls of ' *nan* ' or native bread that he had bought, and gave us each one. This was the first post we had received from the outside world.

The native bread is made in the form of a ring. In the thin middle part there is some ornamentation in the form of a simple pattern, while the thick edges contain the dough.

In this pattern on each roll, Abdul Kaspar, without difficulty, read out the name and address, so to speak, to whom each roll was destined. For the patterns were letters of the Arabic alphabet, and in the dough in the thick edges were concealed letters from friends and relatives.

Our dinners brought from our homes were most carefully examined by the prison guards, sometimes even by the commissar himself. The bread was broken up and everything was cut into pieces. But it would never enter anybody's head to investigate the native rolls brought from the bazaar to the shop for sale to Sart prisoners, and, too, who could ever recognise in the dirty and ragged porter who carried the heavy sack from the bazaar to the shop Abdul Kaspar's own son, a rich young native dandy ?

Two days later this young ' porter ' was relieved by another older and even more ragged Sart, with a hopelessly stupid expression.

" Madamin Bek is asking for our instructions for his further operations against the Bolsheviks," explained Abdul to me when at exercise, taking me a little on one side. " It is his messenger, disguised of course, who is sitting in the store."

The next day during exercise Abdul Kaspar flew into a passion, swearing with all his might both in Sart and Russian, dashed up to the window of the store and savagely flung back the roll he had bought there.

" You are dogs, not good Mussulmen! You sell poor devils of prisoners bread full of cockroaches! You are worse than dogs; eat them yourselves, and may they choke you, and be damned to you!"

Then he called out some expression in the Tadjik language, which is generally known and spoken in the Ferghaná district, but was certainly quite unknown to either of the young Red soldiers on duty by the shop when it was open.

By this means the following instructions and recommendations were sent to Madamin Bek in Ferghaná :—

1. To pull up the railway and destroy bridges and roads leading to Ferghaná.

2. To destroy the oil wells at Ferghaná and so deprive the Bolsheviks of their fuel supply for their railway.

3. To concentrate strong cavalry forces in the Kender-Davan pass which leads from Ferghaná straight through the mountains to Tashkend, and to fall upon the Soviet armies when the rising broke out in Tashkend. The native cavalry could reach the town in a night from there, and inflict a heavy blow on the rear of the Bolsheviks.

From our friends in the town we received good news, too. After a certain amount of confusion caused by my arrest, and that of several of my friends and of people belonging to our organisation, the business of getting ready the rising had been resumed.

A considerable proportion of the workmen were already against the Soviet Government and joined our organisation. I was not particularly pleased by this, as I was familiar with the mercenary character of these people, and had every reason to know that they were capable of betraying us even in the crucial moment of battle and selling themselves to the Bolsheviks.

Still, this good news cheered us up considerably in our

confinement in the condemned cell, where we had been waiting for the fatal day at any moment. The other prisoners were surprised at our carefree appearance and positively cheerful frame of mind. The problem was very simple after all. Would the Bolsheviks shoot us before our rising or not? We sometimes wondered why the Che-Ka was waiting and did not carry its sentence into effect, at least on me. According to prison gossip, I was to be the first.

It was only afterwards I learnt that the explanation was in the progress of the Anglo-Indian contingent which was working its way up from India through Persia and the Transcaspian Region, at the same time that a contingent of ' Whites ' was on the Amu Dariá at Chardjui. In two days' time they might be in Tashkend. From the north, too, as I have already said, Cossacks were making their way down, and in the Semirechie the peasants were rising. The result was that there was nowhere where the representatives of the Workmen's and Peasants' Government could get away. They could expect little mercy from the Cossacks or the peasants of the Semirechie, but it would be less dangerous for them to fall into the hands of educated people like the English, who might even refrain from hanging them. Some commissars were in favour of surrendering to the General who was in command of the British force and so insure themselves against the danger of falling against the Cossacks' swords or of being hung by the angry peasants of Semirechie. Moreover, my friends of the British force had informed the commissars of the Turkestan Soviet Republic that if a single hair fell from the head of any of the political prisoners, they need expect no mercy; that they were all to be hung forthwith.

CHAPTER II. RELEASE.

LIFE in prison went by monotonously, and the long winter evenings were terribly boring for us. We got a kerosene lamp and used to sit up late, whiling away the time with unending conversation. A Soviet hundred rouble note, at that time the equivalent of about a shilling, given to the warder of our section, was sufficient to divert his attention away from our cell.

Voitintseff, head of the Soviet Government in Turkestan, visited the prison, and came into our cell to see the men condemned to be shot. A student of the Electro-Technical Institute in Petrograd, he had not completed his studies. He was a capable and ambitious man, married to a girl I knew well, and I knew him, too, personally. He had been received in our house, and until he joined the Party was a decent fellow. His ambition drove him into the arms of the Bolsheviks in the hopes of making a rapid career for himself as a leader of the proletariat.

I hardly recognised him. Instead of a young, healthy, good-looking student full of the joy of life, before me stood a thin, pale, washed-out, already aged, neurotic-looking man, purposely dressed like a workman, with filthy hands and unkempt tangled hair.

The object of his visit was to talk to me.

He was oppressed by the thought of the possibility of the capture of Tashkend by the British, to whom the Red

Army could hardly offer any serious resistance. Assuming me to be in touch with the staff of the British force and so cognisant of their intentions and plans, he came to me to clear up his doubts.

" Will they take all Turkestan ? Will they add it to their Indian dominions ? " Such were the questions he put.

I tried to explain to him the utter impossibility of the latter, and the uselessness of our Turkestan to the British.

" But the cotton ? Really they are short of cotton for their industry, aren't they ? " he asked.

" Are they really short of cotton in India and Egypt ? Wouldn't it be far cheaper for them to import it direct from the United States than from Turkestan ? " I answered.

" Then why do they come bothering us here ? Why are they advancing on Tashkend ? " he asked querulously.

The repulsive and ignoble face of this renegade was an unpleasant sight. It was hard for me to conceal a smile of contempt when he stood up to go, but it was necessary to be careful.

A month later, during the night of 18th-19th January 1919, when the White troops took the town, Voitintseff with all his comrades who were commissars of the Soviet were killed.

I learnt the circumstances of his death when I happened to meet one of the White officers who had taken an active part in the settlement of accounts with the Bolshevik commissars.

" They are cowards and ruffians," he said ; " they cannot face death like men. Look at Voitintseff, for instance. He flung himself on the ground at my feet and grovelled, imploring pardon and mercy. He promised to abandon his errors, as he called them, and to help us in the struggle with Communism. He cried like a child, and his last words were, ' Mother, mother, mother, how I want to live ! ' I finished him off with a bullet in his brain, the brute, for all the harm he brought on our Turkestan."

Soon after Voitintseff's visit, we were informed by the warders that Captain A. had been brought in from Ferghaná and put in the cellar of the Che-Ka. He was one of those whom I had sent there with Colonel P. G. Korniloff. I was astonished to hear this, and not inclined to believe it, as A. had been with the native guerillas and could hardly have been taken alive. When the news was confirmed, I became aware that the Bolsheviks were arranging to confront us in order to see what our relations were, and this might be fatal for him. For myself, I had long since considered myself condemned.

One morning they took me up to the Che-Ka under a strong guard ; there were ten ruffians who formed the Soviet of this bloodthirsty institution, which now included yet another law student who had not finished his course, Sidoroff by name, who was engaged at the present time in the investigation of all plots against the Dictatorship of the Proletariat.

When they brought in A., we exchanged a very significant glance ; it was evident that he was crushed by his experiences.

I was anxious to know what he had given away at the preliminary inquiry, what line of defence he had taken, how he had explained his presence among the natives of Ferghaná, and where and under what circumstances he had been arrested.

While waiting for the beginning of our examination, the Bolsheviks who were in the examiner's room were carrying on some silly discussion, abusing capitalism, the bourgeois, the persecutors of the working classes and so on. Making use of this, I uttered some provocative expression, and they at once rose to the bait and began to argue with me, quite correctly seeing in me a ' class enemy ' and opponent. During this brief argument I took care to let out what I was accused of, what my defence was and what I had had to do with A. He, understanding my meaning, joined in this lively discussion. Like this we quickly let each other know what was necessary in the very presence of these fools, and when the examiner came into the room, we knew what to answer and how to talk to them.

After this interrogation they brought A. into our cell No. 22, which meant, of course, that his fate was decided—the bullet.

He told us a sorry story of how he fell into the hands of the Bolsheviks. He with another officer and the fourteen-year-old son of the latter had been with Madamin Bek's contingent, which was operating very successfully against the Bolsheviks, scattering detachments of Reds one after another.

One day they heard that Madamin Bek was preparing an attack on the Russian village of Myn Tiubé. It must be admitted that he had grounds of complaint. This village was situated on land taken by force from the natives by the Imperial Government, and the settlers were desperate ruffians who had made Central Russia too hot to hold them. They had certainly done a lot of harm to the natives, who detested them for their insults and damage.

The Russian officers tried hard to dissuade Madamin Bek from this step, which would be fatal in every respect, to say nothing of hopelessly compromising in the eyes of the Russian population the rising so successfully begun by the natives against the Bolsheviks. I think that Madamin himself realised this, but could not restrain his followers. When they saw that all attempts at suasion were useless, and that the attack was definitely decided upon, A. and R. with his son, who had distinguished himself by his courage and the accuracy of his shooting, left the detachment and rode to Myn Tiubé, where they warned the inhabitants of the intended attack. The inhabitants of Myn Tiubé were not particularly confident in their own strength, and sent to ask help from the Soviet authorities. But before this help arrived, in the form of a detachment of the Red Army accompanied by the commissar of the Che-Ka, the attack of the Kirghiz had been beaten off with great loss for the attackers.

The people of Myn Tiubé remained true to type and justified their bad reputation. The first thing they did on the arrival of the Red troops was to hand over their saviours A. and R. to the agents of the Che-Ka as ' imperial officers.' By doing this they hoped to buy the protection and favòurs of the Soviet Government. Even the Communist commander of the Red detachment was surprised at such behaviour.

Two years later the hand of Nemesis did its work. The settlement of Myn Tiubé was taken by a detachment of native guerillas, and all buildings were razed to the ground and all the inhabitants put to the sword.

Poor A. was in a very depressed state of mind, and was astonished at our brightness and even rather cheerful frame of mind.

" Thank you, gentlemen," he said. " I see that you are sorry for me, and hope by putting on a cheerful appearance to encourage me in my depression, but it is useless, for without any doubt we are all condemned to death."

We soothed him by telling him of the preparations for the rising and its progress, and how we all hoped to be soon at liberty unless the commissars decided to shoot us first.

Our postal service by means of the shop gave us information that the day of the rising would soon be fixed. This cheered us up, but still we continued to work out plans of escaping from prison.

Our friends outside had won over a girl who worked as a typist in the Che-Ka office, and she managed to procure them some blank forms with the official stamp and signatures of the commissars. On one of these was an order to the prison authorities to send all prisoners in No. 22 to the Che-Ka. The convoy, consisting of ten of our men dressed in Red Army uniform, was to bring this order to the prison at the dinner-hour, when all commissars of the Che-Ka went to drink vodka. In case of any telephone inquiry on the part of the prison authorities, the typist was to stay on duty and give the necessary answer by telephone. It only remained to choose the day and mark the date on the order.

About this time I had an excellent opportunity of escaping. One morning when I was brought before the Che-Ka for some purpose or other, I was kept there till late at night answering the innumerable more or less stupid questions of the Soviet examiner. When at last they let me go and I went out into the corridor and to the stairs, I found my guards sound asleep, and it would have been perfectly easy for me to have quietly walked out into the street and hidden myself, taking advantage of the darkness of the night, as at that time there was no illumination in the streets. But I remembered that my escape would at once alarm the Bolsheviks and involve my comrades in reprisals, such as ' exceptional measures,' or as a measure of precaution against escape, they would have simply 'charged them to expenses,' as they cynically called the secret execution of prisoners.

During exercise time in the prison yard I had occasion to make the acquaintance of two very interesting Turcomans who had been brought in from the Transcaspian Province. The first was an immensely tall young man who must have stood at least seven feet. He was suffering terribly from hunger, as he had no money, nor, of course, any friends in this part of the world, and the prison fare was intolerably bad. I began to share my dinner with him, and the poor fellow quickly recovered his strength. He came of a rich Turcoman family, and had been fighting the Bolsheviks stubbornly. He told me that with his own sword he had cut off a good number of Bolshevik heads. What a picture he must have presented, this fierce young giant, with his oriental scimitar, mounted on one of those splendid Turcoman horses! He had not been taken prisoner in fair fight, but treacherously seized during an armistice together with his friend, an influential Turcoman named Djanaid Khan, when they were at prayer in a mosque. The Bolsheviks, as true disciples of militant Marxism, did not consider themselves at all bound by their word pledged to 'class enemies.'

Djanaid Khan, a man of considerable age, was the chief of a group of ten thousand Turcoman families which he had brought out from Afghanistan into Russian territory many years previously. He had enormous prestige among his own people. Even here in prison his adjutant never left his side, a fine-looking Turcoman with a long black beard. Djanaid Khan was also penniless, and I was able to help him with money sent in by our secret postal service.

He was admitted to our secrets, and tried hard to persuade me to go with him to the Turcoman steppes as soon as we were free.

" I will give you everything you can want," he promised me : " a felt tent for yourself, with rugs and furniture, cattle and horses." He even promised me a Badakhshan, a splendid breed of horses which is a speciality of Afghanistan. They are extremely difficult to get, as their export is strictly forbidden.

For a time I seriously thought of going with him, but my duties on the staff of the ' White ' movement kept me in Turkestan. Djanaid Khan eventually made his way back to the steppes of Turkmenia and quickly made his presence known to the Bolsheviks. Ever since he has maintained a fierce and uninterrupted war against them for the faith and freedom of his people. Driven eventually by sheer weight of superior forces and armament into Persia and thence compelled finally to seek refuge in Afghanistan, Djanaid Khan is one of those rare heroic souls who, without means or supplies, alone and without help or encouragement, refused to sheath his sword, keeping up the unequal contest for another eleven years, in spite of advancing age, never yielding to the tempting seductions offered him by the Soviet Government, obstinately clinging to his liberty, his religion and his customs, ranging for years over the whole of Turkestan, making it dangerous for the Bolsheviks to leave their towns in the interior of the country, the one district in the whole of Russia where the struggle against Bolshevism has been carried on without interruption. All honour to the peoples of Turkestan for their stubborn refusal to acknowledge the government of the soul-destroying brigands. Their gallant example might well be followed even by peoples who call themselves civilised Christians.

After numerous delays and postponements, which kept filling us with alternate hope and disappointment, the day, or rather the night, of the proposed rising was at length fixed for New Year's Eve, when it was assumed that all commissars would undoubtedly be drunk.

The impatience with which we awaited that day may well be imagined. But there was yet another postponement for some unknown reason, and our hearts sank, for the likelihood of being shot or done to death in some brutal manner increased with every day. The Che-Ka was quite capable of suddenly deciding that it was high time to carry the sentence into effect on the eve of Christmas, so as to instil yet further terror into the inhabitants and poison their holidays. It was just as likely that during Christmas the prison guards would get drunk and settle up on their own account with the " counter-revolutionaries and enemies of the proletariat." Besides that, the fact that some workmen were taking part in the plot made me anxious, as there might easily be a traitor among them who would sell us to the Bolsheviks.

The chief strength of the organisation was in former officers of the old army, the younger generation of the locality and part of the Red garrison under the command of a young Red officer named Osipoff.

On 3rd January our secret postal service brought the good news that the date of the rising had been definitely fixed for Epiphany, 6th January, which is regarded as an important festival in Russia. This night, the people believe, is full of mystical significance; on this night in the villages all doors, gates and windows are marked with crosses, and girls are busy trying to read their fate and future spouses.

We were promised that on the morning of the sixth, which happened to be a Sunday, our prison would be taken by assault and we would be set free.

Now was drawing nigh not only the hour of release, but of the triumph of the Whites, of freedom, order and Christian ideas over the dark forces of Bolshevism.

I fully admit that we all enjoyed the anticipation of the sweet hour when we should be able to wreak vengeance upon the children of hell for all the evil they had wrought upon our country, our neighbours and ourselves.

The tense anxiety with which we sat and waited may well be imagined ; something might go wrong, some unforeseen obstacle might arise at the eleventh hour. But at the same time, no one doubted for an instant that the Whites would beat the Bolsheviks, and our confidence in success was absolute.

At last in the evening we held a meeting and worked out our plan of operations, allotting duties to each of us in case we should be called suddenly to take part in the fighting.

The morning of the sixth broke fine and clear, with a slight frost. At the time of our morning exercise in the prison yard we received our usual ' mail ' through the little shop with the news that the prison had been surrounded all night by a special detachment of Whites as a precaution against any possible reprisals upon the prisoners on the part of the Red guards, and that the assault would begin at ten o'clock.

The prison commissar, as though with a presentiment that something was brewing, was walking uneasily about among the prisoners. At length he stopped, formed a group round him like a sort of meeting, and began to make a long, disconnected and very stupid speech. He told us that Spanish influenza had broken out in the prison, and two prisoners in the criminal section had died the previous day, and so all communication with the outside world was forbidden from that day. The delivery of food from home would not be permitted any longer, and we should have to be content with the prison fare. This to all intents and purposes meant condemning us to starvation.

"You must not blame the Workmen's and Peasants' Government," he said insinuatingly, "for all the misfortunes and deprivations which have overtaken our country. Only history is to blame."

"Hark at him! Who is he throwing the blame on now for all the sins of his fellow-bandits ? " I thought to myself. "Never mind, you ruffian, in a couple of hours you will be swinging on the nearest poplar."

With these thoughts passing through my head I could hardly repress a smile.

"What are you laughing at ? " he asked me sharply.

"I am so happy," I replied. "It is such a beautiful morning, sunshine, blue sky," I answered, smiling more than ever.

"Back to your cells—march ! " rapped out the commissar in savage irritation. "Don't you want to listen to Science ? "

We could not control ourselves at that, and all burst out laughing as we returned to our quarters. The door clanged loudly behind us, and the keys rattled in the lock.

"For the last time," I murmured to myself.

Then I lay down in my hammock and began to read a book of Jules Verne, 'A Voyage to the Moon,' out of the prison library.

Time dragged by desperately slowly. Some of us became restless and kept looking at our watches. The hands pointed to ten. Then a quarter of an hour went by.

"Something must have happened, some accident, everything is so quiet," said one nervously.

"Patience, gentlemen, patience," said another.

Certainly there was a stillness quite unusual for this time of the morning. Not a sound came through from the street outside.

Ten more minutes crawled by.

Suddenly the dead silence was cut by the sharp rattle of a volley from hundreds of rifles, and bullets rattled on the roof of the building.

"Away from the windows, all!" I cried. "It would be a pity to be killed by a friend's bullet."

Loud yells followed the volley, then groaning, strange noises, the clattering of men running, as the Red guard saved their precious skins . . . then an explosion. . . .

"There go the gates of the outer yard," was our thought.

Then more noise, a few isolated shots and the trample of horses' hoofs.

With a crash the gates of the inner yard were flung open, and there burst in a number of mounted men.

"Open cell No. 22! Smartly now!"

We heard the heavy keys rattling in the trembling hands of the warder as he struggled to put the right one into the hole. At length the door opened, and on the threshold stood my old friend Captain B. in full uniform of the imperial army with epaulettes and spurs.

"Welcome, gentlemen," he said, saluting. "The town is in our hands. All the commissars except one were shot this morning, and the Che-Ka with all its contents has been burnt."

We greeted him with loud cheers. Free at last !

Still, we did not hurry to leave our cell. As had been previously arranged, we had still to decide whom to let out of prison, as there was no occasion to release real criminals. They quickly brought us the books from the office, and we set to work.

Meanwhile the two prison yards were filled with White troops and visitors from the town.

But our work was quickly interrupted by the appearance of two officers accompanied by one or two civilians, who insisted that we should at once abandon our task and go out into the street. "The people are very anxious at not seeing you," they said. "They are afraid that you have been caught by the Reds again. Come out and show yourselves. They are so worried about you that they want to see you alive and well." We left the books and walked out.

In the inner yard, among the crowd which gave me a boisterous welcome, I saw a curious scene.

Up against the massive prison wall there stood a trembling figure. It was a man of repulsive aspect, more like an ape than a human being. He was of middle height, sturdily built, with enormous long arms, a clumsy heavy frame, straight black hair, a very low forehead and small, blue, shifty eyes.

Opposite him, a few paces away, on the steps of the prison, young Prince C. was standing, aiming a rifle at the ape-man. The prince turned an inquiring look towards me, as though to ask whether he should pull the trigger or not.

"Pardon! Pardon! Forgive me! Forgive me!" the ape-man was whining in terror. "I was always against cruelty . . . I was always against shooting . . . I protected the bourgeois always . . . I will help you . . . Spare me. . . ."

I smiled, and a laugh went round the crowd standing there, for the ape-man, now trembling in terror at the sight of a rifle, was notorious for his brutality. It was the Commissar of War, Pashkó. On his soul were thousands done to death, some butchered with his own hands, hundreds handed over to be tortured. Before his arrival in Tashkend this creature had won notoriety by his savage cruelties in Sebastopol, where he had invented his famous "Meeting at the bottom of the Sea," when he had thrown several hundred officers of the old navy to the sharks.

Pashkó was the real type of degenerate, half-man, half-brute, to whom the people had so light-heartedly entrusted the government at the time of the revolution.

"Leave him for the time," I suggested to the prince. "We must first interrogate him; he can tell us a lot of useful things."

They quickly bound him and took him away in a lorry.

This surprising cowardice, the baseness and absence of dignity, is characteristic of all these active revolutionaries and leaders. They are miserable scoundrels, and do not even know how to die decently.

When I went out into the streets I found them crammed with people, both Russian and native, all laughing with happiness. They surrounded me, congratulated me, shook my hands and embraced me.

Suddenly there was silence. A whisper of alarm passed over the crowd. At the far end of the street there appeared a detachment of mounted men galloping towards us. What could this be ? Who were they ? Red or White ? Friend or foe ? The crowd stood still, petrified.

Men who had suffered so much, men who had but this moment tasted the joys of freedom, waited in alarm for the return of the nightmare.

Suddenly from a thousand throats went up the cry, Hurrah !

It was a detachment of White cavalry that galloped up, sent by General L. K. to help, as he thought that the prison had not yet fallen.

Very slowly I went home. On the way I was stopped and greeted on every side ; I was overwhelmed by kindness and attention ; friend and stranger alike, they pressed upon me, shaking my hands, embracing and kissing me. The streets were full with people breathing relief after fourteen months under the yoke of the Bolsheviks.

Merrily the church bells pealed their thanks to Heaven for delivery from the hands of the powers of evil. The day was fine and sunny, the sky blue, with a touch of frost in the air, as though Nature herself were taking part in the rejoicings of mankind. It was a moment of triumph when, as we fondly thought, the land had been finally freed from the brigands. A mere thirty-hour train journey separated us from the British force waiting at Chardjui, which would not meet with any real opposition.

And in my home my wife was waiting to welcome me, and with her was Daisy. . . .

CHAPTER III. DAYS OF WRATH.

EARLY on the second morning rifle fire was heard and the roar of a gun. Workmen who had joined the Whites changed their coat and went over to the Soviets. On the third the town was again in the hands of the mob, led by Communists. They were taking their revenge. Looting was in full swing and murder unbridled. I had no horse and could not follow the retreating handful of Whites. Before my eyes I saw the head of the Swedish Red Cross killed and a sister of mercy. The Bolsheviks took off an unfortunate girl I knew, with her mother, to the railway shops, from which no one returned alive. More than five thousand educated people were arrested. They were ordered to dig a common grave, stripped naked and all shot. A little earth was hurriedly scratched over them. Many were buried still breathing. Young Prince C., only a lad, not mortally wounded, fell on top of a pile of corpses ; he lay unconscious for many hours on this fearful bed and at night managed to crawl out and make his way home. His father was already killed, and his mother, when she saw her boy standing there, naked and blood-bespattered, went out of her mind on the spot. His sister washed and bandaged his wounds, put him to bed and tended him ; but the next day, on the reports of their neighbours, Bolsheviks came and shot them both.

A cold snowy winter had set in, and for long pools of frozen blood remained staining street and pavement.

I found refuge in a house where a British officer had hidden previously. Near the bed was a trap-door and a moveable cupboard through which one could get down into the cellar below and wait there while a search was going on. One day there were no less than seventeen domiciliary visits to the house. Austrian prisoners of war particularly distinguished themselves. The government of the ' toiling masses ' was certainly international.

Soon word came through that the Soviet authorities had news of my place of refuge, and I had to seek a hiding-place outside. Towards the evening of 12th January, when the sun had gone down behind the avenue of high poplars, the frozen snow crackling crisply underfoot, the houses enshrouded in a misty gloom, I walked out of the town. I was disguised, had a false identity card in my pocket and succeeded in passing the Red patrol on the outskirts.

I little thought that I was setting forth on a long and distant odyssey that would take me right across Central Asia, to the mysterious land of Tibet, over the Himalayas into the plains of Hindustan. On the contrary, I thought I should soon return home, for was there not a British force on the Amu Dariá, while on the north the Ataman Dutoff was operating with his Cossacks?

I hid for a week with a friend whose house was on the road along which went a constant stream of Bolshevik motors, lorries and Red cavalry. The day was a time of constant alarm. Any minute they might descend upon the house for a search, which would have meant immediate bullets for my host and myself. But the long cold nights brought some relief and repose. By night no one would come here, and it was by no means a pleasure to see the break of the dawn usher in another day of uncertainty and anxiety. While I was there an episode occurred which throws a great light upon the attitude of the middle classes towards the Soviet Government, and provides an answer to many a riddle.

My host asked my permission to invite a relative of his to come with his wife to see me.

" Of course he is not a Bolshevik, quite the opposite, in fact; he is against the Soviet Government, although he serves under them as they mobilised him," he added.

I agreed. I had known his father well, a typical *burjui*, as they call the middle classes. The next evening they came and spent the night with us, as nobody was allowed to move about on the roads after dark. They were a nice young couple; he was serving in the Red Army. After a scanty supper he told us an interesting adventure which had happened a couple of months previously when he was with a contingent at Chardjui. One night there was a terrible commotion. An urgent telegram had come from the station of Ak Kum that the Red force on the frontier, surrounded by British and Indian troops, had surrendered. Then came a telegraphic ultimatum ordering them immediately to choose a committee of respectable non-party inhabitants and hand over the command of the town to them, with all the weapons in the place; resistance was useless; the English were marching on the town, and in the event of failure to fulfil these terms all Communists and commissars would be hung. The Bolsheviks were in a panic, and most of the commissars agreed to comply; but a minority were in favour of asking for a delay till the

following noon, and during that time to send a contingent
with an armoured train to reconnoitre. This party carried
its views, and early in the morning my acquaintance, with
a detachment of Red troops in an armoured train, left on
its risky reconnaissance. They were all in a terrible funk,
he said. Before them waited a formidable enemy, unerring
Indian marksmen, and in the distance were English gunners
who never missed. When the party reached the station
their morale was at a very low ebb, and they wanted to
turn back. Within sight of the station the order was given
to stop the engine, detrain and advance cautiously in open
order. In the station not a soul was to be seen. Obviously
it was a trap. They would let them come quite close and
then suddenly shots would ring out on every side, followed
by the thunder of guns. The Red soldiers, accustomed
to killing unarmed *burjui* and natives with impunity, dis-
liked the situation. It was only by threatening them with
machine-guns from the rear that their leaders were able to
compel the men to advance. They approached quite close.
Still ominous silence. Had but a single shot rang out at
that moment, the whole party would have bolted in a panic.
But all was quiet. In the station not a sign of an enemy.
The Reds, growing bolder, ventured to reconnoitre the
station buildings. Then in one room they found the stationmaster and his assistant, and in the guard-room forty Red
soldiers and railwaymen, all unarmed and locked in. Nobody
could give a clear explanation of what had happened. They
said that during the night there had arrived at the station
a delegate of the White and British forces who declared
that the station was surrounded ; and, in order to avoid
unnecessary bloodshed, they called upon them to lay down
their arms. This was done and the prisoners locked

in. What had happened to the 'delegates' no one knew.

My informant then described how he climbed up the water-tower to look for an answer to the riddle. All he could see was two small human figures in a distant hollow between two hillocks of sand, and a little dog with them. Pursuit was ordered at once, and very quickly one prisoner was brought in. It was a student named Moshkoff; the other, an officer named Bombchinsky, was mortally wounded and left to die in the desert. It transpired that these two Whites, disguised in Red uniform, had arrived in a train from Tashkend, slipped out unnoticed at the station of Ak Kum, cut the telegraph wires, arrested and locked up the stationmaster and his assistant and disarmed and locked up the guard. Then they repaired the wire and sent the message to Chardjui, and another to the Red commander-in-chief informing him that the station of Ak Kum was taken, that British troops were already in their rear, and called upon him to disarm. On the front the officers had difficulty in preventing the men from flinging down their arms in panic. They wanted to shoot Moshkoff on the spot, but his bluff was so bold and so original that even the Reds defended him, and insisted that he be sent back to Tashkend where the Che-Ka would elicit the names of his associates.

"But why did you do the Bolsheviks such a service?" I asked my acquaintance. "Why didn't you pretend that you had not seen those two men in the distance? You are not a Bolshevik and now you have killed two Whites."

"When they mobilise you into the Red Army, dress you in uniform and put you under discipline, then you do everything you are told and forget all your old sympathies," he answered.

This reply is characteristic of that unprincipled mass of Russians who ruined their country by being White one day and Red the next, destroying her freedom and making the people the slaves of the Third International.

It so happened that Moshkoff had been brought into the prison while I was still there, and he had told me the whole story. I knew Bombchinsky well, too, a resourceful, experienced and courageous officer. When living in Tashkend he had succeeded in getting possession of a telegraph apparatus, which he had taken outside the town and with it managed to send the Soviet People's Commissars some telegrams which threw them into a panic. When it had once been necessary to send a man to Kashgar on a very important mission, my choice had fallen on him. Although he could not ride, he mounted a horse for the first time in his life and started on a long and dangerous journey over the mountain paths to avoid the towns and patrols. He succeeded in getting there and making his way back successfully, but by that time I was in prison. A little later, when the American Mission wanted to send an important despatch to Persia for relaying to their government, and the Soviet authorities did not allow the transfer of telegrams on their wires, the task was entrusted to Bombchinsky. He enlisted Moshkoff as an assistant and left in a military train ; when they reached Ak Kum they carried out the bluff described ; tired after their night's work they went out into the desert to rest and there were surprised. Bombchinsky was hit in the stomach and killed almost at once, so Moshkoff surrendered. A Communist soldier shot the little dog.

After a few days I learnt that the Whites were retreating along the Chimkend road and retiring into the mountains by the valley of the Chotkal. I managed to secure a horse and left in that direction to join them. There was a severe frost and the snow lay thick; the marshes were frozen and the irrigation canals too, so I had no difficulty in skirting the village of Nikolsky, where there were Bolsheviks, and cutting through the swamps. My horse was a miserable old crock that could hardly crawl, and there would not be the slightest hope of getting away from the Reds if we met. And I thought, with longing, how many a time I had ridden along that same road on my own good horses, with which I could overtake and leave behind anyone. This was deserted and quiet now, as though some blight brooded over the land. On the faces of an occasional passer-by I could see gloom and fear. The Dictatorship of the Proletariat had left its mark on all.

At sundown I reached the house of an acquaintance, a rich Kirghiz named Yakshi Bai. He was delighted and astonished to see me, as he thought me shot long since.

" Where are you going, *taxir ?* " [1] he asked.

" I am going shooting in the mountains," I answered.

" Good, but you must stay here the night," he replied. When we went into the house and were alone, he said—

" *Taxir*, tell me the truth; you are not going shooting now; you have neither gun nor dog with you and are alone."

" Yes, I am going into the mountains to meet a contingent of Whites who are making their way towards Chimkend ; do you know anything about them ? "

" If you like, I will give you a nephew of mine as a guide ; he will get you by night straight through the steppe into the mountains. But you must sleep here ; your horse is tired. To-morrow morning I will make inquiries in the

[1] *Taxir*, in Djagatai Tartar, is a term of respect, corresponding to sahib.

bazaar about your friends, among the Kirghiz who have come down from the mountains."

I gladly agreed to his suggestion. After some tea and a delicious *palau* I lay down on a comfortable bed, made up on the floor, of a pile of soft rugs, and they covered me with a warm coat of wolf's skin. During the night Yakshi Bai's wife awoke several times to attend to her infant, and she carefully straightened out the fur over me for fear I should be cold.

In the morning Yakshi Bai put on a fur coat and a big cap of fox-skin, mounted his best horse and rode off to the bazaar to collect information for me. He did not arrive back till late in the evening ; he was on foot, without fur coat, cap or even whip.

" The whole road is crammed with Red troops advancing against the Whites," he bewailed. " They are helping themselves to horses, clothing, anything they want. They requisitioned my horse, my coat and cap," he went on with a sigh. " Allah has turned his face away from us and sends us misfortunes such as we had never heard of. *Taxir*, you can never ride into the mountains. Stop with us and to-morrow we will talk it over with wise and experienced men and decide what to do next."

The following day half a dozen Kirghiz and Sarts met and debated the matter a long time, and finally decided that, at least at present, it was impossible for me to go into the mountains : the Whites were hidden in a remote valley on the Pskem, the only way out commanded by the Reds ; all along the road there was a mass of Red troops, both infantry and mounted, and the only thing for me to do was to stay in the neighbourhood.

" You cannot hide among the Kirghiz," they said, " their

life is so open ; their doors are never shut ; their houses are open all the time so that anyone who likes may walk in. In the villages they go on living in the way they are used to in the steppe. You must hide with the Sarts. They guard their families and homes jealously ; their gates are always locked and no one can go in unasked. The Sarts live shut in and you can easily hide among them.

" We will at once send for Akbar Bek. He is an old soldier of Khudoyar Khan, a staunch and experienced man. He has sent many a man to the other world and you can count on him."

Within an hour there came into the room a big-built Sart of immense height, with a black beard, alert grey eyes and a clever, energetic face. After the customary greetings they explained the situation to him ; he simply nodded assent and said—

" All right. I will hide you, *taxir*, at home. I am accustomed to give shelter to the persecuted. I detest the Bolsheviks, Sons of Sheitan ! and am glad to be of service to men of the days of the Tsar. To-night ride over to my house. I have heard a lot about you and am glad to help you."

Late that night a Kirghiz guided me. It was full moon, but snow was falling heavily, which masked me from inquisitive eyes. In half an hour we came to the gate of a Sart's farmhouse standing alone in a field. My guide gave a peculiar knock and the door was opened. Our host met us in a small courtyard and opened a door leading into a room with a mud floor, feebly illuminated by a *chirak*, a primitive little oil-lamp of the same design as those of ancient Greece and Egypt. Not far from the door, round a glowing fire, there squatted a couple of women, a young man, son of Akbar Bek, and a little boy about twelve. They welcomed me civilly and invited me to sit with them. One of the women was young, with big brown eyes and a wistful expression on her pale face ; the other was a good deal older, with a simple-minded expression but not lacking in nobility. They were not in the least embarrassed at my presence, although Mahommedan law forbids women to show the face to strange men, for I was not only a guest but a persecuted stranger, and had come to their home to live with them the same life that they lived themselves. None of them asked me any question. They knew perfectly well whom they had invited into their house, and to what danger they exposed the whole family by doing so.

Soon they prepared for the night. They made me up a bed, and the younger woman took a rug out of a box for me, her dowry, she explained. On leaving the room Akbar said to me—

"*Taxir*, you need not be afraid of anybody. No bad man can come in here at night ; I would slit his throat."

I stayed in this room, together with the little boy and a young Sart woman with an infant.

The walls were simply plastered with clay and the roof was made of reeds ; a few dirty pieces of felt lay about the floor, and they, with a couple of big boxes against one of the walls, formed the entire furniture of this miserable home where I was to take up my abode for an unknown time. The door fastened very loosely ; there were terrible draughts from every side ; there was no glass in the windows and the floor of earth was cold indeed. I lay awake on my couch without undressing for hours, wondering what would be my future fate. And thus began my life among the Sarts.

It has seldom, if ever, fallen to the lot of a European in Turkestan to live in a purely Mahommedan home and to see the intimate life of a Sart family, so it was with interest that I looked round my new home next morning. It consisted of a very small courtyard, one side of which was occupied by the room where I had slept; on the other were two more small rooms and the remains of a brick shed where food for the horse was kept. The other two sides were taken up by a shed and a cart-house. The gate opened directly on to the poplar-edged main road, with a tumbledown wall on the opposite side beyond which ran a big *aryk* or irrigation canal. The whole day long the road hummed with the heavy traffic of lorries taking Red troops to the mountains, the noise of drunken oaths and the jingle of cavalry. Alongside the yard was a primitive oil-press, the property of Akbar and the support of his family. It was very simple, merely a large wooden mortar with a wooden pestle set aslant, to the far end of which a horse was harnessed. The animal went round and round so that the pestle squeezed out from the cotton seeds a black oil with an unpleasant smell; but at that time of general privation and scarcity of everything it yielded Akbar a very respectable return. The horse was very old, bony, ill and covered with running sores. The whole life of the family depended on the work of that poor old screw.

Akbar's family consisted of his older wife, Gul-bibi, a quiet unassuming woman with gentle manners—in fact, a cultured lady; and the second, a young unsympathetic woman with the coarse face of a typical Sart woman; there were two little girls of seven and nine years respectively, and the little boy already referred to. The eldest son, Yuldash, a strapping young Sart, also had two wives. His first, Tahta - Djián,[1] was the woman with the mournful expression whom I had seen the previous evening ; his second, by name Kamar-Djián, was a reddish, muscular, well-proportioned woman with coarse ruddy face that was not pretty but always cheerful. Kamar-Djián was a native of Ferghaná, from the valley of Almaz, which enjoys a reputation, in my opinion quite undeserved, for the beauty of its women.

During the day it was impossible to go out into the yard as I was tall enough to be seen easily over the top of the low walls, and so it was only by night that I could stretch my legs outside. The whole day I had to sit quietly in the little room. We began the day with a cup of tea and a *lepioshka*, that is, a roll, sometimes made with mealie flour ; they were not bad when fresh, but I thought them dreadful, as the Sarts insist on mixing onion with them. Then I sat and read, as fortunately I had brought away with me a couple of volumes of a special work on geology, which had the advantage over fiction that I could read it several times over without getting bored. Thus I passed the time till about one or two o'clock when lunch was ready, consisting only of vegetable soup with another roll and tea.

Yuldash worked on the oil-press and Akbar in the bazaar, where he sold his oil and passed the time getting news and information for me about the movements of Red troops. In the evening we all met at home and at sunset *ash* was cooked; that is, dinner. By this word the natives mean *palau*. It was not the delicious dish of normal times, but made with cotton-seed oil and a tiny piece of dried meat. It was the reverse of nice ; we had to eat it simply to appease our hunger. The family ate in another room, but Akbar

[1] This name means " Stay-with-us," a prayer that the child may not die.

kept me company. In the middle of the floor was spread
a tablecloth, small and none too clean, on which was placed
the *ash*. What spoilt my appetite was to see Akbar, eating
with his fingers as all Sarts do, pick up a handful of hot
rice in his fingers, squeeze out the moisture and knead it
into a firm lump, then put it into his mouth. At first I
divided the dish into two halves and we each ate from
our own portion, but later I succeeded in securing a separate
plate for myself. So as not to hurt Akbar's feelings, I
explained that a law of our religion allowed us to eat only
out of our own plate and to drink only out of our own cup.
As a matter of fact, this is the case with the *Staroveri*, the
Old Believers, to which sect my forbears belonged. On
my wanderings this saved me from the necessity of eating
and drinking out of the same utensils as people who do not
wash, and enabled me to have my own plate and mug
without annoying anybody—a wise and hygienic rule that
is very advisable in Central Asia.

Sometimes, when Akbar wanted to show some special
honour to any of his womenfolk, he would call her into the
room. Modestly taking off her slippers in the doorway, she
would come in barefoot, go down upon her knees and open
her mouth widely, when Akbar with his own hand would
push in a handful of *palau*. It was young Tahta-Dján
who was thus honoured most often. If there were a bone
in the dish, after carefully cleaning off all the meat with
his knife and eating it himself, Akbar would hand it to
his ladies, who, after gnawing it, would pass it on to the
children. Another time he would give it to the dog, a
miserable creature beaten silly, the constant victim of
blows, kicks and any missile that came handy. The Sarts
do not like dogs, believing that their proximity drives away

the Guardian Angel. Cats, on the other hand, enjoy considerable popularity; but one day this did not prevent Kamar-Dján from snatching up one she had been nursing on her knees and stroking affectionately, and throwing it at her husband during a quarrel. He caught the creature in mid-air and used it as a club to beat his wife in the face. The cat resented being made use of like this in other peoples' quarrels and bolted out of the house, not returning for several days.

After dinner Akbar gave me the news of the day. He told me about the fighting taking place at that time in the mountains between the Whites and the Bolsheviks, of the unsuccessful attacks of the Reds on the positions held by the Whites, of the immense losses of the Reds, of their cowardice and of their cruelties to the defenceless and peaceful native population. He told me how the Red Army took away everything from the natives—cattle, horses, corn, clothing, boots—and how they carried off young women and girls, some of whom they killed afterwards; of the despair of the population and universal hatred of the Bolsheviks.

We often heard the mournful tolling of the bells in the Russian village near-by, when they were burying their folk who had been mobilised by the Soviet Government to fight against the White Guards and been killed. Sometimes his stories were embellished with purely oriental fantasies; for instance, the natives obstinately affirmed that the Whites owed their successes to 'Ak Khanum,' the White Lady, who flew aeroplanes round the enemy positions and inflicted tremendous losses upon the Bolshevik armies.

In the evening after supper, when Akbar went to his own room, his eldest son, wives and children came and sat and warmed themselves round the fire. Then the conversation ran on different lines. Yuldash talked about his hunting adventures and of the interesting places he had seen in the mountains, while the womenfolk put questions to me that were very characteristic of their mentality.

"When will the English come to Turkestan?" "When they do come, will it be all the same as before?" "Will there be printed calico in the bazaar again?" "And will there be needles and thread for sale again in the bazaar?" "Where is the Ak Padsha (White Tsar) now?" "How many hours are there in the day now and how many in the night?" "How many days is it now to Ramazan Bairam?" "Which is bigger, Tashkend or Moscow? Moscow or Russia?" "How do you Russians speak to God; as 'thou' or 'you'?" and so on. And when I had satisfied their curiosity, I would receive the compliment in "How clever you are! You know everything!"

Yuldash used to tell me how he had killed two huge boars in the mountains, an otter and a 'wild man.' When I expressed any doubt as to the existence of 'wild men' in our part of the world, he began to give a detailed description of their appearance. It seems that it was a bear, which the natives often call 'wild men.' In fact, the skinned

48

carcase of a bear covered with white fat is dreadfully like a human body, especially if it be a female.

The days all the time were terribly cold and the frosts very keen, yet the Sart women went about the yard with feet simply thrust into goloshes, which they kicked off in the doorway and walked about indoors barefoot. The temperature indoors was no higher than outside, only there was no wind. The women were very scantily dressed; they simply wore a *halat*, the loose gown of the East, shirt and pants, everything old and falling to pieces. When it was washing-day, and they washed in the yard regardless of the cold, the women wore only the *halat*. When their shirts were being washed the children would sit with nothing on, and even a tiny child, which had barely begun to walk, sat on the snow quite naked. But none of them were ill.

All the women, especially Yuldash's wives, begged Akbar to buy them some material to make shirts with. But everything had disappeared from the bazaar long since, and prices for any kind of material were fearfully high.

When young women went on visits the first thing to do was to darken their eyebrows heavily with *surmá*, antimony, or else with the juice of a plant called *ust'my*, that is woad, *Isatis tinctoria;* then the two eyebrows were joined up by a line across the top of the nose. The Sarts do not use powder, but sometimes rouge the cheeks. Then they took their best dresses out of their coffers. These included just the same simple shirt, but of silk, of a pattern, I may say in passing, uncommonly like present day fashions for women in Europe; then they wrapped strips of material, like puttees, round their feet and put on soft high boots. On top, covering the whole figure, they put on the *parandja*, a kind of mantle like a *halat* but with purely ornamental sleeves sown together at the back; they covered the face with a black hair-net, the *chimbet*. This conceals the face from the eyes of strangers, and the *parandja* covers the whole figure of the woman from her head to the ground. As all *parandjas* are exactly alike, of the same colour, shape and material, all women look exactly alike in the streets, and can be told apart only by their height and their girth. Only for young girls are any exceptions permitted; their *parandjas* may be coloured and the *chimbet* is replaced by a white veil.

This full-dress costume of the Sart women has obviously developed in the course of ages from the custom of covering the head with the *halat* when going out, as the Tartar women still do in the Orenburg and Kazan Governments, or did at least until the revolution. They do not veil the face but cover it up slightly with a corner of the *halat*, rather from coquetry than any provision of the law. But with the Sart women of Khiva, Bokhara and Russian Turkestan the *parandja* and *chimbet* are indispensable for outdoor dress, and even Sart beggar women wear this costume in the streets. For a Sart woman to appear in the streets without *parandja* and *chimbet* would be the greatest disgrace, equivalent to admitting herself to be a lost creature, and no self-respecting Sart woman would dream of doing such a thing. For this reason the question of unveiling the native women is by no means so simple as it sounds to Europeans, profoundly affecting the psychology of the Sarts. When eventually the Bolsheviks recruited Communists among the Sart women of a certain profession, armed them with revolvers, dressed them in the typical *frensh*, or leather jacket, and sent them round the houses to preach the emancipation of women as a first step in the unveiling of faces, the Mahommedan women saw in this an insult to themselves, and all the emancipated ones had their throats cut.

Tartar women in Russia long since solved this problem themselves. The educated ones accepted European dress and fashions, and the poorer ones simply stopped wearing the *halat* over their heads. The Kirghiz women never cover their faces, nor do they hide themselves from strangers. The women of the mountain Tadjiks, although they conceal their faces from strangers, do not veil themselves. The best thing is to leave this question of the *parandja* and *chimbet* to the Sart women themselves to solve, especially as they do not really interfere in any way, and a Sart woman wearing them in the street feels herself just as free and easy as her European sister who is wearing a mask at carnival time. . . .

One morning Tahta-Dján brought me boiling water for tea, modestly sat down near me and said—

" *Taxir*, you will not be offended if I ask you something ? What is correct under your law when a man has two wives ; must you love them both equally and give them turn and turn about in everything ? "

"Tahta-Dján, with us in Russia a man may have only one wife ; to have two wives at once is impossible."

"What a good and wise law you have," she said with a deep sigh ; "I am very unhappy, *taxir*. I was born in the mountains, in the village of Kumsan ; there they do not wear *parandja* and *chimbet*. I married and lived on very happy terms with my husband, and he was very fond of me. We were always together. I had dinner with him and used to sit a long time chatting. Then I had a baby, and he decided to take another wife. I raised no objections.

I thought I was older, and the new one would help me with the housework. He brought Kamar-Djan; she had already been married, and so he did not have to pay much for her, only thirty roubles. And now he does not love me any more."

Her big eyes filled with tears, and she went on—

"Now I am completely strange to him. I do not blame Kamar-Djan; she is a good woman and we are friends with her, but he ought to treat us in the same way, but it is only her he loves. For the past year I have no longer been a wife to him, and I am free to go to another. There is a rich Armenian here who offered to marry me."

Not long after this Yuldash came to me and started complaining of his first wife.

"She is a *djindy, taxir*," he said—that is to say, a crazy hysterical woman; "you can see this for yourself."

That evening at *ash* Akbar told me a lot about the difficulties of his domestic life.

"You would never believe it," he said, "how our women are spoilt among us Sarts. You can often see Kirghiz women working in the fields, or Russian women too, but you'll never see a Sart woman doing so. Even in the house they do not do much; they can't even cook a decent *palau*; they only spoil the rice. Some time ago I was well off and had a brickyard where I employed twenty men. My wife did all the housekeeping single-handed and everything went smoothly; meals were always punctual and yet she found time for spinning cotton and wool. Now I have two wives and Yuldash has two more, and they only go gadding about to their friends the whole day and nothing gets done at home. They won't spin and won't weave, and all the time they are pestering me to buy them stuff;

yet they won't do anything themselves. Where can I get the money from? We only live on the sale of the oil; the old horse is nearly done for, and I'm afraid he'll drop dead before long, and then what are we going to do? We shall die of hunger. Kamar-Dján bothers me to death all day long, and even threatens to leave Yuldash if I don't buy her stuff for a new shirt and give her a tambourine. Tahta-Dján is all the time making scenes with Yuldash, and asking for stuff for a shirt, too. My second wife is a lazy slut. Only my first wife is a decent woman and a good housekeeper. I was a good soldier when I was a young man and served Khudoyar Khan," he continued. "They made us work in the iron mines and smelt the ore. We used to work right away in the mountains, behind Gava Sai. No Russians know that place. When they drive the Bolsheviks out, you ride up there with me and I will show you a beautiful place. There is an immense, pure, green lake; all round there are high mountains covered with pine forests. There is splendid shooting. There are tigers, bears and leopards, any quantity of pig and wild sheep and plenty of *tau teke*, ibex, with enormous horns. There are lots of pheasants, too, and other birds. We can all live at our ease, and no one will bother us, as the Kirghiz seldom go up there. It is accessible for only three months, as the rest of the year the pass is under snow. There is a lot of minerals. There is iron ore that gives twenty pounds of silver to five hundred poods [1] of ore, with eleven poods of steel and three hundred of cast-iron. We used to get salt-petre out of it, too, to make gunpowder. There is another ore there that gives silver, lead and tin, very good tin. And at the other end of the lake, where the banks are sandy

---

[1] Three poods equal one cwt.

and a stream runs through, we used to wash gold. Sometimes washed a whole pound of gold in a week. There are trout in the lake, very good eating. There are water-horses there too, but they are very shy and dive into the water directly they catch sight of a man and hide. I saw one killed. It was of a yellowish-grey colour, very fat and quite hairless. Let's go up there, *taxir*, and you'll see what an interesting place it is, what a splendid hunting-ground and lots of rich ores."

Such a lake as Akbar describes actually exists, but it is not known to many of the natives and quite unknown to the Russians, and not marked on the maps. As a matter of fact the maps of the mountainous districts of Turkestan do not even remotely resemble the truth. There is ore of the type described by Akbar Bek yielding iron, silver and saltpetre, but water-horses are a creation of the native fancy. There is a widespread belief among the Sarts and Kirghiz that near remote rivers and lakes there live white, hairless, wild horses. This is a very ancient belief, as it is recorded of their forbears the Scythians, by Herodotus (IV. 53), who relates that wild white horses grazed by the source of the River Hypanis. Probably the fable arose from the *kulan*, *Equus hemionus*, which is now extinct in this part of Turkestan.

While Akbar was telling me about the wonders of this mysterious lake, suddenly Kamar-Dján dashed into the room, blew out the lamp, shut the door and whispered—

" There are two suspicious-looking men standing at the gate, dressed like Russians." A moment later Akbar went out quietly to the road, but the men had disappeared.

A few days later an unpleasant incident very nearly had disastrous consequences for me. I was sitting reading as usual one morning with the door of the room open. Suddenly I had the feeling that someone was staring at me. I looked up and saw a rather pretty young Sart woman, whom I had never seen before, gazing at me attentively. Without showing any confusion at her unexpected appearance I went on reading quietly, without moving. It appeared that this was a friend of Yuldash's wives who had come on an unexpected visit and taken advantage of her right as a woman to walk right in without asking when she found the gate by some chance unlocked. She saw at once that I was a Russian and a Christian, and bombarded the women with questions, who I was and why I was living there. Kamar-Dján's ready wit saved the situation. She held out her hands, all covered with a rash, and said—

" It was I who asked the Russian doctor in to cure my hands, which are very painful, and he came secretly without telling anyone, as the Bolsheviks have forbidden doctoring."

As was to be expected, the woman chattered about the mysterious doctor to her friends, as a great secret of course, and a few days later a native policeman came up to Akbar Bek in the bazaar and said—

" The *Aksakal* has sent me to you to have a look at your place ; they say there is some Russian hiding there."

" You are talking rubbish," answered Akbar quietly. " There are only the four women at home and two little girls, and as a Mussulman you cannot go."

" Right," said the policeman, " I believe you ; you are an old man and respected. Give me a hundred roubles and I will tell the *Aksakal* that there is nobody at your place."

Of course, I had to give the hundred roubles.

After this incident Akbar advised me not to show myself again in that room during the day, so I had to take up my abode at the other end of the yard in a semi-subterranean place where they kept hay; there were no windows, and instead of a door there was a big broken opening in the wall of the yard covered with a piece of felt. It was warm inside, but through the crevices of the old wall only a little light found its way in, so that by peeping one could just see something. Reading was impossible. In this half-underground shed I spent many a long day and night. Only dinner-time and the hours after it did I spend in my old room among Akbar's family, listening to their stories. The rest of the time I had to spend sitting or lying in my den. The weary days dragged out their length. It was the physical inactivity that I found so terribly depressing and the absence of daylight. To kill the time I reviewed in my memory all my past life and work in Turkestan, and gave myself up to philosophical meditation. Einstein's theory interested me immensely, and to my mind remarkably confirms the *a priori* deductions of the Russian metaphysical philosophers such as Aksionoff, Uspensky and others as to the nature of Time.

One evening when I was just going back to my den Tahta-Dján began to say something very abusive to her husband. I must explain that all the members of the family spoke two languages fluently—that is, the Uzbeg dialect of Djagatai Turki, which is the general language of Turkestan, and Tadjik, which is a dialect of Persian. I do not know the latter at all, and so when they did not want me to understand they spoke in Tadjik. The dispute quickly developed into a serious quarrel, so I went off to bed. A little later I heard cries and screams and weeping. Obviously they were beating Tahta-Dján.

The next morning I saw spots of blood in the snow near

my room. The little boy showed me stains on the felt of
the room and then he showed me an iron rod, and explained
to me that Akbar Bek gave Tahta-Djấn a good beating
with it because she had made a fool of herself. She appeared
with her face all scratched and her eyes swollen with crying.

" They have been beating you, Tahta-Djấn," I said to
her.

" Yes, *taxir*, and I deserved the punishment ; I was very
naughty and behaved very badly last night. Oh, it hurts
me so here," she said, and showed me bruises on her arms
and legs.

One day at last Yuldash brought Kamar-Djấn the tambourine which she had been begging for so long and earnestly.
From that day we had concerts every evening. All the
women sang, while Kamar-Djấn accompanied. They had
a book of songs which they made full use of. The Sarts are
not a musical people ; their singing is a wild discordant
howl. Still, some of Kamar-Djấn's songs were not lacking
in melody—of course, of the most primitive sort ; but that
was spoilt by the Sart manner of singing in the throat, so
that a dull and quite wooden sound is produced. The tambourine became the constant toy of Kamar-Djấn, who
played it for days on end. This caused me a great deal of
anxiety. The main road, which was always thronged with
Red troops, motors and commissars, was only a few hundred
yards or so from our yard, with only an *aryk* or canal to
separate us. This perpetual tambourine resounding the livelong day might easily attract the attention of the Red
soldiers, especially Tartars or Sarts. Writing these lines
years afterwards, there still rings in my ears the sound of
that eternal tambourine, the roar of the motors and
lorries, and the hum of the spindle on which all day long

the industrious old first wife of Akbar busied herself incessantly.

All these sounds are associated in my memory with the constant expectation of the appearance at any moment of a Red Guard Bolshevik, which would be the signal for immediately being shot. Fortunately one lucky night the wretched tambourine was gnawed through by mice, and our songstress was in despair. Yuldash consoled her by saying that he would stretch a new skin on to it, but Akbar quietly forbade him to mend the thing, as he too clearly recognised the danger to which this self-willed woman exposed us all.

Not far from us there was a Communist establishment of Bolsheviks. It had been taken from the executors of General R., a splendidly laid-out and equipped estate with a large and very productive fruit-garden. Men and women came to manage the place on Communist principles. The Tashkend Soviet gave these pioneers of proletarian culture huge sums of money and supplied them generously with wine and vodka. Besides that, they had the right of commandeering without appeal anything they wanted from the local agriculturalists. Every day Akbar reported to me how they robbed and took horses and cattle, and how cruelly these pioneers behaved to the helpless Sart population. The head of the business was a notorious Tashkend drunkard and vagabond who had previously dealt in petty thieving.

The spring was very late that year. On 23rd March there was a violent blizzard, after which it turned warm, and on the 26th the doves began to coo. Yuldash declared that he would go into the hills to Kumsan to his first wife's native village and bring back from there a wonderful stone, *zagkhar murra*—that is, serpentine—which is a very powerful medi-

cine against the bite of snakes and scorpions, and that he
hoped to make a lot of money by selling it. He claimed to
know a lot about stones, and told me many tales of the
various specimens he had found in the mountains. He
described one very well-known cavern in the mountains in
the middle of a beautiful grove of walnut and pistachio
trees, a great place for Sart pilgrims. In this cavern there
are several doors, and over one there is an inscription cut
into the rock in Arabic to the effect that this door was
built a thousand years ago. The cavern was looked after
by a dwarf no bigger than a twelve-year-old boy. In a
ravine not far from the cavern there is a doorway in the
rock, carefully sealed by big stones and cemented over,
probably the entrance into some old mine. There are many
old mines in Turkestan which have their adits carefully
sealed. Probably the old miners hid their best mines at the
time of the invasion of the destructive hordes of Mongols.
There was just such an entrance on the mountain called
Maidan Tau, but the Kirghiz opened it, and at the bottom
of a small shaft found a thick lode of native silver. They
still work it a little surreptitiously, coming to the shaft by
night and concealing the lode carefully with stones. " I
have been there myself," said Yuldash ; " it is a very rich
vein. Not far from Tash Khané in the mountains, in a not
very big mine, the Sarts are secretly washing gold. It is a
very rich place. Besides gold they find rubies and sapphires.
A Sart I know sold a sapphire found there to an Indian in
Tashkend for five hundred roubles. All these mines and
other interesting places are described in a very old Arabic
book which belongs to an old mullah living in the mountain
village X. He showed me some pictures in it."

This last information of Yuldash interested me very

much. As as well known, the old Arabic writers—Ibn Khaukal, Ibn Hordatbek, Abul Feda and others—give good and accurate descriptions of the old mining industry in Turkestan in the ninth and tenth centuries of our era in the flourishing epoch of the Sassanid dynasty. There, for instance, are excellent descriptions of mercury, lead and silver deposits in Turkestan very accurately described, as well as mining in Ferghaná, where coal was worked much earlier than in Europe. Not long before the Great War when they began working coal seams in the Shurbad basin of the province of Ferghaná, these old workings were opened up. It is curious that in his description of this coal, Ibn Hordatbek states that its ash was used for bleaching material. This sounds strange, but it is quite correct, as the ash of this coal contains zinc oxide.

It is quite possible that the old book about which Yuldash spoke is some old geography still unknown to Europeans. Some time ago there was discovered in Semirechie a book in the Uigur language which remained unique for years, until Sir Aurel Stein's discoveries in the region of Khotan.

As I have devoted almost a quarter of a century to the investigation of the mineral wealth of Turkestan, I can confirm the truth of the picture Yuldash gave. Whole hills of dump, extensive workings in the mountains, old roads and so on entirely fit in with these descriptions. With the help of those old Arab writers, whose works are remarkable for their accuracy, I have shown among other things that a silver mine found by me in the mountains is nothing less than the famous Kuh-i-Sim,[1] the Mountain of Silver, which provided the whole of Central Asia, Persia and Russia

[1] See my article, " Kuh-i-Sim, the Treasure of Turkestan," in ' Blackwood's Magazine,' August 1921, pp. 184-196.

with silver in the Middle Ages. In the Hermitage at Petrograd there are silver coins with an inscription to the effect that they were struck in the mint of Tunkend from the silver of Kuh-i-Sim. I came across the old mine one day before the war in a remote spot in the mountains. There were great hills of slag covered with grass and scrub, the remains of extensive buildings, old shafts and underground galleries and immense excavations in the rock, all converted by the lapse of time and the action of earthquakes into natural caverns, the walls of which were already covered with a coating of calcareous matter, and here and there from the roof there hung big stalactites. It required a very experienced eye and careful investigation to recognise the work of men's hands, and to see what ores had been worked and from which spots. It was remarkable that in many such mines the chief seams and adits had been carefully sealed, cemented over and masked. A rich and highly developed mining industry had evidently flourished in this place. The spot had once teemed with life, and been such a hive of industry as can be seen to-day in England or Belgium. Her iron and steel were exported to Damascus, where they were worked up into the famous blades. Yes, the soil of Turkestan conceals many a treasure, and the numerous deposits of many kinds of ore, both ancient and modern, which I discovered in happier days would enrich the country and make it prosperous, but as it is they are wasted. Just as the invasion of the hordes of Mongol savages ravaged the country and destroyed its prosperity centuries ago, so their modern equivalents have ruined it, and the exploitation of its mineral wealth has been postponed perhaps for a century or more. The only difference between the two sets of savages is that the Mongols, with all their passion for destruction, spared the educated folk, the philosophers, the learned, the priests and the writers, but their modern successors did their best to exterminate these very classes first. We shall have long indeed to wait before Turkestan blossoms forth once more into a prosperous industrial land as it was in the days of the Sassanidae.

In my wanderings I had also come across the lost site of Tunkend, capital of the ancient principality of Ilak. It was a wintry blizzard on the Kirghiz steppes. Many years ago when riding after a day's pig-shooting to spend the night on the steppe in the *aul* of some Kirghiz acquaintances, a violent blizzard made me lose the way. After struggling for hours through the driving snow, my tired horse and I took refuge from the blinding hurricane under the lee of an obscure snow-covered lump. Hooking the reins over my arm, I tucked myself right into the corner and fell asleep.

When I awoke the storm was past and the sky cleared. I crept out to have a look round to try to pick up my whereabouts. What I saw caused me the greatest astonishment. For a long distance all round, as far as the eye could reach, there lay stretched out before me the *plan* of a great city, picked out in black lines against the white background, of natural size. Whole streets were clearly marked: the sites of houses, buildings, irrigation canals, cisterns, towers, walls and the city walls. The dry snow, driven by the wind, had filled in all depressions in the soil, throwing out into relief the protuberances, thus marking out the town, which had at some remote time been razed to the ground. Thus the plan of the ancient city, long since destroyed, lost and forgotten, appeared once more, like a photographic negative, in this strange fleeting fashion.

CHAPTER V.   PERSECUTION AND ALARMS.

PRESENTLY the weather turned warm.   In April the apricots and peaches were in full blossom, but it was only through the chinks of the old wall that I could spy bits of blue sky and the twigs of trees, and only at night that I could come out into the open and inhale their fragrance.   Spring and the warmth combined awoke some stirring in my veins, and life seemed somehow easier, though I had no plans at all for the future.   Sometimes Akbar and I would debate how I could best make my way through the mountains to Ferghaná, the greater part of which was still in the hands of native guerillas who were keeping up the battle with the Bolsheviks.   Besides, there were many friends of mine among their leaders.   But the news Akbar brought in from his friends among the Sarts and Kirghiz in the bazaar were the reverse of encouraging :   Bolshevik patrols were out on the roads everywhere, and there was a pair quite near us. I must wait on.

Yuldash came back from the mountains and brought a few small pieces of serpentine, with the news that a White detachment had successfully repulsed Bolshevik attacks, inflicting severe losses on them, and then retired towards Ferghaná, making their way over almost inaccessible passes through the snows.   Meanwhile the movement of motors, lorries and mounted troops along the road became rarer and rarer.

With Yuldash's arrival, Tahta-Dján became more and more depressed and restless. Choosing her moment, she told me that Yuldash had gone to Kuman not only for *zagkhar murra*, but to a place called Katanalykh to see a famous old witch, and bought some *mar gurush* from her—that is, arsenic—to poison her with, that she had found it in the pocket of his coat, but was afraid to take it away.

"But how can he poison you like this when we all eat out of the same dish ? " I asked her.

"I am not afraid that he'll do it by day," she replied, "but by night."

"But how can he poison you by night ? "

"I see you don't know us, *taxir :* husbands often poison their wives and wives their husbands with us, and even parents get rid of unwanted children. When anyone dies with us, he is buried at once and quite quietly ; nobody looks at the body and nobody knows what he has died of."

"But how can he poison anybody asleep ? "

"That is easy. You pound the arsenic into a fine powder, put it into a hollow tube made of a reed with one end closed and the other open, creep up close to the person asleep and gently pour some into his nostrils ; he then inhales the poison without knowing it."

"Then you had better bolt the door where you sleep," I suggested.

"So I do," replied Tahta-Dján, "but still I am very frightened."

A couple of days later Yuldash came and complained to me that Tahta-Dján intended to poison him, as he had found some *mar gurush* in her box, and she was a real *djindy*, a witch.

I do not know which of the two was right. The strange

thing was that relations between Yuldash's two wives were perfectly good and friendly.

One evening Kamar-Dján came and put a lot of questions to me—

" Why doesn't your wife come here to see you ? "

" You know that is quite impossible, Kamar-Dján."

" Then if your wife cannot come to see you, why don't you take another from the Russian village ; there are plenty of nice girls there."

" But we mayn't have two wives."

" Then I tell you what : you'd better take a Sart girl. You can marry a Sart, I suppose. I know a young widow, quite nice-looking too, who would marry you."

" Stop talking rubbish, you great fool," broke in Akbar, who had at that moment come into the room.

After a pause she started again—

" What book is that you are reading all the time ? "

" It is a book about the precious stones and ores that are found in the earth."

" Show me the pictures," she asked.

Everybody in the room came over to have a look at the illustrations in my geology book.

But, like most Kirghiz and Sarts, they were utterly unable to understand the pictures or illustrations of anything at all : scenery, a plan, drawing of an animal, design of a machine, they took them all for ores and kept asking, " What kind of ore is that ? " although the picture in question was not an ore at all, but a view of a mountain or a river or something like that.

One day Akbar came back to lunch, a very unusual thing, in a great state of agitation. He said that a young Russian, very well dressed, kept on asking him if he did not know where I was hidden, saying he was a great friend of mine and wanted to send me greetings and to help me with money or anything else I needed.

" I told him that I did not know anything about you," said Akbar, " or who he was talking about, as I did not know any Russians."

I thanked him, and told him he could not be too careful.

A few days later Akbar did not come back from the bazaar until very late at night, which caused me considerable anxiety, and I began to fear he had been arrested. It had been a beautiful sunny day, and through the chinks of my prison I could see the tops of the distant mountains, the snow turning purple in the rays of the setting sun. The glimpse brought on a terrible feeling of homesickness, a craving to be once more in my beloved mountains where I loved to live and shoot. If only I could get through to them I should be in safety and in freedom.

And then I would sit listening attentively to every sound, thinking that at any moment Bolshevik soldiers might come or agents from the Che-Ka. They would catch me in a trap in my stone box, and there was nowhere to escape to. And the thought that not only I, but these good souls who had treated me so well, would be shot, too, made me desperately unhappy. Long after dark Akbar arrived in a very excited state.

" *Taxir*, it was almost a disaster ; I was frightened terribly, but, glory be to Allah, He saved us," he exclaimed.

He went on to explain how two Red Army soldiers came to him in the bazaar and took him off to the Russian village to the *Ispolkom*, the Executive Committee, where there were some men from the Tashkend Che-Ka, commissars, and a guard of soldiers. They at once asked him where was I hiding. They advised him to tell them the whole truth or they would shoot him on the spot. Akbar kept perfectly cool and answered quietly that he was not hiding any Russian, that he did not know at all who was hiding or where, that he was an old man and had not been to town for twenty years, which was the truth, and did not even speak Russian.

"Don't tell lies!" roared the commissars and pointed revolvers at him, one to his forehead, the other at his temple.

"Speak at once and don't deny it! We've been hunting for this Nazároff for ages, as he has done us a lot of harm. We have sent parties to find him in Pskem, in Chinaz and Chimkend, but now we know he is hiding here."

"If you are so sure that he is in my house, go and look for yourselves," answered Akbar with dignity.

"Of course we know he isn't with you in your house, but you must know where he is and you must tell us."

"I don't know anyone named Nazároff and never heard of him."

The ruffians went on interrogating Akbar, with threats of shooting and even of torturing him. They threatened to pour kerosene over him and set light to him, or to beat him to death; but these scoundrels could not shake the staunch heart of the old warrior, who stood true to his word and his honour, and looked with the deepest contempt on his persecutors.

After exhausting their threats the commissars gave him a little rest and then put a huge pile of money on the table in front of him, not their own Soviet rubbish, but the old imperial bank-notes, which were very highly prized by the natives then, and said to him—

"Look, here is a whole fortune for you; only tell us where Nazároff is and you can have the lot."

"If when you threatened me with death I could not tell you what I do not know, how can I tell you now when you offer me money? I say again, I know nothing."

It is now a recognised fact that the Bolshevik reacts to only two stimuli: fear for his own miserable skin, and greed. Other motives for human action are unknown to him.

When at length they let Akbar go and he came out into the street, the headman of the Russian village came quietly up to him, took him by the sleeve and whispered into his ear—

"Bravo, Akbar. You're a sportsman!"

The spring wore on. The blue rollers (*Coracias* sp.) arrived, a sure sign that it was time to work on the vines, and for days on end Akbar was busy tying his up to the trellis on the house. His little boy managed to catch a little fish in the *aryk*, cleaned it and roasted it on the ashes and brought it to offer me. Naturally I declined the morsel, which he promptly ate himself with much relish. One morning they brought me some pies filled with some herb which smelt like orange; they were very good indeed, and I asked what the herb was. They called it *djulpys*. Later on the little girl brought me some of it, which turned out to be *Melissa officinalis* or balm, which grows here and there on the banks of the *aryks*. Another herb they used was the young leaves of some kind of sorrel; this was not particularly nice, but after all it was fresh vegetable and a pleasant change in the dull and coarse diet on which I lived.

One day Akbar brought home a great armful of material

which sent his women-folk into the seventh heaven, as their shirts were all in rags and tatters. They at once set to work cutting and sewing, but it was all very simply and quickly done. They just cut it out roughly and tacked the pieces together, and within an hour the whole family was wearing new shirts, and the faces of the women and little girls were radiant with happiness. At the same time they pierced the nostrils of the little girls and hung on nose-rings. It was a great festival for everybody.

I ought to explain that it is not considered the thing for a respectable Sart woman to go to the bazaar. Anything she wants must be bought by her husband or brother. Akbar's women-folk were free to go about by day wherever they liked, and were often away for days at a time on visits, but it would not be considered good form in a Mahommedan family for them to go to the bazaar.

One evening Akbar told me that he had decided to divorce his second wife, who had been with him three years and had a little boy.

" She is quite useless to me," he explained ; " she does not do any of the housework, does not help at all and is thoroughly lazy."

The next day at twelve o'clock the mullah came. They sat round in a circle and the mullah read the appropriate prayer, and then they ate a *palau*, and that finished the ceremony. An hour later Yuldash drove the divorced wife with her baby and things to Tashkend, where she had come from. It was all as simple as dismissing a servant.

The same evening the children brought me a handful of ground nuts, *djiryanchak*, and very good they were. They are highly nutritious and are considered good for stomach troubles. The leaves are small, long and laciniated, but I did not see the flowers, so cannot say what the plant really is. This is a pity, as I had not seen it nor heard of it before.

About this time Kamar-Djän sent an ultimatum to Akbar through her husband; he was to buy her a piece of real calico print for a new frock, a new *halat* and new boots with goloshes, or she would leave Yuldash and go away. Her poor husband, who was hopelessly in love with her, was terrified of losing her, but perfectly well understood the impossibility of fulfilling her demands under present circumstances. She abused him and went away from home for a whole day, coming back late in the evening, when she made scenes with Akbar and cried.

"The woman is mad, *taxir*," said poor Akbar to me. "It is quite impossible for me to buy the things she wants. Under the Bolsheviks everything is crazily dear, and anyhow we can hardly make both ends meet. And if I did buy her stuff for a dress, I should have to do the same for all the women. Why should I offend my poor first wife? She works twice as hard as all the others put together, the good woman; she never complains nor asks for anything."

His first wife certainly was a remarkable woman : intelligent, industrious, with simple dignified manners astonishing in a Sart family. Tahta-Djän suggested a simple remedy. "Give her a good hiding," she said. "When I was naughty, Akbar gave me a beating and then I was good." But, as we shall soon see, she did not stay good long.

Meanwhile the wretched old horse, on whose work the whole family depended, grew weaker and weaker. I cured a huge running sore on his back with permanganate of potash, which I used successfully, too, to stop diarrhœa in the children, so the whole family looked upon it as very wonderful medicine. One night a wild shriek from Kamar-Djän woke us all. She was sobbing hysterically by the poor old creature, which lay on its flanks, grunting hoarsely. The whole family started crying and praying. This was, in fact, a very serious blow for them all, as they were losing a friend that fed and had served the family faithfully and well for many years. The next morning Akbar skinned it, cut the dry, bluish, sinewy meat into strips and hung it up to dry.

" You don't mean to say you are going to eat that meat, Akbar ? " I asked him.

" No, of course not, but I'll sell it," and seeing my reproachful look he added—

" It is all right ; I cut its throat properly and repeated the proper prayers."

All that day everybody was depressed and wretched; even the little girls stopped playing. I gave Akbar some money, and the next bazaar day he bought a good young horse, and the old one was forgotten. When he was buying the horse he met one of the commissars of the Che-Ka riding back with some Red soldiers from the mountains from Chimgan. The commissar stopped Akbar and said to him—

" We have been into the mountains to look for Nazároff at Chimgan, but there are no signs of him there. All the time I'm quite sure you know where he is, damn your eyes, and you won't tell us."

Not long after that Tahta-Dján came to my den and said—

" Kamar-Dján is up to mischief, *taxir ;* she has threatened to go and tell the Soviets that Akbar is hiding a Russian in his house."

" But she knows we'll all be shot if she does ! "

" She says she doesn't care. *Taxir*, give this fool of a woman a hundred roubles and tell her to be quiet."

Of course I agreed and gave Kamar-Dján a hundred roubles. She brightened up at once and promised not to tell anybody anything. The next day Akbar sent for the mullah to try to persuade her to stop her nonsense and remain with her husband. I could hear how gently and persuasively the mullah spoke, and at last the business ended in a compromise : she consented to go on living quietly with her husband if . . . they bought her new boots and goloshes ! After this we had perfect peace and quiet in Akbar's family for a time.

Easter was drawing near. At the beginning of Passion Week the rumour went round that on Easter Night, when the services were in progress in the orthodox churches, a state of siege would be proclaimed and curfew rung, while patrols on the roads would be doubled. Akbar, who told me this, suggested that on Easter Night I should go with him to Tashkend to see my wife. " Your beard has grown now," he said, " and you look like a Sart, and in Sart costume by night no one would know you ; we can come back in the morning." This idea pleased me, and I began to think out how to work it.

But it was not ordained to be. Suddenly the news came that a special search was going to be carried out in all the villages, all along the main road, even in distant farms, a detailed house-to-house search ; there would be whole detachments of troops with commissars from the Che-Ka ; they would surround all the villages and houses and ransack every corner, even open all the boxes ; they were determined to find their man. This search was clearly meant for me. On the Wednesday, Akbar returned from the bazaar very early and came straight to me in my den and told me that it would begin early next morning, that the Red troops were already arriving and the patrol on the bridge was reinforced.

"What shall we do, Akbar?" I asked him. "Where can I hide?"

"I don't know, *taxir;* the situation is terribly dangerous; let's think it over."

"If all the roads and the bridge are held by sentries, the only thing to do," I said, "is to swim the Chirchik and hide with the Kirghiz on the other side among the reeds. Your horse can carry me and we can swim the river together."

"The river is full of water and you'll have to swim nearly a mile."

"Better drown than fall alive into the hands of those brutes," I said.

"It doesn't make much difference whether you drown or not, for, of course, the Kirghiz will take you in and give you shelter; but they are tremendous talkers and live quite openly, so it will be known to everybody in a moment that you are there, and you will fall into the clutches of the Bolsheviks at once."

"Then what can we do?"

"Dinner is ready; come and have something to eat, *taxir,* and then we shall think of something."

I must admit that I had very little appetite. We ate in silence. When we had drunk our tea, Akbar made the following suggestion—

"You stay here where you are, *taxir,* and during the night Yuldash and I will brick you up in the wall, plaster it over with mud, smear it well with dust and then make it all black with smoke. It'll look just like an old wall, and nobody will guess that it is a place where a man can lie down."

There was nothing else to do but to consent to be buried

alive. We put in a whole bucket of water and a good pile
of rolls and set to work. The walls grew rapidly and cut
me off from the outside world. Then there remained only a
tiny hole that disappeared, and in my den reigned darkness
as of the tomb. I could hear Akbar and Yuldash as they
worked in feverish silence.

Presently I fell asleep. During the night I awoke several
times, and feeling myself thus shut off by the wall as of a
tomb from the New World of the disciples of Karl Marx,
I felt absolutely calm and at peace in my heart.

The next morning Akbar's little girl amused me; she
came up close to the wall and asked me in her childish
voice—

" *Taxir*, how are you going to drink tea ? "

About three in the afternoon a volley of oaths and cursing
was audible in the courtyard and the stamp of feet. The
search was evidently in progress. I learnt afterwards that
the brutes interrogated the children, asking them if there
were not a Russian man hidden about the place or with
some of their neighbours. The clever Sart children, well
brought up, all answered that they knew nothing. On the
Friday evening Akbar reported that all the Red soldiers
had left the village and that it was quite safe to come out.
He broke down the wall, and it was with the greatest satis-
faction that I crawled out into the fresh air from my volun-
tary temporary tomb and stretched my cramped legs.

On Easter night I did not sleep, but climbed out on to
the roof and listened to the sound of the Easter bells pro-
claiming the Glad Tidings from the Russian village near-
by. I greedily filled my lungs with the fragrance of the
fruit-trees, reminding me of the happy days when I had
celebrated the feast in my own home among my own family

circle. It is the Feast of Spring, associated with so many happy remembrances of childhood. "And now," I thought, "in the celebration my people are praying for 'those in travail, suffering and captivity, and for their salvation,' and thinking of me cut off from them, living so strange a life in a Mahommedan family."

After this the days passed quietly enough. The weather turned hot, and all Akbar's family slept under the eaves in the yard, but I moved into their room, the door of which was kept shut. The trees budded, the acacia flowered and the nicest time of year set in, the full spring tide in Turkestan. The nights were warm and the air full of the fragrance of the flowering trees.

The younger women, and more particularly Kamar-Dján, set themselves to dig a deep hole in the yard, and dragged in some great thick logs. "We are going to give you something very nice," they explained to me. Then over the top of the pit they had dug they fixed a huge cauldron that would take a dozen buckets of water. Into this they poured wheat, linseed oil, flour and a few well-washed cobblestones. They lit a fierce fire underneath, and stirred unceasingly with special wooden shovels. "This must go on boiling all day and all night," they explained to me. I, too, spent the whole night in the yard, as it was nice to lie in the open air near the big bonfire, while the women took it in turns to sleep and to stir. The result of all this effort was to produce a thick sweet mass like treacle, very pleasing to the children, who had not had any sweets for a long time, since sugar had by now gone quite out of use. The Sarts in the villages make this stuff every spring.

About ten the next morning I was suddenly disturbed by wild cries, howls and lamentations. All the women were weeping and wailing and the little girls crying and yelling. This startled and upset me, as I thought something dreadful must have happened, yet I dared not leave my shelter. The noise lasted about half an hour and then stopped suddenly, and all was quiet. A little later Tahta-Dján came and explained to me that this was a requiem for a child which had died a year ago. I heard afterwards that the Sarts who lived near my house in the country had honoured me with just such a requiem when they thought I had been killed. But afterwards an old Sart fortune-teller, after doing her mysteries with some round pebbles, told them that the requiem was quite unnecessary, as I was not only alive but not very far away and living not with Russians but with Sarts. The howling of the women was so intense and the sobbing so real and acted so much on the nerves that my wife, who was present at the requiem and knew perfectly well that I was alive, could not restrain herself, and was carried away by her emotion and burst into hysterical weeping.

When spring came in Yuldash's domestic bliss went out. Tahta-Dján began it all. One day at our usual scanty lunch, consisting of the inevitable vegetable soup and rolls, she suddenly leapt up and, without even waiting to put on her *parandja* and *chimbet*, dashed out to the gate to run round to the *kazi* to demand a divorce. Yuldash sprang up, bolted the gate in front of her, caught her by the arm and made her return to the table in spite of her opposition. She refused to eat anything, but all the time kept nagging at everybody, irritating them to the quick, until they all jumped up and shouted back at her. This made her worse than ever, and she replied by shrieking the wildest abuse at them until the whole place was in an uproar. Suddenly

Tahta-Dján seemed to go quite mad : she flung herself upon the most innocent, gentle, harmless woman in the place, Akbar's first wife, and seized her by the hair, her lips drawn back and her eyes blazing like those of a wild beast, the jaws open as though to bite the unfortunate woman, who shrank back in terror. This was more than Akbar could bear, and with a sudden energetic movement he knocked the raging virago down and gave her a vigorous kick. I was afraid something even worse might happen, and took Tahta-Dján away to my room, near which this wild scene had taken place. She had hardly taken breath when she tried to dash out again, but I barred her road and begged her to sit still and calm herself or something terrible would happen.

" This isn't your business, *taxir !* " she cried, and dashed out before I could stop her. The others crowded round her at once, when she said something which drove them into a frenzy. Yuldash in a fury picked up a heavy iron bar and dashed at her to smash her skull. Murder seemed inevitable, when Kamar-Djan flung herself between them and seized his arm, while I took off the screaming woman by force to my room, where I locked her in. Yuldash started to break down the door with his iron bar, but I called to him sternly to stop ; he obeyed at once and went away. It was no easy job to deal with Tahta-Dján. She frantically struggled to jump out of the window, but I was able to stop her and force her down to the floor ; then I poured a big mug of cold water over her head and succeeded in forcing her by threats to drink some. This steadied her a little, though it was a long time before she was really quiet. Her teeth chattered, her whole body shivered as in a fever and her eyes glittered like those of a mad woman. It was not for another two

hours that she calmed down. Then, making sure that
Akbar and Yuldash had cooled too, I let her out. A temporary peace reigned. Yuldash told me afterwards that
Tahta-Djǎn in a frenzy of rage wanted to go not to the
kazi but to the *aksakal* to report that there was a Russian
hiding in the house.

Not long after that it was Kamar-Djǎn's turn to make a
fool of herself. Once more she began to make scenes with
her husband, threatening to insist on a divorce if her demands
were not satisfied. Yuldash took the part of his beloved
wife. He stopped having his meals with his father, and
began to demand money from him to buy his wife a costume.
The wretched old man came to me in despair, declaring
that Yuldash and his wife were plotting to poison him,
that Kamar-Djǎn had long ago told all her own friends that
they had a Russian hiding in the house, who had given her
a hundred roubles to say nothing about it. The next morning
Kamar-Djǎn went out early without telling anyone where
she was going, and Yuldash was distracted. She did not
come back for a couple of hours, and then said quite definitely
that unless her demands were satisfied she would go straight
to the Soviet authorities and tell them that Akbar was
hiding a Russian.

I offered Akbar the money to satisfy her demands.

" *Taxir,*" he said mournfully, " to-day it is quite impossible to buy what she wants, and besides, if I did she
would want double as much to-morrow. And then all the
other women would begin to ask. No, you'll have to go
away."

Needless to say, I saw that quite clearly myself, but the
question was, Where ?

CHAPTER VI.   HOME LIFE AMONG THE
SARTS AND KIRGHIZ.

THE domestic life of the Central Asiatic peoples is very little known to Europeans, for few have had the opportunity of observing at close quarters the family life of the Moslems, so jealously screened from outside eyes. Quite apart from my prolonged stay with a Sart family already described, I have had many an opportunity of seeing their intimate affairs during my numerous wanderings in Turkestan and the Kirghiz steppe, and so I venture to interrupt the thread of my story with an account of some of what I have seen.

Not Europeans only but even Russians who live in the towns of Turkestan are inclined to look upon the women-folk among the Sarts, Kirghiz and Turcomans, and the women of Khiva, Bokhara and Kashgar, as nothing more than slaves completely subject to the caprice of their lords and masters, sitting all their life in harems. They think that the natives treat their wives like cattle, that in these lands there is a regular slave trade in women, and they even quote cases where girls have been sold.

This view is entirely wrong. In order to understand the position of women in the East, and here I am speaking of Turkestan, it is first necessary entirely to disabuse the mind of our ordinary European's ideas about marriage. In these countries the very institution of marriage is totally different

79

from ours, which has grown up and been elaborated under the influence of Christian ideals, according to which marriage is not looked upon as an ordinary civil contract but as a sacred mystery, a bond sanctioned by the Church. In the language of the Uzbeg Turki, in the Kirghiz, Kashgar and Tartar dialects and the allied idioms, there is no word conveying our idea of ' to marry.' They can only say ' to take a woman.' Neither is there any true equivalent to the word ' to love '; there is only the paraphrase *yakshi karamyn*, literally, I look favourably upon, that is to say, I love. The verb *karauga* means to look, to observe, to keep, to control.

The family life of the settled population—that is the Sarts on the one hand, and of the nomads, that is the Kirghiz and the Turcomans, on the other—is totally different and so consequently is the position of their women-folk. Let us first consider the Sarts.

The Sarts take their women and get rid of them as lightly as we dismiss a servant. The payment made by the bridegroom to the parents of the bride—that is, the *kalym*—varies according to the position of the parents, her youth and beauty ; it is higher for a girl and less for a woman. In the latter case it may be a purely nominal amount, merely four or five roubles. They regard the woman as a servant, a convenient sort of thing to have about the house, and that is all. Naturally sometimes human feelings assert themselves : devotion, love, children may cement the bond, but, generally speaking, the attitude of the Sarts towards marriage is just the same as towards any other civil contract. True, the bargain is concluded with the blessing of the spiritual authority, the mullah, but this is a pure formality. Any good Mussulman begins everything with a prayer, whether it is slaughtering a sheep, felling a tree, beginning to harvest his rice, bringing in the grapes, buying a house or selling a horse. Consequently upon this attitude towards marriage, a Sart woman regards her position relative to her husband as that of a servant. Often enough she will indulge in petty thieving at his expense, secretly selling domestic things or provisions to make a hidden store of money. Divorce, as we have seen, is the simplest thing in the world. If a Sart woman is not satisfied with her husband, if he treats her badly, does not feed her properly, or does not give her sufficient clothing or neglects her, she simply goes to the *kazi*, asks for a divorce and gets it easily. Often enough a woman will get a divorce because she has not had new clothes for a feast day. The only restraint upon it is the purely material question, how she will get her keep afterwards. A woman will move from one husband to another just the same way as a servant in Europe, provided there is a demand for her.

A divorce is no obstacle to remarriage on either side and further divorce, though after having divorced her seven times a man may not remarry the same woman. Remarriage is also forbidden if at the occasion of the divorce the husband repeats a certain formula, completely banishing her on his oath for ever. Still, the accommodating law provides a loophole in both these cases. All that is necessary is for the divorced woman in the meantime to have married another man, even if only for a single day, or merely gone off to another man and the original husband satisfied himself of the truth with his own eyes. Then he may begin all over again from the beginning and go on marrying, divorcing and remarrying the original wife.

Harems, in the sense in which Europeans associated with

the word, as they used to exist in Turkey and Egypt, were known in Turkestan only with the khans, emirs and high court officials. Rich Sarts often marry young girls for a time and then pass them on to some poor relation or employee. But all this is done in a perfectly correct manner and all formalities are strictly observed—that is to say, with the blessing by the mullah and the indispensable invitation to *palau* and tea afterwards. Neither law, religion nor custom put any restraint upon these short-term marriages. The later Emir of Bokhara employed a whole staff of women whose duty it was to find brides for him ; they ransacked the place for pretty young girls of thirteen or fourteen years for him. After a few days of wedded bliss this exalted personage transferred their charms in due order to his officials and courtiers.

Such manners and customs as these hardly encourage the growth of tender and romantic feelings. The poetry of the Sarts, as would be expected, is very poor, and this matter-of-fact people have but few songs. They are capable only of a kind of coarse sensitiveness which completely dulls the more elevated æsthetic feelings. This physical sensitiveness leads in turn to an extraordinary laxity of morals. The strength and sanctity of the marriage bond depends entirely upon the degree of jealousy on the part of the husband, who entrusts the custody of his honour to purely material considerations.

The Kirghiz, on the other hand, are a poetic race. They love music and song, and are fond of improvising. A well-known Russian writer and poet, V. Krestovsky, some years ago published a book of charming verse under the title ' Songs of Spain.' As a matter of fact, these were translated not from the Spanish but from the Kirghiz. They were collected in Western Siberia and translated for Krestovsky by an educated Kirghiz, Cholkan Valykhanoff.

In our part of the world there was one very strange custom. It so happened that there was always a surplus of unmarried girls among the Kazan Tartars and in Persia. Often enough in those districts some enterprising and highly respectable mullah would organise a party of brides and take them to Turkestan to the Kirghiz or Turcomans, where the bride's price or *kalym* was very high, sometimes reaching really large sums. It was easy to get them married there in return for a very substantial *kalym*, part of which went to the bride's parents and part to the mullah as a form of commission. At one time this was regarded as a genuine slave trade, and there was a regular hue and cry about it in the press. But it cannot be called a slave trade, for if the girl was dissatisfied with her domestic life she had only to go to the mullah for protection, and he would divorce her so that she could marry another man. As a matter of fact, the position of Sart women was in many respects better than that of Russian peasant women, who until quite modern times was a creature almost without rights; divorce was quite out of her reach; her husband could treat her as cruelly as he liked; he could flog her to death, and still she was quite unable to leave him. Some time before the revolution the hardness of the peasant woman's position was recognised by the authorities and relief was granted to her; she could leave her husband, live away from him and receive her own independent passport.

Among the Kirghiz of the steppe there is a very remarkable game which the most determined efforts of the Moslem clergy have been unable to suppress. It is played as follows. All the young folk in the community mount their horses;

the fastest is given to the prettiest girl, together with a good thick whip. They then start galloping like mad. The game is for the young men to catch the girl and give her a kiss, while she gallops as fast as she can to escape, and, what is more, defends herself with her whip, which is heavy enough to break a man's arm or even crack his skull. Is it necessary to add that the victory does not go necessarily to the man with the stoutest heart or swiftest horse ?

Among the nomads of Turkestan, the Kirghiz and the Turcomans, the position of the women is totally different. It has remained unaltered through the ages as it was in antiquity, and Islam has not affected it. The *kalym* paid for a bride is very high, sometimes running to hundreds and even thousands of roubles, sometimes paid in instalments spread over a great many years, as was the case in the days of the Old Testament. As a rule the betrothal takes place when bride and bridegroom are still in the cradle, and the payment of the sum agreed for the *kalym* begins. The consent of the betrothed couple, of course, does not arise.

A Kirghiz girl enjoys the most complete liberty up to her marriage. She is under no restraint. She may love whom she will and have as many romances as she likes. Not only is her behaviour not discussed by the public opinion of the *aul* or community, but it is considered unpardonable to betray a girl's secrets or discuss her behaviour. The prospective bridegroom has no claim upon the favours of his fiancée ; his turn will come in due course ; the number of her lovers, in fact, testifies to her charms ; for what is the use of a girl that nobody wants ? Even the appearance of a baby does not detract from her value. Children are valuable, and every sensible man wants them. The only discussion that can arise is about the destination of an infant, whether it shall belong to the clan of its mother or go with her to the clan of the bridegroom.

When a Kirghiz girl is married she becomes not only the property of her own husband and his family, but also belongs to his clan, which she cannot leave. The clan system is very strongly rooted among the Kirghiz. By it, after the death of a husband, or even of a fiancé, the widow does not become free ; she is subject to the law of succession and passes to the brother or other male relative of the husband —that is to say, to his legal successor, whose age, moreover, does not come into question. Once in the Turgai steppe I was invited to a very elaborate wedding. A girl of two-and-twenty, daughter of a Kirghiz friend of mine, was being married to a nine-year-old boy who inherited her from his elder brother, who had recently died. The *kalym* had been fully paid up, and the relatives of the late bridegroom did not want to pay it back. The poor girl was sobbing bitterly at the idea of having a nine-year-old child for a husband. Meanwhile he, in his Sunday best, was playing happily, utterly unconscious of the importance of the events taking place around him.

As born cattle-breeders the Kirghiz attach great importance to blood, not only in beasts but in man. One Kirghiz friend of mine used to complain of the stupidity of his young son, and was genuinely surprised where he could have inherited it from. " His mother was of very good stock," he said, forgetting that he, too, could transmit moral qualities to his son. Another time a rich Kirghiz whom I knew well had no children. He often used to visit a Russian friend of mine who had lovely children, two boys and a girl. The Kirghiz often used to ride over with his wife, who could not tear her eyes off the little Russian children, who completely won her heart. The result was that one day the Kirghiz invited my Russian friend to stay a few days with him in the *aul*. " I shall be going away for a short time," he said, " to another *aul*. My wife desperately wants to have such splendid children as yours."

In spite of her subordination to her husband, a Kirghiz woman plays a very important part in the family life, especially the eldest wife. Without her consent and counsel, which is usually given secretly, no important decision is made. She enjoys the respect not only of her husband's family but sometimes throughout the clan or even district. A famous example of the influential position a woman may command among this people is afforded by Kurban Djàn Datkha, the ' Empress of the Alai,' who died comparatively recently. In the 'seventies of the last century she was the head of the Kipchaks or Mountain Kirghiz of the Alai and Pamir. Under her rule these mountain nomads put up a very stout resistance to General Skobeleff, the famous conqueror of Ferghaná. It was only thanks to the superiority of modern arms and methods that the Russian general secured the victory. Afterwards her sons long held official posts under the Russian Government as heads of *volosts* or districts. At the beginning of the present century Kurban Djàn Datkha, at that time over ninety years of age, received as a gift from the Tsar Nicolas II. a magnificent diamond necklace which must have cost tens of thousands of roubles.

Another ' *Datkha*,' a Turcoman woman, is, I believe, still living. She was the head of the Turcomans in the Transcaspian Province. She did not hold any official post, nor was ever elected by anyone, but enjoyed immense popularity and extraordinary influence among all the Turcomans.

Thanks to her, the Turcomans kept up a prolonged resistance to the Bolshevik invasion and introduction of Communist principles.

In the history of the Turki peoples such women of marked personality have played a very important part. There is not the slightest reason to cast suspicion upon the story of Herodotus about the Queen of the Massagetæ, Tomyris, who beat the conqueror of Asia, the Persian Emperor Cyrus himself. Historians regard the whole story as a myth, but it fits in perfectly well with everything we know about these nomad peoples of Asia. There is no doubt, as Professor Mischenko thinks, that the Scythian tribe of Massagetæ were nothing more nor less than the ancestors of the Kirghiz of to-day in the Turgai Province, where the name survives in the River Massagatka and the mountain Mussagat.

But for our great superiority in armament, who knows but that our great hero General Skobeleff would have met the fate of Cyrus. The name of Tomyris, like other Scythian names, is of Turki origin. This name, Tomyris, means ' crush iron ' or ' bend iron,' from *temir*, iron ; and recalls another famous warrior out of Asia, Temir-leng, Temir the Lame, or Tamerlane, a remote descendant of his famous compatriot Tomyris. If one carefully reads Herodotus's account of the Amazons and their origin, the inevitable conclusion is that these Amazons were the wives of just the same Turki nomads whose menfolk had gone off on some military expedition to some remote district. The first syllable of their very name is a Turki word, conveying the idea of woman. In the same way his remarkable description of the Scythians, their manners and customs, does not leave any room for doubt that he was describing the ancestors of that same people which is to-day called Kirghiz, and from the most remote dawn of antiquity has inhabited the steppes of Southern Russian and Western Siberia.

From the above sketch of the position of women among the peoples of Turkestan, which has endured for thousands of years, it will be seen that polygamy is so deeply rooted in the customs of the peoples and the nature of the family that their women have obviously entirely lost any feeling of jealousy, while on the other hand the feeling of envy of each other is very acute. They look upon it as entirely natural that their husband should spread his love among several women, but that one of them should receive a more beautiful kerchief or finer dress is more than they can stand.

It is characteristic that the legislation of the Soviet Government dealing with marriage, as in every other department, contains a mass of inconsistencies. By their edicts about marriage and divorce the Communists have decreed the knell of family life among their Christian subjects, but they dared not touch the marriage rights and polygamy of their Mahommedan subjects. And undoubtedly in their attitude of denial of all religion they have divided their subjects into two categories by a purely religious characteristic. The Christians may change their wives as often as they like, provided they do not have more than one at a time, while the Mahommedans are subject to no restrictions at all.

To be logical, these Marxian adepts ought to remove these inconsistencies and equalise the rights of the two groups, especially as they have removed not only the religious and moral foundations of the institute of marriage but also its æsthetic basis.

After which digression about the domestic life of the tribes among whom I have spent so many years, I must return to the story of my wanderings.

IT was obvious that I must leave Akbar's home as soon as possible. After talking it over with him, I decided to go back to my Kirghiz friend Yakshi Bai, take his advice again and find another refuge. I should have to do the journey at night, of course, but even then it would be very dangerous, as I had to cross the river by the bridge, where there was always a Bolshevik guard on duty to stop and interrogate anyone who crossed over. True, if I went late he might be asleep ; but, on the other hand, if he did happen to be on the look-out, he would be more than ever likely to stop me, as the natives never ride about late at night. If I went. earlier, when there was plenty of traffic on the road, the guard would be all the more alert and I might easily attract his attention. After some hesitation I chose the middle course. About ten one evening I mounted Akbar's horse, and his youngest son took up his place behind me. His business was to bring the horse back again. Besides, it looked more natural, for the natives often ride two on a horse, though Russians never do, and I intended to pass as a native. I am a good weight, over fourteen stone, so when the boy's extra five or six stone was added, the poor horse began to stumble, but he quickly pulled himself together and stepped out bravely. I wore a shooting-jacket, with high boots, a Sart's *halat* on top and a Sart fur cap. At a distance I easily passed for a native ; at close quarters anyone could tell from my face that I was Russian. To dress completely as a Sart would have been dangerous, as though I was definitely trying to disguise my nationality. A mere *halat* would not arouse suspicion, as Russians often wear them instead of an overcoat on grounds of economy.

When we rode up to the bridge the boy quietly slipped off the saddle and followed on foot, hiding himself in the shadow of the trees and watching to see what happened to me. Of course the poor little chap was quite right ; why should he be dragged into my risks and dangers ?

The Red guard, exhausted with his efforts of the day, had relaxed and was enjoying a game of cards. He paid no attention to the solitary horseman who slowly rode across the bridge and turned off sharply into the steppe on the far side.

When we were close to Yakshi Bai's farm I pulled up in the shadow of the trees and sent the boy on to find out the lay of the land. I had to wait a long time. At last the little chap came back in a terrible fright. He said that Yakshi Bai was lying ill and there were Red cavalry in the yard who had come to help themselves to forage. It was too dangerous to stop there.

The boy took me farther into the steppe to another rich Kirghiz, a friend of Akbar. The night was very hot ; there was a vivid flash of lightning, followed by a violent storm. The Kirghiz received me in the most friendly way. I explained that I was a surveyor working on the steppe overtaken by the storm, and asked to be allowed to take shelter with him and stay the night. He arranged a couch under a sort of verandah opening out directly upon the steppe. The storm became more violent, and the horizon was illuminated by almost continuous flashes and the thunder was crashing unceasingly. In Turkestan storms are not rare in the spring, but they are usually quickly over. This one did not bother me, for my head was entirely occupied by the problem of my next move and immediate future. My position was uncomfortable. Here was I, in an absolutely exposed place, with Red guards and commissars on every side. I had very little money left and no means of transport at all. My trifling but indispensable luggage was left behind at Akbar's; it was not much, only a native *kurdjum* or pair of saddle-bags, but it was my all. What with the unceasing noise of the storm and the gnawing anxiety I did not sleep much that night.

Early next morning I heard my host's voice and that of some unknown man asking him who was this guest of his.

" It is a surveyor; he is working in the steppe near here," replied my host.

There was silence. Then after a moment or two I heard the voice of a man reading the Koran aloud, and noticed that the Arabic words were pronounced in a strange accent. It was evident that the reader was not a native. The reading lasted a long time, and I guessed that they were praying for the recovery of someone sick.

I pretended to be asleep, and waited for the mullah to finish his reading and go. It was not till it was quite quiet that I ventured to have a peep, and, seeing nobody, I stood up. I looked round and saw extending away into the distance fields of clover and other crops on a hummocky plain studded with native farmsteads, marked by clumps of lofty poplars.

My host's farm consisted of a courtyard and a few small dark rooms in it, with a broad verandah on the outside. It was exposed on every side. The Kirghiz are accustomed

to the expanse and freedon of the steppe, and even when
they adopt a settled mode of life they keep the ancient
customs and usage of their nomad days and build their
homes in open places.

My host brought me a roll and some milk and asked me
where I was working, where I lived previously and so on.
I told him that I had surveyed that district before.

" Why, yes ! I remember," he said. " I remember getting
the samovar ready for you."

Then I remembered him. Some five years previously he
and three others had rented a piece of land from me for
growing cotton. Luckily, my beard had grown and completely altered my appearance. Still, it was very odd that
he did not know me, as the Kirghiz have a wonderful memory
for faces and can often recognise people whom they have
seen only once and that many years ago.

It was a beautiful day, fine, bright and sunny. All
around was green ; even the roofs of the buildings were
covered with green grass, dotted with scarlet poppies.
After my long confinement what a delight it was to wander
freely about the place and to fling myself on to the grass
alongside the canal ; it was perfect bliss to revel in the
beauty of nature, in the freedom of movement, and to drink
in the clear pure air, but the pleasure was marred by the
consciousness of the danger of my position and the uncertainty of my immediate future.

About mid-day, when I was sitting on the bank of the
canal pondering various schemes, wondering where and
how to make my way, a thin swarthy man with an aquiline
nose came up to me. He was dressed like a Sart, but had a
red fez on his head. He greeted me civilly, sat down and
began to talk about himself.

" I am a mullah," he explained. " I am reading prayers
for the recovery of our host's little boy ; he has been ill for
a long time, but is much better now. I am not a Sart," he
continued, " but an Arab. I was taken prisoner with a
lot of others by General Yudenich at the capture of Erzerum
and sent off to Siberia. It is very cold there, and I managed
to get away through the Kirghiz steppe and came to Turkestan. Here the Bolsheviks took me and sent me to the
front against General Dutoff, but I got away from there,
and now, you see, I am wandering about among the Sarts
and the Kirghiz. They treat me very respectfully here
because of my spiritual capacity and learning, and always
receive me well and pay me for the prayers I read. I see,"
he went on, " that you are having just as bad a time as all
decent educated folk. Come away into the mountains with
me ; there we will find food and shelter ; we shall be out
of danger and be able to live comfortably among the Kirghiz."

" No," I answered him, " I am afraid I cannot do that.
I have some work to do and I cannot abandon it."

" It is not good to live among these cruel brutes; they
are worse than dogs. Don't serve the Bolsheviks," he went
on earnestly. " Listen to me and let's be off into the
mountains. . . ."

I could not accept his suggestion, tempting as it was. I
could not give up contact with my friends in the town,
as I kept in touch with them, though with the greatest
difficulty and caution, occasionally getting news through of
the position there, nor could I abandon my luggage at
Akbar's. Besides, a wandering life like that did not fit in
with my plans. My main idea, which really hardly seemed
to be practical, was to make my way through to Chinese
Turkestan, to Kashgar, where the old Russian consulate was

still in existence, where there was a British Consul-General, and communications, remote but still communications, with the civilised world.

Towards the evening our host told us he was going off to his flocks in the mountains and there would be only women-folk left in the house. This was a polite hint that we could not spend another night there. Naturally he had guessed that I was not a surveyor but really in hiding from the Soviet authorities.

So the Arab and I went off to hunt for some place where we could spend the night. First we came to the house of a Kirghiz who had been rich but was now completely skinned by the Bolsheviks. The commissars had taken away all his cattle and all his stocks of corn and fodder. When we explained the situation to him he answered mournfully—

"The Bolsheviks have robbed me of all my property; if they find out that I have given shelter to two Whites they'll take my life into the bargain and my family's too."

Then we called on a Kirghiz I had known, but before we reached the door a relative of his came out and recognising me at once was in a great state of alarm.

"For God's sake, *taxir*, . . . aren't you frightened to go walking about openly when the Bolsheviks are all looking for you? You can't stop with us. Commissars and Red guards from the Russian village keep coming here."

We had to move on.

The Arab said philosophically, "If we cannot find shelter among the rich, let us have a try among the poor," so off we went to an acquaintance of his, a poor Kirghiz who lived by the road.

"I will take you in gladly," he said. "Although I live right on the roadside where there are hundreds of commissars always riding along, I am too poor for them to pay any attention to me."

He gave us rolls and eggs and played the balalaika to us. His entire home consisted of a verandah alongside a small dark hut. But I slept soundly and undisturbed through the night, though in the morning the merest chance saved me.

After breakfast I was standing having a look round when suddenly I caught sight of my host running towards me across a field, silently, but frantically waving his arms. I looked up the road, and there, to my horror, I saw a cart with a pair of horses being driven at a rapid pace by a couple of men dressed from head to foot in black leather, at that time the full-dress uniform of Bolshevik commissars. Ten mounted Red guards followed at a smart trot. In a flash I sprang behind the upright that supported the verandah and the whole party drove swiftly past without having noticed me. I crept into the hut, where my host came in very perturbed.

"They were commissars from the Che-Ka," he said. "A neighbour of mine told me and I came hurrying to warn you, but was not in time. You sit and wait here while I go and have a good look round. While I am away don't go outside; it is terribly dangerous."

My position was desperate, and really it seemed that there was no way of escape.

A Sart I knew named Devlet dwelt near-by, a very resourceful fellow, and he would surely be able to find me a hiding-place, but I did not know where he lived. The only way to find him was to go to the bazaar and ask for him in some *chai-khané* or tea-shop.

When my host came back with the news that the commissars had driven off into the villages and would not come back by the same road, I suddenly decided to go to the bazaar myself and look for Devlet at any risk. I gave my host a little money, which I had the greatest difficulty in persuading him to accept in spite of his poverty, said good-bye to him and went off towards the village. The Arab kept me company as far as the outskirts of the village, pressed me warmly by the hand in farewell and followed me with his gaze until I disappeared round a bend in the road.

When I arrived in the village I confidently went to the biggest tea-shop. As I went in a young Sart sitting there stood up and came straight towards me. " Now I'm for it," I thought. " This is an agent of the Che-Ka ; he'll interrogate me and then call up the guard."

He came straight to me and asked—

" Why did you come here ? "

" My work is here ; I am making a survey of this neighbourhood," I answered. " I am looking for a Sart named Devlet."

" Oh, the contractor. I suppose you want him to supply provisions for your men," he said in a loud voice so that all the Sarts sitting round could hear. " Sit down and wait in this back room and I will send for Devlet. It is market-day and he is sure to be in the bazaar."

He took me into a snug little room at the back over the terrace ; there was nobody there, and he said to me—

" You can't think how glad I am to see you alive and well, *taxir !* "

" But who are you ? " I asked him.

" Of course you don't know me," he answered, " but I know you well. I am a nephew of Said Akram, whom you know well."

My new friend insisted on giving me tea and rolls, and did everything in his power to show how glad he was to see me and to make me comfortable.

Devlet came in a little later, and in his usual business-like way asked me if I were not in need of money.

" How much do you need ? I'll get it for you," he said.

" I do want some money, but most of all it is a hiding-place that I want," I answered.

" Good ! We'll arrange that. Don't you worry ! The owner of the tea-shop is a good fellow ; he'll hide you, and to-morrow I'll find a place where you'll be out of danger."

I sat in that little room until quite late that evening, and my young friend refused to leave me. Occasionally a Sart or two would come into the room, and twice some Russian peasants came in, but we sat quietly in the corner and no one paid any attention to us. After a supper of an excellent *palau* the owner of the tea-shop took me out into the court-yard, opened a shed where he stored clover and told me not to worry, as I could sleep there undisturbed. For further safety's sake he locked the door and put the key in his pocket.

I lay down on a bundle of lucerne and slept the sleep of the just. Next morning I was aroused by the cheerful twittering of a swallow. The bird, sitting on the door, which did not reach the ceiling, was busily pouring forth its not particularly musical though pleasant little song. It had built its nest under the ceiling, and many a time during the long dull day that I spent shut up in that hot shed the little bird flew in, perched on the door and cheered me up with its twitter. I could not help feeling that it was there for the purpose of helping me to bear my troubles, as it seemed to say : " Don't give way ! Don't despair ! You'll

come out all right!" It definitely did help me, as I lay
listening to its soothing, caressing little song. And I needed
its help, for this was one of the most depressing, blackest,
most hopeless days of my life, sitting there, locked in a
miserable shed, with no hope nor ideas of the future, but just
a blank in front of me. . . .

Another living creature came, but this was a crafty and
pitiless robber. Silently, swiftly, with astonishing agility a
weasel climbed up the vertical wall, winding its way like a
snake along the ceiling of boards and thin slates towards
the swallow's nest. But the parents had built their little
home so artfully that it was absolutely inaccessible even to
this agile little pirate. After hunting over all the ceiling
trying to find a way into the nest, the weasel climbed down
the wall again and disappeared.

Late at night, when everybody had gone to bed, the
owner of the tea-shop came with Devlet and Said Akram's
nephew, and they took me off to the new hiding-place chosen
for me. We walked a good long time, then entered a dark
avenue of poplars and came to a gate which was opened
by a Sart who was waiting for us. It was a very dark night,
and I followed him feeling my way, apparently on to some
sort of verandah, where he said to me: "Here you are.
You can lie down and sleep here, and I will lock the gate
and go to the mill." There was nothing else to do, so I felt
with my hands for the rugs on the floor and went to sleep.

I dreamt of a great victory of the Whites, of the smashing
of the Bolsheviks, the triumphal march of the victorious
army on full parade; I could hear the shouts of joy while
the band played the last scenes from Glinka's opera, 'His
Life for the Tsar.' And when I awoke to reality, the sound
of music and of bells continued. I opened my eyes and

peeped out : the great wheel of the mill was squeaking and creaking as it turned, and that was the triumphal march I had heard !

The mill was situated in a very secluded spot, surrounded on three sides by irrigation canals, open only on the fourth, where was the approach through the shady avenue of poplars. Huge willows were growing all round, massive elms and quantities of white acacias.

Adjoining the mill was a small yard with a small dark hut and a terrace in front of it, where I now transferred myself. The yard communicated with the mill only by a small opening through which a full-grown man could hardly pass, and it was kept closed by a special shutter. A very small low doorway, through which one had to crawl, led out from the yard to the banks of a big canal. When it was dark I could go out this way for a stroll along the banks of the canal or in the fields.

Compared with my former den, this was luxury, as I could walk about the yard even in the daytime, could revel in the sunlight and the pure air, have a good wash in the canal, watch the birds on the trees and read at my ease. On one of the big elms there was an oriole's nest, and several little red grosbeaks (*Carpodacus rubicilla*) enlivened the belt of willows. Our Turkestan dove (*Peristera cambayensis*) flew down into the little courtyard together with a few white wagtails. Now at last I could live again, breathe comparatively freely, and enjoy the light and the sights of nature around me.

Devlet brought me my luggage before very long, together with an Easter cake and some red Easter eggs from Tashkend, better late than never, and some newspapers and letters. The Bolshevik papers were full of alarms. Admiral Kolchak's army was already approaching the Urals. The letters from my friends told me that Ataman Dutoff's Cossacks were not far from Kazalinsk. The Soviet commissars in Turkestan were drowning their fright in drink. It really looked as though my dream might come true. All this combined to encourage me and inspire me once more with hope and fortitude.

Sometimes the owner of the tea-shop would come and pay me a visit in the evenings and bring me the latest news and gossip which he learnt from the Sarts and Kirghiz, and tell me about the guerilla fighting against the Bolsheviks in Ferghaná and about the Kirghiz rising in the valley of the Chotkal. One day Devlet came to say that a certain B. wanted to see me. I did not know him very well, but knew his reputation as a good honest man. The next night he arrived, coming secretly from the mill through the little doorway. He was the first Russian I had seen since I had left Tashkend. He told me all the latest happenings, and offered his services to help me in any way he could.

" I did not take any action against the Bolsheviks, and so consider it a moral duty to help those who staked their lives in the struggle with them," he said.

We discussed the position in detail, and finally decided that he would help me to get away into the mountains to some secluded spot in the valley of one of the tributaries of the Chotkal, where I could live till the winter. He said he would get me the necessary documents of identity from the Soviet Government, made out in a false name, so that I could get past the Bolshevik guards and sentries.

Although the Communists pestered the life out of their subjects by their red tape, countless permits, certificates, passports and mandates, and no one could leave a town or

go to any village or even out on to the main road without
a document, the Bolsheviks are so stupid, uneducated and
corrupt that it was not difficult to arrange for any paper
in a false name. A good example of their officials was
afforded by the Chief of the Police of the town of Tashkend,
the Chief of the *Okhrana*, as they called him, the Guardian
Angel of the town, as he called himself, a Lett named Tsirul.
He was formerly a baker, could scarcely read and write,
and had been condemned to twelve years' penal servitude
in the old days for robbery with violence and homicide and
then released by Kerensky. Tsirul did not hesitate to do
his executions with his own hand in his own office ; even
his own Communist comrades, if he considered it necessary
in his own interests to have them removed. This was the
gentleman from whom my friend arranged to secure a
' mandate ' for me to go into the mountains—of course,
under an assumed name. In the document issued by the
Che-Ka it was stated that I had reported personally to
receive it.

I spent three weeks in my secluded little mill, and when
everything was ready B. came for me late one night with
a couple of saddle horses. I went out of the little gate,
across the canal and rode away secretly from them all. I
heard afterwards that when the miller brought my breakfast next morning he was astonished to find me flown. The
door was locked and the key in his pocket. Terrified at my
disappearance he had run round to Devlet to tell him that
his guest had gone. Devlet reassured him : I had not been
spirited away by the Bolsheviks, but had quietly disappeared
without leaving a trace, which was quite in order.

This secret departure was absolutely necessary. I had
already lived too long in the locality, and it was quite time

that I hid myself so completely that even well-disposed people would not know where I was, so I covered up my tracks and simply disappeared. By this time the Bolsheviks had given up looking for me here. They were bewildered. One of my friends had arranged for them to receive news from their own agents that I was hiding in Bokhara.

The second morning found me riding at the head of a caravan of seven camels loaded with bee-hives. I was dressed as a ' comrade ' in a shabby old soldier's coat, with a dirty shirt, and on my head a black leather cap, a repulsive form of head-dress to which the Communists are addicted. In my pocket was a Soviet passport in the name of Nikolai Ivanovich Novikoff, with a whole bundle of permits, certificates and mandates, giving me the right of riding into the mountains in charge of a caravan of bee-hives. Now I was a peaceful and loyal citizen of the Soviet Autonomous Republic of Turkestan. Wherever necessary I could produce to the guards and officials my legal documents with the seal of the sickle and hammer. Thus for me began a new life.

ONE thing caused me anxiety. The friends who had organised
my disguise considered that I should have difficulty in concealing my ' non-proletarian ' origin in spite of the beard
which I had let grow freely, as my face certainly did not
have anything like a ' proletarian ' look. I had learnt, too,
under interrogation, that these savage ' proletarians ' are
angered and irritated by the appearance of an educated man.
Later, during my wanderings in Semirechie, I was unable
to conceal the fact that I belonged to the educated classes.
Bolsheviks and Russian peasants and Kirghiz could all
scent out that I was not a ' proletarian,' and behaved
accordingly, their attitude being hostile or friendly and
respectful, as the case might be.

And so I rode away into the mountains, giving rein to my
fancy and meditations.

But in the very first village, right in the market-place,
the girths came loose, and it was necessary to unload the
camels and reload them. And all this took place, to my
great anxiety and impatience, in full view of the Red patrol
that was standing by. Two of them strolled up as though
to ask me questions, but I said sharply, " Don't come close
to the hives, comrades ; the bees might come out and sting
you badly." The Red soldiers withdrew hurriedly.

The day was sunny and very hot. That disgusting leather
cap was heated through by the sun's rays, and had no

ventilation. It seemed as though my head was in an oven. It became unendurable, and at times I felt that I was going to faint and fall off the horse. Many a time in happier days had I ridden along this same road in the very hottest weather and never felt any inconvenience when I had been wearing a topee or light felt hat.

On the road I met mounted Red guards and commissars in comfortable carriages splendidly horsed, all stolen, of course ; but our peaceful aspect aroused no suspicions, and the Bolsheviks did not want to make too near acquaintance with hives full of angry bees.

Spring was in full swing : everything was green, the birds were singing, the air was clean and clear, the sky dark blue without the trace of a cloud. As I rode along I came upon a curious spectacle, which I cannot describe as anything else than a sparrow's prize fight. At many points along the road were groups of these birds sitting in a circle on the road, while in the middle of the arena thus formed two cock sparrows were engaged in deadly conflict. The audience was obviously absorbed in the fight with intense interest. Even when my horse was on the verge of treading on them they would hardly fly away. In Turkestan we have the Indian sparrow (*Passer indicus*), which is somewhat different from the European species. I had never before seen or heard of these sparrow-fights conducted formally in the presence of an audience, although similar duels are known to occur with blackcock, and particularly in the case of the ruff (*Machetes pugnax*), which is notorious for its pugnacity.

Late at night we reached a river valley, where the camels could not go any farther, and we had to hire donkeys. We stopped on the banks of a mountain torrent, unloaded the camels and sent them back at once. I was left alone. Incautiously I lay down to sleep on the verandah of a half-ruined building that stood on the banks of the stream. During the night I was tortured by the stings of great black bugs (*Reduvius fedschenkianus*, Oshanin). These dreadful creatures are about an inch long, with a long sharp beak which they plunge into the skin, leaving a red spot which aches and burns like fire for a long time after. In the old days the khans of Turkestan used to put criminals into a deep pit crawling with these loathsome insects. It was into such a pit that the Emir Nasrullah threw two British officers, Colonel Stoddart and Captain Conolly, who went to Bokhara on a diplomatic mission in 1842. Their sufferings must have been terrible before they were pulled out and executed in public.

Next morning I walked up to the nearest mountain village ; its inhabitants were Tadjiks, descendants of the original Persian inhabitants of Turkestan, among whom I hoped to find an old friend, Osman, a companion of many an expedition in the neighbouring mountains, where we used to shoot *tauteke* or ibex (*Capra sibirica*), which formerly were very numerous in the district. The following morning we left early to go farther into the mountains. There began at once a steep and fatiguing˙ ascent, and then the road followed a valley full of fields green with clover and corn, interspersed with groves of walnut trees. On one side of the road were the shady gardens of the natives with their summer huts among them. The sweet briar was in full flower and the mulberries were ripe. I had a good feast on them. In the spring these mountain valleys are extraordinarily beautiful ; rains are frequent, and the air is pleasant and fresh but not really cold, even at night ; the green of the fields and trees is brilliant, and there is an abundance of wild flowers on every side. The sheer cliffs, where not covered with vegetation, have a reddish tinge, recalling the laterite of the tropics. The red tint of the soil harmonises with the green of the fields and forest, and the deep blue of the sky with the white fleecy clouds. The whole scene offers an enchanting picture of nature unspoilt, and this escape into the depths of the mountain country, away from communistic experiments, brought peace and consolation to my aching soul.

We crossed a deep ravine at the bottom of which a torrent tumbled over its bed strewn with boulders. Here the track came to an end, and it cost us a good deal of hard work before we could make a road through the stones passable for the donkeys, and then up the steep banks of the ravine, and no sooner were we out of that than we had to attack a stiff climb up a lofty mountain. Delightful flowers and interesting plants became more and more numerous. After crossing several gorges we rode into a dense dark forest, consisting of immense walnut trees, with crab apples, sloes, maples and iron-wood or nettle trees (*Celtis australis*) and hawthorn. This forest covered the entire flanks of the mountain and extended right down to a brook bubbling at the bottom. A very narrow path, half grown over, used nowadays only by wild animals, wound capriciously along the slopes, but always in the shade of the trees. Clearings and open spaces in the forest were covered with varied and delightful shrubs and other plants, and the whole scene produced the impression of a cultivated park-land.

It was pleasant and cool, and the air was saturated with the fragrant aroma of the wild flowers. We rode for some time along this path. Sometimes it took us into open spaces, sometimes through almost impenetrable thickets, sometimes along the edge of steep cliffs, while in places it was washed away by the rains and in others blockaded by the trunks of fallen giants, so that we had to clear a road for our laden donkeys. Then we descended into another deep ravine full of trees and shrubs, the flanks covered with briars with white and yellow fragrant blossom, the walls of white limestone, with a bubbling torrent below. We crossed the stream and laboriously climbed up the far side, where the path was washed away, and came to a small clearing in the shade of an immense walnut.

Osman promised to send me bread and other necessities, so I let him return with the donkeys and remained behind with my bee-hives. The locality was singularly beautiful and the vegetation exuberant. The brook bubbled busily below and the forest was full of interesting birds and plants. I had been here before on shooting expeditions for wild pig, but that had been in the autumn, when there was nothing like such a variety and quantity of plants and flowers, as the summer heat killed them all. It was dark before I started making my bed on the ground under the tree, and threatening clouds were coming up from the west. I broke off branches and cut grass and made myself a couch, so as not to be caught on the wet ground when the rain came. With a few branches, my overcoat and a little tarpaulin which I had with me I managed to fix up a sort of tent over the bed, and lay down for the night. Then the rain began to patter at first, but rapidly turned into a regular downpour. Roll after roll of thunder echoed among the rocks until it was one continuous roar, while the constant flashes of lightning lit up the fantastic picture of the storm in the forest. Down in the gorge the brook was roaring, the noise of waters growing louder and louder as the torrent overflowed its banks. The water streamed under my improvised tent and bed, and I was quickly drenched to the skin. The forest had really met me with a most inhospitable reception. About midnight the thunder died away, but the rain lasted until dawn. I slept fitfully, dropping off into an unconscious slumber for a few minutes at a time. In the morning I was aroused by the penetrating song of a nightingale. Our Central Asiatic bird (*Daulias hafizi*) is not such a finished songster as his European brother, with neither its length nor variety, but its voice is extraordinarily loud and penetrating. The morning was charming, clear and warm. The grass was wet through and so slippery that it was impossible to walk about on it, and it was only with the greatest difficulty, clinging to bushes and leaning on a broken branch I used as a stick, that I could make my way down the sides of the ravine to the brook to have a wash. The water was muddy, with broken branches swirling down, but half-way up the far side, under a briar in full flower, I found a delightful spring of pure fresh water. I built a rough shelter round it and fenced it in with stones and branches.

As I had not been able to lay in a store of dry firewood overnight I could not light a fire nor brew myself tea, as everything was sodden, so I spent the day drying my bedding and clothing in the sun.

It was not until the second evening that the ground was dry enough for me to be able to go for a walk and have a look round. In places, especially where there were crab apples and hawthorn, the forest was an almost impassable thicket, while in others there were delightful open spaces where stood an occasional huge walnut, affording a wide area of shade around. Farther down, among the rocks on the flanks near the brook, were almond trees, and higher up, near the top, where it was drier, on the steepest parts of the cliff, were pistachios with their broad, curious, leathery leaves and handsome bunches of the fruit, still unripe and green.

Beneath the trees, where there was thick deep shade, the ground was entirely covered with a soft, pale-green, so-called ' shooting grass ' ; it is low-growing, with fleshy stalk and pointed leaves. The fruit is a thin small pod, which, when ripe, splits open at the slightest touch with a crackling sound into several narrow strips, which soon shrivel up into a spiral and expel the seed like shot out of a gun. If you draw your hand across the grass you can hear a continuous crackling, and your hand feels a tickling as though of a gentle electric current. This interesting grass is one of the few which reacts mechanically to contact, and creates the impression that it is a live animal.

In some places there were sweet-smelling white tulips on long stems. Also two very interesting kinds of *Arum :* one, *Arum korolkovi*, has green flowers with a yellow pistil, which turns into red berries later in the season ; the other, *Eminium lehmanni*, is of a very unusual colour. The flower is entirely of a velvety dark purple, sometimes with a violet shade, so strange that the natives will not handle it, as they attribute all sorts of dangerous properties to it. Among the rocks along the brooks there grew quantities of ferns, including the maidenhair, which is a great rarity in Turkestan. Then there were the handsome clusters of *Eremurus*, with huge spikes of pale pink flowers : two species, *E. robustus* and *E. kaufmanni*. Both these noble flowers have been introduced from our mountains of Turkestan into the gardens of Europe, for I have admired their beauty at Hampton Court and in the windows of London florists.

An interesting shrub was a species of *Cotoneaster*, the hard white wood of which is excellent for walking-sticks and handles of tools and instruments. Then there was a special kind of honeysuckle, called *isa mussa* by the natives, which is highly prized for walking-sticks, especially by the mullahs. When the bark is peeled, a pretty pattern as though engraved shows up clearly on the hard, yellowish, ivory-like wood.

Balm, *Melissa officinalis*, was growing in abundance on every side, filling the air with its aroma of orange. I found this herb very useful, as by rubbing my face and hands with it I could work with the bees without using a net. It will also keep mosquitoes away, though I had little trouble from them, and I used the dried leaves as a flavouring. Rice boiled with *Melissa* leaves and raisins makes a very good pudding. I was interested in this forest as a naturalist, and I studied it also to see what it could give me in the way of food, of which my supplies were extremely scanty.

On the very top of the mountain, above the zone of trees, on the short Alpine turf, I found *Eremurus spectabilis*. The young leaves are edible and quite nice. There was another Turkestan plant, *Korolkovia severzovi*, with round fleshy bulbs, which make an excellent vegetable if well boiled. In one field at some distance from my camp was abundance of sorrel, very good for soup, and now ready for picking. Somewhat lower down grew a kind of rush (*Cyperus longus*), its bulbs very good seasoning, a very important thing when one is confined to a coarse and monotonous diet. In fact, in the case of absolute need, I could keep alive on roots and leaves, and I thanked Providence for having given me the opportunity of making the acquaintance of the resources of the country and learning to make use of the natural wealth of Turkestan.

Fruit was even more abundant. Lower down, among the trees and shrubs, there were vines, some of which were immense, with great thick stems, creeping over the trees and sometimes entirely covering them, at others stretching like garlands from one tree to another or creeping along the face of the cliff.

It took me several days to explore the whole forest and all the ravines in the neighbourhood, some of which were very interesting and picturesque. This particular type of forest, known as the Fruit Forest of Turkestan, is frequent in the mountains, especially of the Ferghaná province. I had no doubt that later in the year, in the summer and autumn, it would provide me with a quantity of fruit ; but then there would be the danger that the natives would begin coming in numbers to collect it, and I did not quite like the idea. It might involve the very undesirable visit of an agent of the Che-Ka, and they look with the greatest suspicion on all Russians who are not under supervision.

It is hard to say what was the origin of these fruit forests. Walnut trees are very widely distributed in the mountains of Turkestan, and undoubtedly are relics of the immense forests which covered the country and the Kirghiz steppe almost to the Urals in the Pliocene period. The pistachio and almonds, with their excellent fruit, are obviously endemic species in Turkestan. The wild almond has an excellent flavour, but the shell is extremely hard. Pistachios used to cover all the drier parts of the foothills of the ranges of Turkestan, but were nearly exterminated by the miners and metal-workers of the ancient period, as they preferred charcoal made of the wood for smelting their ores. Camels, too, destroy this charming and useful tree mercilessly, greedily browsing off its leaves and young shoots, so that nowadays pistachios are to be found only in districts inaccessible for camels.

It is not so easy to account for the apples in these forests, as within the memory of man there have been no gardens in the places where they grow now, and their fruit is in no way inferior in flavour to the cultivated sorts. Besides, apples are seldom to be seen in the native gardens, and when they are it is a totally different variety. Neither can they have arisen from gardens of the ancient inhabitants of the country before the Mongol invasion, as the trees are common in places where there has never been any settled population. The trees themselves are covered with thorns, and have all the characteristics of wild and not of cultivated forms. We can only conclude that it is a natural wild apple. The form of the fruit varies a lot : small and round, elongate, brown, yellow and red. Often the fruit is far too acrid to be edible, but sometimes sweet and juicy, even exceptionally so. Evidently the taste does not depend only upon the variety but also upon the soil and position of the tree. Some ripen at the end of June, others in July and in August ; and there are winter sorts too, which hang on the trees until the frosts. These are fragrant and full of flavour. Sometimes they are indistinguishable in appearance and taste from the cultivated varieties. When they are transplanted into gardens they react at once to culture, and with a little attention and care give most excellent results.

It is believed that most of our European fruits originated in Persia. More likely they came from Turkestan, which for centuries was a portion of the Persian Empire. Here there occur in the wild state rye, wheat, barley and oats, growing in the fields in the hills in such masses that they look like fields cultivated by man.

My diet was not distinguished by its variety. It consisted of rice and rolls of wheat or barley meal ; the latter was very indigestible and not at all nice. Very rarely I had an egg as a dainty, and still more seldom a soup or *palau*, as both eggs and mutton were very scarce and expensive.

Rain was frequent, and I was not always able to light my fire in spite of my stock of firewood and tinder. My matches were bad, and in damp weather refused altogether to light, and so I built a special oven of stones, where I always kept a supply of smouldering charcoal.

Through the good offices of a Sart who used to bring me bread, I employed a couple of men to build me a little verandah in an open sunny glade and a cellar near it for firewood and stores. I made a bed out of a layer of branches with a thick heap of grass on top, and it made a most comfortable and aromatic couch.

The forest teemed with birds. At night and in the early mornings the nightingales maintained their song, then came the warbling of the thrushes and blackbirds. I especially like the song of the maina (*Myophone temminckii*), a rather large bird of an ashen colour. All day long I could hear the deep but rather loud cooing of the pigeons, which the doves accompanied on a more delicate note. A very beautiful bird there is the paradise flycatcher (*Chitralia paradisea*). The cock has long slender tail feathers widened at the ends, which give him a very strange appearance on the wing. It is really a native of the hot parts of India, but nests in a few wooded valleys in our mountains, migrating to India for the winter.

There were a few clumps of big thistles near my hut which were the delight of flocks of our eastern goldfinch (*Carduelis orientalis*), which also used to entertain me with their music. Beautiful but very undesirable guests were the bee-eaters (*Merops apiaster*), with their brilliant gold-and-green plumage ; they are ruthless destroyers of bees, of which they consume enormous quantities. The insects know their enemy well, and directly the melodious chirrup of the bee-eaters was heard the poor bees refused to leave their hives. These birds do very serious damage to the apicultural industry, as each one consumes several hundreds of bees a day. For that reason the natives of Semirechie place their hives in the most open spaces without a tree or shrub, as the bee-eaters do not like places without a perch to sit and rest on.

One evening, rather late, when I was sitting under an enormous walnut tree admiring the play of the moon-beams on the green even turf, I heard a slight rustle and cracking noise in the wood. I was alert in an instant and froze where I stood, waiting what would happen. A moment later I saw a whole family of pigs slowly walk out of the forest. First went a huge boar, in his proper place in front, his great tusks glistening in the moonlight ; behind him the sow and half a dozen piglings, already quite well-grown. The whole family strolled quietly by, at a distance of about fifteen paces from me, disappearing into a neighbouring ravine to the brook, where they took a bath. I had no weapon and so lost a splendid opportunity of securing some good fresh meat, a delicacy I seldom saw on my table.

Another evening, not far from my hut, when out for a stroll in the woodland, I met a female porcupine with a family of eight comical little ones. They were not in the least afraid of me and went quietly past.

After a time the rains stopped and splendid weather

set in. The nights were mild, and I used to enjoy strolling about in the bright moonlight among the forest paths. The pale rays of light made their way through the foliage, giving a fantastic, unreal appearance to the scene. I loved to stand under a tree and gaze out on to a strongly illuminated glade where everything was calm and still ; it looked like a fairy world, and every moment I half-expected to see a party of elfs and goblins come whirling and spinning in their headlong dances.

CHAPTER IX.   THE WHITE LADY.

ONE day B. came to pay me a visit. He brought some letters and papers and the latest information. The news of Kolchak's advance pleased me enormously. B. and I discussed at length whether it would be better for me to stay where I was or to make over the mountains into Semirechie, where I could spend the winter in less discomfort and danger. We had no doubt whatever that in the spring the efforts of Kolchak and Denikin would set Russia free for ever from the international crooks, degenerates and German agents who bore the resounding title of the ' Workers' and Peasants' Government.'

We decided that it would be best to make my way through to Semirechie ; the chief point was to manage to slip past the extremely dangerous place of Chimkend, where they arrested everybody who passed by and kept them in prison " pending investigation into the causes of their arrest." My friends in Tashkend were to get everything ready for my journey and procure me the necessary documents and ' mandates.'

He gave me sad news, the arrest by the Bolsheviks of my friend Colonel P. G. Korniloff, brother of the famous General of that name. The Colonel had been hiding in the neighbourhood of Tashkend. He had a strong resemblance to the Kirghiz type, spoke Sart fluently and was in fact in every way so much like a native that when he came to see

me dressed as such, when we were plotting against the
Bolsheviks, nobody in my household suspected that he
was a Russian Colonel, but took him for a Kirghiz who
had come to see me about some shooting or mining business.
He could easily have hidden in Ferghaná, or anywhere he
liked, but he wanted to remain as near as possible to his
unhappy family, consisting of a wife and four little children.
These were living literally as beggars, the Soviet authorities
having taken away every single thing from them, including
even the children's linen and bedding. A postman had
recognised Korniloff by some chance and reported his
hiding-place to the Bolsheviks. The joy of these scoundrels
was unbounded, and it only required my arrest to complete
their triumph. P. G. Korniloff's arrest depressed me
unutterably, coming as a bolt from the blue just when my
peaceful contemplative life with nature had soothed some
of the wounds in my heart and brought me a certain amount
of contentment.

An unexpected visitor turned up before my departure,
and came to see me every day. This was a great, big, white
Kirghiz sheep-dog. She appeared on the scene by some
chance, and I made a fuss of her and petted her. This so
completely won her heart that she came every morning
and stayed all day, keeping me company in my strolls
through the woods and all my walks abroad. She was not
hungry and would not accept the rolls which I offered
her ; evidently well fed, but not very fond of her masters.
Every evening she went home, and I suppose was on night
duty, but at daybreak was sure to be outside my hut. She
was obviously attracted by the fuss I made of her and the
nice walks I took her in the woods, attention which she
would hardly get from a Kirghiz.

One morning a Sart came to see me, brother of the one who brought my bread. Unendurable toothache had been torturing him a whole week. In the eyes of the Sarts every European is necessarily also a doctor, and always has a whole pharmacopœia with him for all kinds of sickness. I had to disillusion him and tell him that I was no doctor, nor had I any medicines with me in the forest. But instead of going away and leaving me, the wretched fellow lay down under the tree and stayed there, occasionally uttering a groan of misery. The poor devil was evidently in great pain. I felt sorry for him, and racked my brains to think whether I could not find something among the herbs growing locally which might give relief. Suddenly I remembered a bottle of mint alcohol that I happened to have in my *kurdjum*. A drop of this on the hollow tooth instantly relieved the pain, and the man went home in delight. It is extraordinary how rapidly and effectively all medicines act on Sarts. The next day he brought me three eggs and five rolls as a fee for my services.

A little later I had occasion to doctor a young girl whom Osman brought to me suffering from a bad cough. As there was any quantity of liquorice growing on the hillsides, I pulled up the long, sweet roots and gave them to her, telling her how to use them. Osman told me afterwards that the treatment did her a lot of good. Another day he brought me a patient with a tumour and running sore on her hand, and I succeeded in curing this too, with a hot infusion of some herbs that grew in profusion along the banks of the streams.

I soon found, however, that my practice as a doctor was bringing me unmerited fame, as the Sarts and Kirghiz are very fond of medicine. I forbade Osman to bring me any more patients, and explained to him that all this advertisement was dangerous.

" Yes, that is true," he assented. " Nowadays it is dangerous to get talked about. I, too, want to leave this locality, give up my farm and go somewhere farther away, to the valley of Kaftar Kumysh (The Silver Pigeon), for instance ; it is difficult to get through ; the place is absolutely secluded and the forest is still finer than here, and the whole place delightful. Let's go ; I will get my rifle, and you can go shooting *kiik* (kids) and pig. There are bear too, and rich silver ore."

" I have heard of that deposit of silver," I replied ; " but before we can work it, it is absolutely necessary to hang all the Bolsheviks first."

" That is so," agreed Osman. " Last year in the bazaar at Hodjakend they found about a pound of gold dust on some Sarts, who had washed it in the valley of the Chotkal ; of course, they took it away and put the Sarts in prison."

One afternoon, when I was collecting firewood, I heard a woman's voice calling, obviously Russian. The call was repeated. Someone was coming towards my hut. To hide deeper in the wood was awkward, as it would arouse suspicion : it would be wiser to go out boldly and meet my unexpected visitor. Picking up a bundle of undergrowth and carrying it on my shoulder, so as to conceal my face as much as possible, I walked out of the thicket into the open in front of my hut, where, to my astonishment, I saw Mrs P., wife of a good friend of mine who had been very helpful in securing my various ' mandates,' a man who had done a lot for the Whites. When she caught sight of me she seemed surprised and disappointed, for she did not recognise me, so completely was I disguised by my beard and costume. But when I spoke she knew my voice.

" How did you find out that I was living here in this forest ? " I asked her.

" I am spending a few days in the mountains for my children's health, at a village not far off. The Sarts told me there was a Russian high up in the forest, and that he knew all the herbs. I felt sure this must be you, and asked a man to show me the way. You can imagine my surprise when I saw a strange face, as I did not recognise you at all, although in my heart I knew it must be you ; but my eyes were quite deceived, and if you had not spoken I should never have made up my mind that you were the man I know."

I was very glad indeed. We sat and talked for a long time about affairs in Turkestan and in Russia. But the incident clearly showed the real danger attached to my amateur practice as a doctor among the natives. I asked Mrs P. to come again to see me, and to bring her daughters. They could ride on donkeys, and pass a whole day here. The apples were beginning to ripen, and the children could have a good feast on them. A few days later they came, and Mrs P. brought me some presents that I very much appreciated : some wax candles, a first-rate smoked sausage, a bottle of Madeira and a pound of real tea. Tea, at that time, was one of the very scarcest luxuries. The Soviet Government, according to its socialistic principles, absolutely forbade private trade, undertaking itself the responsibility of supply-ing the population with all necessary foodstuffs ; they made their own ' soviet ' tea out of dried apples, cut fine and roasted ; in colour it resembled China tea, but the taste reminded one of a compôte of rotten fruit. But even this

miserable substitute was far out of my reach, as the price
was high, and it was put on the market only in strictly
limited quantities. The natives refused to have anything to
do with this so-called tea, considering it harmful. Others
made tea from the dried skins of peaches, which had a
pleasant aroma.

A good drink was made from a mixture of dried flowers
of the yellow briar, wild yellow everlastings, blue sage and
balm. Another mixture with the advantage of not requir-
ing sugar, which was available only for commissars, consisted
of mulberries, dried and roasted, with raisins. Living in
the forest I drank the tea of the natives made from the
young leaves of *Sisimia loeseli*, which grew in abundance
in the forest clearings and glades.

The natives, not having sugar but wishing to make sweet
cakes, collected the berries of the *katranga* or nettle tree
(*Celtis australis*), dried them, pounded them and added them
to wheaten flour.

Thus it was that the Universal Social Revolution compelled the population to turn to wild nature to find new
products, new forms of food and substitutes.

There is one native plant in particular that I cannot pass
over, as it ought certainly to be introduced into European
horticulture. That is the Pskem onion (*Allium pskemense*,
Fedsch). The bulb, which is not round but long and bottle-
shaped, has a delightful spicey flavour, and makes an excellent vegetable for soups and stews, to which it imparts
a peculiar delicate flavour, entirely free from the unpleasant
element in the common onion to which so many object.
The stem is branched, hollow inside, rather tall, and this
original shape gives the plant a peculiar and attractive
appearance, so that it would be a welcome addition to

English rock gardens. It grows among the rocks in the most inaccessible parts of the mountains, and it has not infrequently happened that natives, when gathering it for a delicacy, have lost their lives, crashing down the precipitous slopes, like some unfortunate collectors of edelweiss in the Alps. I brought some bulbs down from the mountains in the old days and began to cultivate it in my own garden, where it grew very well, flowering and delivering seed. I did not succeed in raising it from the seed, unfortunately, but was successful with cuttings by dividing the root. Still, I think that with a little experiment the conditions could be found by which this valuable vegetable could be raised from the seed ; it is worth a little trouble.

For days on end I used to wander about the hills and observe nature in the mountains around, and in the ravines. Low down at the river's edge there was an exposure of red marls, with conglomerates over them. Above my hut there were huge masses of crystalline limestone, cut in places by thick veins of hornblende porphyrite. I found several interesting minerals characteristic of the so-called zone of contact metamorphism, and a little later, in one gulch, I found pieces of copper ore and galena, indications that there may very likely be valuable deposits of these ores in the neighbourhood.

In one valley falling away from the same massif, there is a mineral spring at which the natives drink to cure their rheumatism. In another, in palæozoic shales, I came across thin layers of carbonaceous shales and pistachio trees growing around. Here I found, also, lumps of old scoriæ and pieces of magnetic iron ore. Evidently these were old workings where the ancient inhabitants had burned charcoal of pistachio wood to smelt their iron ore.

In the gulley where the mineral spring is there are some mysterious old ruins, almost round in outline, something like the remains of some old fortress or castle, but it is more likely that these were *dakhmas*, that is, Towers of Silence, places where the Magi of old used to expose their dead to be devoured by vultures, according to the teachings of Zoroaster, whose faith was very widely spread in Central Asia before the Arab conquest.

Facing the village of Hodjakend, picturesquely situated at the mouth of the gorge of the River Chotkal, on the edge of a lofty cliff, there are ruins of an ancient castle or fortress, obviously the stronghold of a Dek Khan, as the feudal aristocracy was called in this district in the Middle Ages. Unfortunately, here as everywhere else in Turkestan, these interesting monuments of the hoary past are ruthlessly pulled down by the new hordes of savage invaders from the north—Russian peasants.

On the high peaks of the mountains formed by the crystalline limestones, and in similar localities in other parts of Turkestan, the natives collect a very interesting substance which they call *mumy* or *mumiya*, to which they attribute the most magical powers. They take it internally for broken bones in the form of pills about as big as a pea. It seems as though it has a stimulating effect upon the vitality of the organism. I have known Russians who have taken it in the case of broken bones and hernia, and they have reported that it accelerates healing and the growth of the new matter in the bone to a remarkable extent. It is given to animals too, for the same purpose. *Mumiya* oozes out of the limestone rocks and solidifies into lumps. Ibex are very fond of eating it, so the natives who collect it in the mountains cover up its outcrop with big stones so as to protect its

rare and valuable substance. It is greatly treasured throughout Turkestan. When I first heard about it I was very
sceptical, doubting even its existence ; but once, when I
was shooting in the Hodjakend district, a Kirghiz took me
to the very tops of the crest to the marble peaks and showed
it to me *in situ*. It is of a dark brown colour, inclined to
reddish at the edges ; in hardness and brittleness it is like
camphor ; it tastes somewhat like over-cooked meat, and
has a not unpleasant smell like balsam. I thought at first
it was a form of bitumen, but *mumiya* is easily and entirely
soluble in water. In my extensive collection of Turkestan
ores and minerals, afterwards stolen by the representatives
of the " proletariat of the whole world," I had a considerable quantity of this mineral, which is not yet known to
systematic science. I had intended submitting it to ex-
haustive examination with a view to a detailed description,
but that is one of the things which I have left undone.

August arrived. The plums ripened in enormous quantities ; they were small and of several colours—red, dark
red, black and yellow. The trees, loaded with them, looked
extraordinarily beautiful, but very few were eatable ; most
were far too acid.

Then came the apples and wild vines, which afforded
quite good fruit. The latter were of two kinds, black and
white ; the bunches were small, and the grapes varying
from the size of a hazel down to that of a currant.

The wild flowers underwent a transformation, too, at this
season. The 'shooting grasses' disappeared, as also the
various ferns ; quantities of mallows appeared, white and
yellow ; some enormous mullein (*Verbascum*), seven or eight
feet high—beautiful things with a big rosette of fluffy,
greyish-green leaves at the base, and magnificent plumes of

yellow flowers on top. This flower would be a fine addition to European gardens.

Wild pig came by fairly often to feast on the fallen fruit ; they used, too, to pay nocturnal visits to the natives' fields and devour a great deal of their corn and melons, but unfortunately I had nothing to shoot them with.

Very late one extremely dark night I came out from under my verandah and strolled down in the direction of the stream. Suddenly, at the edge of the forest, where the path led up from the ravine, I saw a strange white thing moving slowly and noiselessly ; presently it assumed the form of a tall figure. This unusual and mysterious phenomenon aroused my curiosity ; I took a few steps towards it, when I was petrified with astonishment. Before me stood the famous phantom, the White Lady, just as described in the novels and drawn in illustrations. I distinctly recognised her tall, slim, woman's figure in a white dress, but it was difficult to make out her features. My first impression was one of astonishment : why should a ghost want to appear in such an outlandish spot ? Why should the spectre of the White Lady want to go wandering about the mountains of Central Asia when her proper and respectable place was in the ancient castles and moated granges of Western Europe ? I determined to investigate this remarkable phenomenon, to study it at close quarters, and began to make my way slowly towards it, afraid that at any moment the wraith would vanish.

The phantom stopped and stood still. It stood out sharply against the background of dark trees. The nearer I approached, the more clearly and definitely did I see that it really was a White Lady. When it unexpectedly asked, " Pavel Stepanovich, is that you ? " I was dumbfounded. I could reconcile myself to the appearance here at midnight of a spectre from the Other World, but a living woman of flesh and blood at such a time and place was unbelievable.

" I am the sister of the student G. We were coming to see you, but got lost and are late. My brother will be here in a minute ; he is scrambling about in the ravine. I found my way up by the path, feeling for it with a stick."

G. brought me important news ; he did not want anyone to know where he was going, so did not take a guide but set off with his sister, following the directions which B. had given them. They stayed the night with me, and then I made my preparations to leave this beautiful and richly endowed spot where Nature had been so lavish, where I had made my home so long.

In the mountains of Turkestan there are many such beautiful forests and valleys. They are admirably suited for horticulture, market-gardening and vineyards. Apples grow better here than in the plains, where the heat is too great for them, and the most delicate sorts could be culti-vated successfully.

These valleys produce the finest apricots in the world for drying. The vine gives an abundant harvest and yields a finer wine, and fermentation follows a more normal course than in the heat of the plains. The vine grows splendidly and does not require protection in winter. Almond trees flourish and yield excellent crops, and the cultivation of the pistachios would be very profitable, as the fruit is valuable ; moreover, it gives rise to a gall which is used in medicine and as a dye. And many other useful and valuable plants could be grown here successfully.

But the natural wealth of these wonderful valleys is little

known ; it is even difficult to find access into some of them, where there are no roads or bridges over the rivers. Perhaps it is as well.

The former Russian Government had a curious system of colonising Turkestan. It endeavoured to populate this rich land with beggars and drunkards not wanted in Central Russia. It hardly made it possible for a man with any capital to start farming here, yielding to the Socialist tendencies of the Russian intelligentsia. The present Government of ' peasants and workers ' knows how to do only one thing, to rob and ruin this rich and beautiful country.

It was not long before B. arrived and brought me all the documents necessary for my journey into Semirechie, together with some money. I was now armed with papers stating that I, Nikolai Ivanovich Novikoff, civil engineer, was sent on duty into Semirechie on 'hydrotechnical investigations,' a rather artful term which would be incomprehensible to the half-educated Bolsheviks and place me in a position of superiority. Special 'mandates' required the Soviet authorities to afford me every possible co-operation in my work, and to forward me on my road by the mail-carts and horses. Nevertheless, ordinary caution demanded that, for the time at least, I should avoid the main roads and make my way over the mountain footpaths past the district and town of Chimkend, where I might easily be recognised or merely detained 'pending orders,' as was the custom with the proletarian authorities in their dealings with educated people.

The evening before my departure a Sart arrived with a small donkey for my baggage, and on the next day, 19th August, before sunrise we started. I was sorry to leave the peaceful secluded spot where for three months I had lived alone amid the beauties of nature ; where I had become so used to my surroundings that I had become part and parcel of them myself. I felt sad at heart. I was tearing myself away from well-tried friends and going into the unknown, an unknown full of dangers and alarms.

A heavy shadow still hung over the valleys, but the rays of the sun were already illuminating the peak of the great Chimgan (12,000 ft.), throwing up the granite in a purple light, while the pockets of snow shone like burnished gold. We made our way by a faint track along the slopes of the mountain among shrubs and trees, rocks and crags, at one moment down to the banks of a brook, at another rising abruptly by the cliffs and crags of the escarpments. The morning was fresh and dry, for in this part of the mountains there is neither dew nor fog.

We dropped down into the main valley, crossing the lateral ravines, covered with fresh turf and other delightful vegetation, irrigated with brooks and streams of crystal water which bubbled in the shade of the trees and bedewed the water-plants upon the banks. Everything was fresh and unspoilt by the hand of man, just as though no human being had passed this way before. When the sun was well up and had begun to burn, I greedily quenched my thirst with luscious bunches of ripe grapes, which hung in abundance from the creeping vines that covered the bushes and trees along the path.

About noon we had to cross the narrow abruptly sloping edge of a dangerous crumbling crag. Our poor donkey stumbled, lost its balance and crashed down the almost sheer flanks. Fortunately the thick shrubs broke its fall and held it, so that when the guide and I, by great effort, succeeded in reaching the poor creature, we found it lying helplessly on its back with its legs sticking up in the air. Luckily it got off lightly with only a few scratches on its legs and a torn ear. My baggage had come off and rolled on one side, where it lay unhurt, and even the bottle of Madeira, which I kept in reserve as a 'hospital comfort,' was not smashed. It took us a long time to get the wretched donkey back on to the path, as the slope was very steep and rugged, a mass of boulders, covered with dense thorny thickets of *Berberis*.

A couple of hours after this adventure we forded a river to the far side of the valley. This was the only place on our way where the current was gentle and the bottom even. We stopped on a shady patch of grass near the bank to give the donkey a feed, and have a bite and drink some tea ourselves. Our lunch was a poor one, consisting only of native rolls, and we had to be very economical even with them.

Farther on the valley narrowed into a deep ravine, and the path zigzagged up to a lofty hill above the stream and wound its way among the limestone crags. Then, again, we came down to the river, where we passed a cave which was used by tigers forty years ago. These have now disappeared from the district, but bears often make use of the same cave for their winter sleep.

We mounted again sharply once or twice and down again to the river itself, which here flowed smoothly in its narrow valley among thickets of willow and sea buckthorn (*Hippophae rhamnoides*), covered with a mass of aromatic yellow berries. The typical forest vegetation came to an end. The steep slopes were covered with a luxuriant turf, forming an excellent pasture on which great herds of sheep and horses used to graze, but now everything was deserted and empty. The methods of the Communists had not taken long to ruin a rich country ; the stocks were gone, the owners, the Mountain Kirghiz, impoverished, and hundreds and thousands of acres of splendid grazing land gone to waste.

The day had sunk into the evening, and the valley was in shadow. It was time to bivouac, but my guide succeeded in persuading me to push on a little farther, and then still a little farther. At last I realised his stubborn dislike of a bivouac ; he insisted on pushing on, for surely we should soon come across the camp of some wandering Kirghiz with his family.

"But what do you want a dirty tent for," I asked him, "when we can spend the night in the pure air on the grass, and we have everything we want ? "

"But don't you see," he replied, "there are people there, and here is only wilderness. . . ."

There spoke the settled town-dweller's eternal dread of passing the night alone with nature. For the Kirghiz there is nothing terrible in this ; the only attraction to him in the *aul* or camp is the opportunity of drinking *kumys* and having some mutton to eat. But for a Sart a night in the open is full of alarms and terrors. Apart from the fear of robbers, his imagination peoples the darkness of night in the wilderness with all sorts of terrors : children of Shaitan, *djinns*, most fearful among whom is *djys tyrnak*, a monster in the form of a woman with claws of steel, against whom even prayer has no avail and exorcisms are useless.

In spite of all these dangers of the night on the banks of a lonely stream in a remote deserted mountain valley, I insisted on stopping to bivouac in a corner among high grass. I brewed tea, a pot of real fragrant tea, and that inspired my guide with a wonderful courage and reconciled him to the danger of spending the night among such terrors. This was the first time for two years that he had tasted the real thing. The grass was so luxuriant that when I lay down on my ground-sheet it was like a feather bed and spring mattress.

The next morning was fresh and the grass covered with dew. We made our way up a lofty hill in order to avoid a deep and narrow ravine in which the river wound like a barely discernible ribbon, overhung with sheer limestone cliffs. In the distance we could see the tops of the Ugam ridge, covered with snow.

Before we reached the crest our attention was attracted by the peculiar behaviour of a pair of bee-eaters hovering in a state of agitation over a somewhat elevated patch of rock, screaming and wailing as though distraught. Directly they saw us they flew to meet us and then back to the patch of bare rock, and then again back to us as hard as they could fly, just as though they wanted to attract us to the place where there was something disturbing them so much. I went up and saw a viper basking in the sun. I smashed its head with my stick and the birds at once quieted down. Snakes are very serious enemies to bee-eaters, as they make their way easily into the holes in banks where these birds make their nests and devour the eggs and young. The curious thing was that the bee-eaters should have recognised in us an ally that could kill their enemy.

We crossed the ridge and descended into the broad, level, fertile and attractive valley of the Kizil-tal. The river here was flowing slowly and split into several branches, in this way forming islands covered with shrubs and bushes and marshy spots with bright green grass. All around were scattered fields of clover, diminutive water-mills and the gardens and tents of Kirghiz. At the first mill I dismissed my guide, a Sart, with the donkey, and, waiting until he had disappeared over the crest, took a Kirghiz, with a saddle-horse, and rode off farther along the valley. Thus my first guide could not know in what direction I was travelling.

In the swamps there were a lot of ruddy sheldrake (*Casarca rutila*), which stood out splendidly in their brilliant deep golden plumage against the green grass. On our approach they rose and deafened us with their ringing cry. On our right and on our left were the grassy foothills, behind which there reared up the lofty mountains with alpine meadows and crags.

This was a splendid locality for shooting ibex. It is a curious thing that in summer and winter the does and kids stay in flocks on the mountain on the eastern side of the valley, but the old bucks on the west. The horns sometimes attain a huge size, up to fifty-eight inches. In the autumn the bucks come over to the does, and in the spring they all go down to the foothills together to enjoy the luscious grass. At that season they are not difficult to shoot.

In many parts of the valley wild oats with a black barb were abundant. This interesting grass grows everywhere on the mountains, on the dry slopes or in the moist meadows ; it grows in colonies, and is specially fond of old grazing ground, which it fills up in a solid mass as though sown by man, and no other kind of grass can gain a footing in it. It almost seems to ask for cultivation. There was one field, walled in with stone, which was chock-full of these oats, so much so indeed that it seemed incredible that it had not been sown and tended by man ; it was higher than my waist and extremely dense. They tried collecting the seed to cultivate it, with brilliant results. The grain was bigger and fatter than common oats, but whether it is as digestible for horses' stomachs remains to be proved. In any case it is excellent feed in the green stage.

I stopped twenty-four hours in this valley and then took a guide and a saddle-horse and rode through the mountains to a locality populated by Russian colonists on the main road to Semirechie. Our path rose by zigzags and capricious bends to a very lofty steep pass over massive limestones, the ascent taking us two and a half hours. On the heights there were growing some stunted junipers, *Juniperus pseudosabina, archi* in Turki, among the fantastic shapes of the columnar limestone rocks which were relics of the eroded cliffs. A wonderful panorama was spread before us from the top of the pass. On the east, in a narrow ravine far below in the abyss, there wound a silvern ribbon, the River Ugam, and beyond, tier upon tier, disappearing away in the distance, rose crest after crest capped with perpetual snow. This was the mountain ridge of Tian Shan, fading away towards the east into the depths of the deserts of Dzungaria. On the west our road led down to the undulating foothills, and the eye could take in, in the remote hazy distance, the sun-dried valley of the Syr Dariá.

At the first *aul* I sent back my guide and took on another Kirghiz with a horse. This time they gave me an old one, but it was a splendid animal of the Turcoman breed, with a good walk and first-rate trot. It was a real pleasure to ride this horse; it made me forget for the moment that on the next day I should ride into a Russian village and meet the Soviet authorities.

After spending the night in a Kirghiz *aul* we came to a straggling Russian village called Doroféevka or Djangali, from the Turki word *djangal*, meaning a thicket, whence the English word jungle, which the observant and quick-witted Kirghiz had nicknamed Djanganchi, that is to say, Swindlers.

We stopped at a large peasant's hut over which hung a large red notice-board, ' Rural *Revvoenkom*,' that is to say, ' Rev-Voen-Kom,' Revolutionary Military Committee. I had to wait quite a time for the ' Comrade ' President of this establishment. He was, of course, a Communist and also, of course, a member of the Red Army, so wore a brand-new uniform recently invented in Turkestan, dark-blue jacket with yellow braid and red breeches. By physiognomy he was clearly a rogue and cut-throat. Long and slowly he read my ' mandate ' and attentively examined the seal. I was not worried, as all my papers, with their signatures and seals, were the real thing.

" Why, Comrade, do you ride over unfrequented paths instead of following the Chimkend mail road ? " he asked inquisitively.

" How can I conduct hydrotechnical investigations on the main road ? " I answered with a condescending smile.

" H'm. . . . Yes. . . . Of course . . ." the President answered in some confusion. " Of course, there is nothing on the roads . . . of course . . . you want mountain districts. But still, you must have your route laid out." And he looked up with a bright smile.

" How can I lay down a route for the investigation of the hydrogeology of the region and determination of the debit of the arterial streams of its drainage system ? " I answered again with a superior smile, using as many long words as I could in order to make a fool of the fellow.

" H'm . . . yes . . . of course . . . that's so . . . I quite understand . . . quite right, Comrade. You see . . . to tell the truth . . . I have not the time to study science, as I have a natural talent for politics and so have only studied the science of the platform." He broke off, and then, " Well, that's all right. . . . Here, Comrade Hromoff ! Arrange for the Ispolkom to supply the Surveyor Novikoff with saddle-horses and a guide."

Ispolkom, I should explain, is ' Portmanteau word ' for Executive Committee, a favourite expression among the Communists.

I went off with my Kirghiz to the caravanserai, and on the way bought a large fragrant melon which had a double advantage. Not only did it afford me an excellent and most refreshing breakfast, but saved me from a danger which might well have been very real. As I was going to the caravanserai I suddenly caught sight of a surveyor I knew from Turkestan coming straight towards me. He was not a Bolshevik but had entered their service. He was walking along deep in conversation with another man who was dressed from head to foot in black leather, a sure sign of a Communist. A face to face meeting was unavoidable. I raised the melon to my nose to appear as though inhaling its aroma, and so covered my face completely. They glanced my way, but could only see my leather jacket and dishevelled beard. But suppose they had thought of speaking to me . . . well . . . I should certainly not have lived to write this.

I was kept waiting ages for the horses, so much so that, in spite of the danger of going about openly in the village, I was obliged to go back to the Ispolkom to ask them to hurry the horses up. I found the members sitting in the yard with some peasants lazily discussing whose duty it was to get the horses and who should go with me as guide. They kept repeating that it was harvest-time, that it was the hot season, that it was working-time, that everybody was frightfully busy—all this contradicted by the very presence of these country-folk in the village and the fact that half of them were drunk.

Tired of waiting and anxious to get away from this dangerous spot and unpleasant company, at last I went up to the President and said to him firmly—

"Look here! It is not for my own amusement that I am risking my neck riding about the mountains, but to carry out the orders of the Workers' and Peasants' Government, which we've all got to obey ; and so, Comrade President, please get a move on with your subordinates and give orders for them to get me the horses at once."

"Now then, get a move on, there, you fellows! It's nothing to squabble about. Get those horses along at once, or else . . .," cried the President to the peasants sitting round, who were still disputing who should do it.

Within an hour I rode off, and towards evening came to the village of Trokhsviatskoe, situated in a fertile valley on the foothills. Here again I stopped at the house of the President of the Ispolkom, a young man who had been a soldier in the old army. He was very busy threshing the result of an abundant harvest. This was the first village on my road where there was plenty of corn and abundance of food supplies generally. It was the beginning of a district full of corn and cattle, not yet ruined by communistic experiments and the plundering of the Bolsheviks.

In view of all this plenty, I wondered why they did not send corn from here to starving Tashkend, where a pound of bread already cost a hundred roubles. Owing to their unbelievable stupidity, coupled with stubborn obstinacy, the Communist authorities, who had taken over the whole problem of supplies and food, forbade not only export from the hungry localities, but import into them! There were Red patrols on all the roads who took away from passers-by even such trifling parcels of flour as they might have with them, which, perhaps, they might be smuggling into the town to help their friends and relatives stave off the pangs of hunger.

While we sat and drank tea, my host held forth at length on his political views. In his opinion there should not only not be any Soviet or Bolshevik government in Russia, but also not any Tsarist nor even any *burjui* republic ; the proper form of republic should be ' democratic.' Surprised at such lofty political views on the part of a simple yokel, I questioned him a little closely on his political opinions, and found, to my disappointment, that by a ' democratic ' republic he meant one where the Russian colonists in Turkestan could help themselves freely to all the land of the Kirghiz and divide it among themselves.

" There'd be plenty over for them, the swine ! " was the conclusion of his political credo.

His wife brought me tea, which she served with delicious *smetana* or sour cream, butter, eggs and lots of lovely white bread, such as I had not seen for getting on for two years; in Tashkend people had given up thinking about it.

" Eat away," she said. " Don't be afraid of it ; I am sorry we've only got common bread and no white rolls."

I slept that night on a pile of fresh straw, which was as soft and warm as could be, although it was a very fresh night. Next morning, at the orders of the President of the

Ispolkom, a young Kirghiz brought round the horses and we started on the road. We followed along the foothills of the mountain range which extends away eastwards. The road was through gently undulating country cut by ravines and torrents bustling down from the mountains, and covered with fields of corn, clover, meadows and Kirghiz and Russian farms. I spent the night in the Russian village Mai Bulak, which in Kirghiz means the Oil Spring. The owner of the house where I stayed, an oldish man, invited me to go on an excursion into the mountains to inspect an old mine with extensive workings, where a quantity of ancient tools had been found. He told me, too, that before the revolution the Kirghiz used to bring down first-class coal from the mountains for the blacksmiths. " Now they've gone off God knows where, and we haven't any coal," he concluded.

Here, as everywhere else among the Russian settlements in Semirechie, I was struck by the dependence of the Russian colonists on the Kirghiz. Everything was done by the Kirghiz : they worked in the fields, tended the cattle, hauled the coal and charcoal and so on. Sometimes even they rented back their own land from the settlers—land that had been taken from them by the former Government and granted to colonists from Russia. Such was the system of colonisation of this country, which grew into the chief cause of discontent among the Kirghiz against the Russian authorities which led to the rising of 1916. They tried to justify such measures as these with such catchwords as the beneficent influence of the Russian colonists on the rude nomads—a beneficent influence which expressed itself in teaching the Kirghiz to drink vodka and so co-operate in the swelling of the imperial revenues, the Kirghiz, of course, like all true Mahommedans, being an extremely sober people.

As it was essential for me to leave the dangerous neighbourhood of Chimkend, I declined the tempting invitation
to visit the interesting old mine, pleading lack of time.

" Then come back again afterwards," said the old man,
trying to persuade me. " There are a lot of interesting
places near here : for instance, you are going to cross the
River Ak Su ; in one of the gorges running into it there is a
whole mountain of ' steel ore.' In the next village there
used to be a blacksmith who found gold in one of those
ravines. He used to go off for two or three days and bring
back a pound of gold dust, and then go on the spree until
he had boozed all his money away. Eventually he disappeared."

Next morning a native boy of about fourteen brought
me round the horses. The one meant for me was a typical
Kirghiz animal, powerful, with a straight neck, a long thick
mane and a great thick tail. She was a good mare with
some life in her, and stepped out at once at a good pace,
not asking for whip or spur. After a few versts at a good
smart trot we began a steep descent into the valley of the
River Ak Su, which runs at the bottom of a deep and narrow
cañon between vertical cliffs of conglomerate. The path,
which was enough to make one's head swim, dropped sharply
down to a bridge over the stream, which roared and raged
as it plunged down its abyss. The bridge consisted of long
timbers, the ends of which were supported on abutments
of short stout beams and big stones. Bundles of brushwood
were laid on the timbers, on which were scattered handfuls
of earth. There was not a single nail, not one single scrap
of metal used in building this structure. This was typical
of the bridges built by the natives in the mountainous
districts of Central Asia, and they are to be seen throughout

Turkestan to the mountains of India. This particular one was exceptionally long, and the sight of it was enough to make one shudder. The Kirghiz boy, who had been riding ahead all the time up to now, stopped at the bridge and stood aside to let me pass, as though offering me the honour of being the first to crash down into the abyss yawning beneath. Now I knew that between my knees was a good stout Kirghiz mare that knew her way about very well and had seen all sorts of things in her life; at the same time, the constant peril of falling into the hands of my enemies blunted the sense of danger, and I rode unhesitatingly on to the bridge. My good horse stepped out boldly and strode ahead. The bridge danced as though on springs, but she never paid the slightest attention to that, and started cheerfully climbing the steep slope on the far side. The young Kirghiz followed. In the afternoon his horse began to give way, so we rode into a neighbouring *aul* and exchanged it for another. Then we rode on, making our way through a small valley up to the top of the pass, where we found ourselves on an immense perpendicular cliff, below which there extended a plain, flat as a table, right away for miles towards the north, to another lofty ridge, Kara Tau. We were standing on the upthrow of a big fault formed by limestones, which are the main mass of this part of the mountains. We did not take long finding our way down, and then we set off across the plain. My mare stepped out in the most gallant style; she required no spur; she rather wanted holding in.

Just after sunset we rode into the village of Vysókoe and stopped at the inn. That day we had ridden forty-five miles in ten hours over mountain roads, so I bought the horses a double ration of oats, a great luxury at that time.

Next morning, while I was waiting for the horses, the innkeeper began complaining about the hard times which had set in for everybody since the Bolshevik revolution, of the insults, the ruin of everyone and the robbery of the peasants' corn. He complained that the Soviet Government forbade the hiring of labour, which was as good as prohibiting agriculture.

" In the old days our young folk were full of life and were often troublesome, but they are quite impossible now; you can't do anything with them at all. The Kirghiz youngsters are better than ours; they at least have some conscience," he concluded.

I had previously heard that somewhere not far from this village, in the mountains, among some almost inaccessible rocky cliffs, there is a cave where there used to stand an idol in terra cotta; that some Russians had succeeded in making their way into this cave, had smashed the idol and beneath it found a silver dish with some very old gold coins. I asked if anything were known about it.

" Of course, I know it well," he answered. " The cave was almost inaccessible; our fellows got in by letting themselves down on a rope; they broke the idol up and found the old money under it, just as you say."

" What did they do with the money? " I asked.

" They melted it down and got drunk on it. Why, they got enough money to be able to keep drunk for ages," he said.

" What did they want to go and break up the idol for? " I asked. " They could have sold it for a good price; the dish alone was worth more than the coins."

" Just laziness; the idol was heavy, and it would have meant a lot of trouble to get it down out of the cave. It was just the same with the mechanic from the pumping station on the Arys, who shot the china statue to bits."

" What statue ? "

" The mechanic and a friend were doing some excavations in secret in the ruins of Otrar and they found an underground room ; they are said to have got some good things out of it and done pretty well. They brought back a china statue nearly four feet high ; it had a halo on its head and holes in the feet—for screwing it down, I suppose. It lay about for a long time in the mechanic's yard, but one day when he had a birthday and some friends came to the party, they all got blind and started target practice with their rifles and shot it to bits."

Obviously, some old relics of Buddhist art had fallen victim to the drunken stupidity of the Russian peasants. Buddhism was a very widely spread religion in this district before the conquest by the Arabs. Otrar was a rich mediæval town not far from the junction of the Arys with the Syr Dariá, the trade centre between China, Persia, Byzantium and Europe. It was destroyed by the Mongols, but recovered from the ruins, and under Tamerlane was very flourishing. It was here that he died. Its ruins cover a large area and lie in a district which has to-day reverted to waterless desert conditions not far from the station of Timur on the Tashkend railway.

In the afternoon I reached the postal station of Burnoe, reported to the local authorities, produced my mandate and received a carriage and pair of horses, with which I drove on, taking full advantage of the privileges of a Soviet official on business for the Workers' and Peasants' Government.

All around extended fertile lands, splendid pastures, fresh meadows along the river valleys; on the right of the road rose mountains with snow-capped peaks, out of which flowed a whole series of streams.

It was a long time indeed since I had driven in a post-carriage, and the cheerful sound of the bells on the *duga* and the thud of the hoofs on the grassy steppe evoked memories of my early youth, when I used to drive about a great deal in post-carriages in the Lower Urals and Orenburg steppe, of which, too, the district reminded me.

Many of the streams here are gold-bearing.

In the gorge of one of them, Talas, on the face of the cliff there is a mysterious inscription incised in an alphabet which does not resemble any known Asiatic scrip, either ancient or modern. I learnt afterwards that it was identical with the writing of the famous Orkhon inscriptions on the distant Yenisei. These were eventually deciphered by the Danish archæologist, Professor Thomassen, who showed that they were in the Uigur language, the ancient tongue of the Turki peoples whom to-day we call Kirghiz. The interesting thing about it is that the letters of the Orkhon inscriptions are identical on the one hand with the *tamgas* of the Kirghiz—that is, the tribal signs and brands used on their stock, while on the other they very closely resemble the old Aramaic alphabet, in which was written the language spoken in Palestine at the time of our Lord, which had replaced Hebrew as the vernacular. It is hard to say whether these *tamgas* were borrowed from the Aramaic or are even older. The inscription of isolated *tamgas* is far from rare on the rocks in the Kirghiz countries, and is attributed to a very ancient epoch. The Turki themselves are a people of the most ancient culture, and it must not be forgotten that the oldest known civilisation, older even than the Assyro-Babylonian, was that of the Sumerians, who are considered a race of Turki stock.

What thoughts and reflections about the remote past of mankind can the sight of a simple *tamga* arouse, just the brand of ownership on the flanks of a Kirghiz horse!

CHAPTER XI.   PISHPEK.

By nightfall I came to Aulie-Ata, which means the Tomb of the Holy Father. Like the majority of the new Russian towns, it sprawls over a disproportionately wide area. One would think it had been designed as a rival to Petrograd or Paris itself. The market-place was bigger than the Place de la Concorde, and very tiring it was, too, walking across it. Of course, there was no attempt at planning. On the other hand, every house was a complete homestead, with a huge farmyard and garden. All the houses are built of raw bricks. There was no pavement nor footpath nor water supply. All buildings of any pretence and the workshops of the postal station were in an abandoned half-ruined condition. Horses and carriages were in a shocking condition of neglect and collapse. The management of the posts for the district had been taken out of the hands of the original contractor and passed into those of the " Proletariat of Workers and Peasants." The whole day long there were carriages with pairs and troikas dashing about with half-drunken workmen and cabbies, cursing and swearing horribly and flogging the poor horses mercilessly. The wretched animals were covered with sweat and foam, all their tormented bodies quivering, with wild looks in their starting eyes, trying to bolt in terror. The air was filled with the din of mad yells and wild cries.

" Why don't you stop torturing the poor brutes ? " I asked the manager of the station.

" How can I ? " he answered. " This is the proletariat exercising its powers and breaking in afresh the horses ' nationalised ' from the Kirghiz. All our old horses have been done to death or completely ruined."

It was not till the evening that I was able to secure a pair and to get away from this awful place. Just before I started a young girl came to me with her mother ; she was teacher in a village which lay on my road, and they implored me to take them with me ; they were to go to the village where her work was, but had no ' mandate ' to order a postal carriage and horses. As there was plenty of room in the carriage, and their presence gave me a more peaceful and respectable appearance, I gladly assented.

As soon as we were clear of the town we forded a river with wonderfully clear, clean and rapid water. It was so deep that it nearly flooded the carriage, and my companions took a cup, bailed some up and eagerly drank the crystal water.

We spent the night at the nearest station, and the following day drove almost all the time along a dry and dusty valley, coming in the evening to the village of Lugovoe, where we met with a special military mission of Bolsheviks from Kopal, right away on the boundary between Semi-rechie and Siberia, where ' White ' Cossacks and Kirghiz from Siberia were invading.

In that remote, isolated and rich agricultural district there had never been either landlords or landowners, no proletariat, no factories nor industrial labour, nor ' exploited masses,' not even landless men, and so it is quite incomprehensible why, how and what for Communists arose there.

The members of the Bolshevik commission—the ' delegates,' as they called themselves — were antediluvian in appearance—in fact, savages reverted to type. When the serving girl was late bringing the samovar for tea, two of the ' delegates ' decided to " go and sock her one on the jaw." They actually stood up to go and do it, when I persuaded them to give up the idea of punishing the girl in that way, as she must be of proletarian origin just as they were.

" We have got lots of everything," they told me, " both meat and bread and everything cheap, only we've not got any goods. We are glad to accept anybody into the Party, but they've got to go to the front and fight the Cossacks. If he doesn't want to go and fight for the socialistic fatherland, we will give him a damned good hiding." They themselves were obviously delighted to be on their way back to Tashkend, where they were counting on spending a long time—that is, as far as possible from the front and ' post of danger.'

The next night we spent at Merke, once a rich and prosperous community, now in a state of desolation. Here, for the first time on the road, we had eggs to eat and *palau*, which put us in a much better frame of mind. Merke is situated at the very foot of the mountains, which are full of good game, such as ibex, wild pig and sheep, including a very rare and interesting wild species, *Ovis heinzii*. It was an excellent shooting centre.

In the morning we stopped to lunch at a village where the engineer in charge of the road was brother of the schoolmistress who was travelling with me. The young man quite openly told me that he simply could not go on serving the Bolsheviks, and was seriously considering escape across the Balkash steppe to join Kolchak's force, and he was already making his arrangements. He told me that in the village

there was a secret organisation to help people who wanted
to escape from the Communist paradise to freedom. His
sister and mother approved the idea, and the old lady gave
her son her blessing for the long and perilous journey. He
asked me to join him, but I refused, as he himself had not
any clear and well-thought-out plan.

All this day we drove through splendid meadows and
pasture-land, often meeting wandering Kirghiz, which gave
us the opportunity of drinking first-rate *kumys* (mare's
milk), a most refreshing and sustaining drink that is really
nutritious and invigorating. Then came Russian settlements, arranged in a very strange way ; nothing more nor
less than a single street extending over thirty miles ! It
was a series of villages with various names, such as Kara-
bata, Belya Vody, Alexandrovka, Dunganka and so on,
but they had all fused into this one immense uninterrupted
street through which ran the postal road. Even at this
dry season of the year it was in places impassable owing to
slime. The wheels of our carriage sank up to the hub into
the mud, and the horses had the greatest difficulty in dragging us out. Each house consists of a separate homestead,
often quite extensive and scattered without any system
whatever. The road was bordered with trees ; behind the
houses we could see spacious yards, gardens and fields of
clover, all against the deep green of elms, poplars and
willows.

At the time of the Kirghiz rising in 1916 the village of
Belya Vody was attacked by the rebels ; many inhabitants
were killed and some women taken away by the Kirghiz.
But when the rising was crushed, the villagers took a cruel
revenge on the Kirghiz. Over seven hundred were killed,
including many who had taken no part in the rising. Feeling

ran high, and the Russians were so exasperated against the Kirghiz that even women gouged out prisoners' eyes with pitchforks.

The cause of the dissatisfaction of the Kirghiz with the Russian authorities was the unfair way in which their land was taken from them and given to Russian settlers ; there were also various irregularities in the requisitions by the local authorities during the war, such as the seizing of their cattle, horses, tents and so on, on the grounds of making a sacrifice in the national crisis. The rising was, of course, prepared and organised by German agents and Turkish prisoners of war, with the benevolent co-operation of the higher so-called ' Russian ' administration. The Government at Petrograd could think of no one better to whom to give the appointment of Governor-General of Turkestan in war-time than a German, von Martsohn, and of Military Governor of Semirechie to another German, Folbaum !

Von Martsohn provoked the rising of the Mussulmen in Turkestan deliberately by suddenly calling them to the front line for military labour.

The confiscation of land from the Kirghiz for the benefit of the Russian settlers was not only entirely unjustifiable, but was a grave economic blunder. Owing to the Kirghiz cheap methods of stock raising, Russia occupied a privileged position in Europe, having at her disposal millions of horses, cattle and sheep, which gave her immense supplies of cheap meat, hides, dairy and similar products. The Russian peasants could produce only corn, for which there was no means of transport from this region.

Later on, moreover, the Bolsheviks, true to their custom, corrected the mistake made by the Imperial Government, according to their ideas. By the time I was in Semirechie

most of the Russian settlements had been burnt down, ruined
or completely destroyed, and the settlers either done to
death or fled from this land of plenty, which, under reason-
able administration, could have produced enough for
everybody.

In one of the villages along the road the ladies left me,
and I went on alone. In the first station where I had to
change horses, the postmaster told me that he had only one
troika, and that they were called for by a couple of Red
commissars bound for Verny.

" Show me their 'mandates,' " said I in an authoritative
tone.

I examined them and then said—

" Look here ! Their 'mandates' were issued by the Ispolkom in Verny, but mine by the central authorities in
Tashkend, and consequently have priority. Give me the
troika, therefore, as you are in duty bound."

" Quite right," replied the postmaster. " I will give
orders for the troika to be harnessed up in your carriage."

Presently the commissars turned up and began to dispute
my right to the horses, but I reminded them firmly and
authoritatively of " the discipline of the revolution," and
they quieted down. They proposed, however, a compromise,
that they should harness the horses to their carriage, which
was a bigger one than mine, and all drive along together, as
they had a lot of military baggage and I had very little.

To this I agreed, and we all three drove off to Pishpek
together.

" Your name is Novikoff, isn't it ? " asked one of the
commissars. " There are some Novikoffs in Verny ; perhaps
they are relatives of yours ? "

" Are they Staroveri, Old Believers ? "

" Yes."

" Then they are relatives all right. Remember me to them when you see them."

So I riveted my false name firmly on. It is worth mentioning, as a pure coincidence, that at this time there was in Verny a commissar, Communist and very proper rogue of my name, Nazároff.

The town of Pishpek received its name from a Kirghiz whose flocks and herds used to be in this region. It is pleasantly situated in a smiling grassy valley, almost at the feet of the imposing Alexandrovsky Range, which is part of the system of Tian Shan. This crest rises sharply from the foothills to the snow-line, and in the clear air it is easy to distinguish from afar the numerous defiles, separated by massive crests, the glistening glaciers and brilliantly white snow, unfolding a wonderful panorama. Numerous streams of cold clear water come tearing down the flanks of this great crest. The bottom of the streams seem to be laid out in a beautiful mosaic of jaspers, pudding-stones and other variegated rocks washed down from the mountains. The streets of the town are cut by these streams in many places, which gives it an original appearance. Pishpek sprawls over a wide area, just like the other towns of Semirechie. There are broad streets bordered with trees, endless open spaces, sometimes grown over with grass, numerous gardens and irrigation canals full of water on every side. As we drove into the town I saw a pair of sandpipers walking about quite unconcerned.

We drove up to the only inn in the town. While a room was being prepared for me I went out on to the stairs, from which post of vantage I was witness of a curious incident. A woman neither very young nor very beautiful but quite well dressed for that time, in white, was nervously walking to and fro by the staircase, evidently waiting for someone. Then she picked up a good-sized cobble-stone out of the street and held it in her hand. A few minutes later there came out of the door of the inn a young girl, poorly dressed and of homely appearance. Like a tiger the woman in white flung herself upon the girl, hitting her on the head with the stone. Blood streamed from the poor girl's head, and both women screamed and yelled like mad things. I was just going to intervene when both combatants, pulling each other's hair, screamed out something and went out into the street. People came running up from all sides, the *militioner*, the equivalent of the policeman, all out of breath, and I thought it wiser to slip off to my room. Even then it was my fate to witness the finale of this extraordinary scene. After tea I went out into the corridor of the inn and I saw the two women sitting side by side. Before them, in the position of an orator haranguing a meeting, with two pistols in his belt, fully dressed in the black leather of his kidney, stood the commissar, who turned out to be the husband of the lady in white. Striking an imposing attitude, he held forth to the two women upon the Communist system of ethics, eloquently describing how by their unseemly behaviour they had lowered his dignity and prestige as commissar, Communist and commandant of the local militia. He explained how, in a society of collectivised Communists, there was not and never could be a place for so vulgar a feeling as jealousy. Jealousy ! What a *burjui* thing ! Dreadful ! The proper punishment for having created such an unseemly scene was to shoot them both, but he, in the great mercy of his heart, as a true son of the proletariat, would magnanimously pardon them. The eloquence of the commandant of the local militia evidently produced its effect upon the combatant rivals, as in the evening I saw all three sitting on the foot of the stairs, peacefully nibbling sunflower-seeds.

I then went for a stroll to have a look at the town. Once rich, with a thriving trade, Pishpek now was dead. The bazaar was empty, the shops shuttered and barred; people had a depressed look on their faces, with an expression of fear and of wretchedness. I never heard a snatch of a song nor saw a smile. Not only the Russians, but the Kirghiz, Sarts and Dungans were just as sad, just as woe-begone. The Dictatorship of the Proletariat had placed its heavy hand on this remote but wealthy province, where formerly, with the exception of a handful of soldiers and officials, everyone had been his own landlord, every townsman had his own house and garden, every countryman his own field and farm, where before the revolution a pood [1] of wheat had cost ten kopecks, where they used honey to grease the wheels of the peasants' carts, as a pound of honey cost only seven kopecks, but a pound of cart-grease cost double. This was a land where the Kirghiz had their herds of tens of thousands of horses and flocks of hundreds of thousands of sheep, where it is literally true that beggars went on horse-back among the *auls* to beg for alms.

The architects of the communistic paradise here were the dregs of the towns of Turkestan, together with the local criminals.

Huge posters on the walls and in the windows of the empty shops informed the toiling masses about the successful progress of the world revolution; great pictures showed a map of the world painted red where the revolution was

[1] A pood was about 36 lb.; ten kopecks was about 2½d.

successful. All red were Russia, Germany, Hungary ; dark red were France, England, Italy. All ablaze were Ireland, Afghanistan, Egypt and India. The United States had caught fire, and red spots appeared in New Zealand and Australia. Only the seas and oceans remained white.

As I was strolling about the empty bazaar, wondering where I could buy some fresh bread, I unexpectedly heard the sound of military music, and from the corner of one of the streets there appeared a procession with red flags. As a precaution I took up my position behind one of the columns of an empty shop and stood there to watch the procession. As usual, it was headed by small boys and dogs, then behind came a group of Communists with a red flag, among whom I recognised a certain Alexandrovich, a former director of a technical school in Tashkend, who had been dismissed for stealing and therefore considered himself aggrieved by the ' bloody imperial régime ' ; then came Red Army soldiers and the band, playing the ' Internationale ' out of tune, and behind them again they were dragging an old gun and a couple of machine-guns. The procession concluded with a detachment of Red cavalry. The common folk, passers-by and citizens of the " freest country in the world " timidly hid themselves in their houses and behind doors.

On the second day after my arrival, when it was getting dusk, I went out on the pavement near the inn. I chanced to look up into a window which was brilliantly lit by wax candles, a luxury at that time available only for commissars, and there I saw a face I knew. It was the Commissar Grinevich from Tashkend. He had been a German spy during the war but now was a full-blown Communist, a member of the Che-Ka and had some work in connection with the Proletarian University. Grinevich knew me by sight, and therefore it was essential for me to get away from this neighbourhood as quickly as possible.

On the next day I moved to the house of an acquaintance who had made his way through to Pishpek from Tashkend some time previously. His house stood over the broad valley of the River Chu, covered with an exuberant growth of grass, which in places stood higher than a man's head. In a lake in the valley there were always plenty of duck, and quantities of pheasants were to be had in the thickets on the banks, and every morning, always in the same direction, there flew heavily by a flock of great bustard, and in the autumn there appeared huge flocks of lesser bustard (*Microtys tetrax*), an interesting game bird that is very good eating.

It was during a day's pheasant shooting in this valley that our famous explorer, N. M. Przewalski, incautiously drank unboiled water, with the result that he developed typhoid fever and died on the banks of Lake Issyk Kul. The valley of the Chu, which was named by the Chinese, is uncommonly fertile. Nowhere else have I seen such wonderful vegetables and such immense potatoes.

The climate of Semirechie is not so hot as that of Tashkend; the winters are longer; snow falls every year, lying for a month or two; there is abundant rainfall in the spring; the summer is not so long as it is there, but still it is dry, and in most localities artificial irrigation is indispensable for agriculture and market-gardening. Cotton cannot be cultivated here, but it is a wonderful country for corn and for the vine, which gives excellent results, especially in some of the mountain valleys on a slightly stony soil. There the vine produces a wine that is not so strong as that of Tashkend, but lighter, with a better bouquet, an excellent table wine in fact. A good friend of mine, A. N. Ivanoff, who had studied viticulture in France, laid out a splendid vineyard and started making wine near Pishpek. He invested a very substantial capital, but in January 1919 he was shot by the Bolsheviks as a *burjui* and exploiter of the toiling masses. On the plateaux and in the valleys among the mountains apples and pears grow splendidly, and in some of the valleys sheltered from the north winds apricots and peaches do very well indeed.

Up here melons do not attain such an immense size as they do in Tashkend, but in aroma, sweetness and flavour they are in no way inferior ; there is, perhaps, a greater variety of sorts. Water-melons give such an immense harvest and are of such sweetness that, as we shall see later, they have even been a source of misfortune to this much favoured country. Excellent results have been had with tobacco in the mountain valleys, and the Semirechie leaf is in no way inferior to the Crimean kind. The opium of Semirechie has the best reputation in Kashgar. A bountiful nature has also endowed the country with a whole wealth of useful plants.

I left Pishpek and went to Verny, where, thanks to my official recommendations, I entered the service of one of the departments and was detailed to conduct ' hydrotechnical investigations ' in the valley of the Chu. They gave me the use of a light cart and a pair of horses with a driver. This was excellent, as it made possible for me a free and independent life in the midst of the nature I loved so well.

My first expedition was into the mountain forests up the valley of the Chu and in the valley of its tributary the Keben. It was a glorious September day when we drove out of the town and headed for the east. The horses were fresh and made a good pace at a brisk trot along the level road, and the light cart bowled along easily. I felt relieved in my mind, and looked around with interest at a country that was new to me. On my left was the Chu with its water meadows and thickets ; on the right the mountains stood out sharply and clearly in the clean morning air, their snowy crest glistening like molten silver, cut by the dark and mysterious clefts of the numerous gorges. After driving through several Russian villages with their inevitable quagmires of mud we came to a slight elevation covered with the extensive ruins of an ancient town, Balasugun. In the dry, clayey, barren soil I could clearly pick out the traces of streets and places where houses had once stood, the irrigation canals and larger buildings. The remains of the city walls were quite distinguishable, and of the towers, fortresses and palaces. In the Middle Ages this was a populous and prosperous city, a mass of gardens and handsome buildings, conducting a busy trade with Western Europe on the west and distant China on the east. Its warehouses were crammed with costly merchandise, embroideries of the east and other rich treasures. . . . But in the twelfth century, after a long and obstinate siege, the town was taken and sacked by the Kara Kitai, who came out of the east. More than forty thousand inhabitants, including women and children, were massacred in the streets of Balasugun ; the ground was drenched with blood, and the once prosperous city converted into a cemetery and a desert, and thus it has lain for eight hundred years in the midst of a rich and fertile country. Interesting things are often found buried among the ruins, especially after heavy rains, such as ancient utensils and works of art, gems and precious ornaments. Fortunately the dry soil of the elevated hill where the city stood has jealously hidden these archæological treasures from looters for the benefit of future generations, just as it has protected them from the barbarism of the Russian peasants and the greed of those most thorough robbers, the Communists.

This part of Semirechie is rich in the remains of antiquity, kurgans, old buildings and old fortresses, as this fertile and pleasant land has attracted a settled population from the earliest days. One of the most remarkable forms of ancient relics are the ossuaries. These are elongated boxes made of baked clay, with a lid, about two to two and a half feet in length and from one and a half to two feet in width. The outside is decorated with a very primitive pattern, and occasionally with designs of the human figure, pigeons or animals. Inside there are always found human bones and nothing else, and they have always been carefully cleaned, with no trace of flesh left adhering to them. Sometimes the bones are stained red. No inscriptions have ever been found on these ossuaries.

Who were the people who adopted this remarkable form of interment and when did they live ? These strange burial urns are met with everywhere in Turkestan where there is settled population, and they clearly are referable to various epochs. Occasionally, but very rarely, specimens are found with the Nestorian cross on the lid. There have been many attempts to account for these urns, all more or less speculative. It seems to me that the answer to the riddle lies in that deep-seated desire of man that his bones shall repose in his own home. To the present day in Central Asia it is customary to bring home the remains of a rich or distinguished man who has died abroad, to bring them back to repose in the earth of their own home. A well-known naturalist, the late N. A. Zarudny, once told me how he had come upon a couple of Kirghiz in the Kizil Kum desert busily engaged in carefully cleaning the bones of a half-decomposed body in order to carry them home. In former days, they say, this method of interment was widely spread in our country, and the people, not Mahommedan, who buried their dead in tombs and sarcophagi made these funeral urns for the bones of their friends and great ones who died abroad, in order to bring them home.

As I drove into the large and prosperous Russian village of Ivanovka, where I stopped to get something to eat and to rest the horses, I was surprised to find an atmosphere of general merriment. Men and women were walking about the streets arm-in-arm; wild singing echoed around, and here and there some drunken man reeled about, while others lay in a stupor, peacefully sleeping it off on the ground by the edge of canals, and others, drenched to the skin and clinging to the fences after wallowing in the mud and slime, brawled with difficulty out of the canals into which they had evidently tumbled, overcome with their lightness of heart . . . and of head. The air resounded with drunken cries, ribald songs and the filthy swearing so characteristic of the Russian peasant. Evidently there was some big celebration in full swing, and the whole scene was a remarkable contrast to the sad and depressed town I had left. In many of the houses there was great activity : women chattering by huge piles of *arbuzy* or water-melons, which they were chopping up, throwing the pieces into vats. . . .

" What extraordinary festival of yours is this ? " I asked the hostess of the post-house where I stopped.

" Festival ? There isn't any festival," she answered contemptuously. " They've been brewing poteen from watermelons these three weeks past and having a good drunk. They have managed to make some sort of vodka out of watermelons and so now they have given up doing anything else."

" And how long is it all going to last ? " I asked.

" Naturally they won't stop till they have distilled all the *arbuzy* into vodka. I'm afraid they'll go on drinking and howling for another month yet. . . ."

The good woman gave me some splendid apples and did not want to take any payment for them.

" I have a job here, you know," she said, " in the office of the Irrigation Canal Commission as a caretaker, and I get a big salary, and tea too, probably more than you do."

" I get twelve hundred roubles a month," I told her.

" Ha ! but I get three thousand six hundred."

" Why, that's more than our chief ; he gets two thousand altogether. And what is your job that you get so much ? "

" They don't pay by the job but by your family needs ; I have four children. My job isn't much ; I have only to do the lamps and sweep the floor, and not too much of that.

I spoil them, though. I sweep it once a week ! " she said with a cheerful laugh.

Such were Communist principles, the position of the individual as a basis for calculating salaries. A talented engineer with plenty of experience behind him, bearing all the responsibility of his duties, receives less than a simple charwoman who sweeps the floor. Each according to his wants, yet these wants are reckoned on a starvation basis. Bread then cost twenty-five roubles a pound and meat a hundred and fifty.

Near the village of Ivanovka there is an interesting spring containing saltpetre in solution ; the local sportsmen distill it and recover the salt, from which they make quite good gunpowder.

The road to the town of Tokmak runs through low-lying grassy country, in places covered with shrubby vegetation and studded with haystacks. Hundreds of pheasants were running freely about the road and among the bushes ; a flock of duck on the way to their feeding-grounds flew overhead ; while the telegraph wires were weighed down with countless flocks of swallows mobilising for their autumn flight to the distant south. I looked wistfully at them. " Lucky little birds ! " I thought. " Free as the air ! If only I could fly away with you to the magical land of Hindustan ! " But unfortunately there was no freedom in my poor country, only slavery and violence.

We spent the night in Tokmak, a frightfully dirty town situated in a low-lying marshy district. In rainy weather some of the streets are closed to traffic, as there is a real danger that carriages may get hopelessly and inextricably stuck in the mud ; there were actually cases where horses have thus been bogged with their carriages and perished.

Yet there is any quantity of stones and cobbles in the immediate neighbourhood of the town, admirably suited for paving the streets; but, bless your soul! who on earth would think of such a thing in this happy land?

Only thirty years ago tigers still lingered on the reed-beds near-by, and they used to do some damage in the town, but now they are forgotten, and the only wild animals in the neighbourhood are the jackals.

In Tokmak the Bolshevik revolution had not involved very profound changes. Here the Soviet officials were all local men, who were by no means disposed to Communism, and simply turned Bolshevik outwardly in order to save their town and district from the invasion of criminals and murderers. For this reason Tokmak was spared the cruelties and horrors which had caused so much misery and terror in Pishpek and other towns in Semirechie, and often enough the commissars, like the augurs of old, could barely repress a smile when executing their communistic obligations. But even this did not protect them entirely, as a few genuine Communists appeared on the scene who had pretty bad records. As a matter of fact, several of these real Bolsheviks had been shot under some pretext or another by the local false Communists. This was a very advantageous arrangement, as by this means they satisfied the blood lust of the Central Soviet Authorities, proved their own activity and at the same time avoided the influx of notorious ruffians.

I took advantage of this liberal spirit in Tokmak and succeeded in procuring a rifle, an old army *berdianka*, and drew ammunition from the military stores.

A veteran of the old army who was a real Bolshevik occupied the post of commandant of the arsenal. Knowing doubtless from bitter experience what wonderful and mysterious things reading and writing are, he naturally doubted that the fellow before him in a tattered old military cloak and leather jacket would be capable of such heights, and said—

" Comrade, if you can't sign your name here, run and ask somebody to come and sign for you."

" That's all right," I replied. " I'll manage it after a fashion," and laboriously scrawled out my assumed name, Novikoff, thinking to myself, " If only you knew who it is you are arming ! "

In the ' Rev-Voen-Kom,' where I had to receive my mandate to carry arms, the President declared that he could not issue the necessary document sooner than three days, as the secretary was ill and there was nobody else who could draw it up.

" But," I replied, " you've got an office full of staff ; why . . . look what a lot of girls you've got . . . ! "

" Yes," he assented ; " but, you know, they can only copy complete documents ; they aren't capable of drafting one themselves."

" In that case, let me draw up my own certificate," I said, and offered my services.

" Could you really do it ? " asked the President incredulously.

I quickly dashed off the requisite mandate authorising me to have a rifle and to draw ammunition for it from the State arsenal, and forbidding anyone else to take it away from me.

The style and contents of the mandate pleased him very much, and he signed it at once, adding the formal stamp with the hammer and sickle, the arms of the Socialist Soviet Republic.

Then he shut the door of the office firmly and turned to me with a question—

" I see that you are an intelligent sort of fellow ; tell me, for heaven's sake, when will all this be over ? "

" What do you mean by ' all this ' ? " I asked in turn.

" Why, this precious liberty of ours, all the nonsense going on now ; good God, I'm fed up . . . nobody can stick it any longer, all this the damned scoundrels are doing to us and our poor unfortunate Russia, these Soviets . . ." and the President's voice rang with sincerity.

" Just look at that ! " he went on. " Look at that and admire it ! Look at the damned mug of that blasted Jew ! " and he pointed to the portrait of Bronstein, *alias* Trotsky, hanging on the wall. " In the old days we used to hang sacred ikons in public rooms, military offices and so on, or portraits of the Tsars, or national heroes such as Suvoroff or Skobeleff . . . but they ordered us to take them all down and put up that God-forsaken muck . . . ! "

As a matter of fact, Trotsky is not exactly a beauty, and his portrait looks more like some caricature than the likeness of a real man.

As I went out I thought to myself what an extraordinary thing it is. What is it that could compel the Russian people, always considered so religious and patriotic and so devoted to the imperial family and system, to forget everything it used to respect and to bow down to everything it used to despise ? Did it only want a stick in the hands of Lenin and Trotsky to drive the Russian people into the arms of Communism, just as it wanted only the cudgel of Peter the Great to force them into European culture and the world of civilisation ?

It took me nearly a whole day to drive from Tokmak to

the village of Samsonovka. I kept passing large Russian settlements alongside the road, and in all of them half the population was drunk; then Kirghiz villages, completely ruined and razed literally to the ground—villages where, but three short years previously, there had been busy bazaars and farms surrounded with gardens and fields of lucerne. Now on every side a desert. It seemed incredible that it was possible in so short a time to wipe whole villages off the face of the earth, with all their well-developed system of farming. It was only with the most attentive search that I could find the short stumps of their trees and remains of their irrigation canals.

" Our country-folk pulled down the buildings, hacked down the trees, dug up the gardens, cut the *aryks* so that everything dried up quickly and the fields of clover were ruined," my driver explained to me.

" But what did they want to dig up the gardens and cut the canals for ? " I asked.

" Because they were fools. They are sorry themselves now. All that clover that they went and ruined would have come in very useful for themselves now." He meant lucerne (*Medicago sativa*), usually incorrectly called *klever—i.e.*, clover—by the Russians.

The destruction of the *aryks* or irrigation canals in this district quickly reduced a highly developed farming district into a desert and blotted out all traces of cultivation and settlement. Only in the water meadows and low-lying ground near the streams is any cultivation possible.

When they rose against the Russian authorities, the Kirghiz, in a general conference of their leaders, passed a resolution not to kill any of the peaceful non-combatant population nor to loot their property. The intention, doubtless, was a noble one and reflected great credit upon them, but it is difficult to curb the animal instincts of human nature once aroused, even among peoples who are generally considered civilised. The rising broke out, and straightway killing began and looting and various atrocities, rape and rapine, and there is no doubt that Russian women and children were captured and taken away into Chinese territory. The Kirghiz detachments were under the command of Turkish officers, prisoners of war escaped from Siberia. The Kirghiz fought gallantly, attacking recklessly, undertaking even cavalry charges against our quick-firers and heavy guns ; but they were lacking in steadiness, determination and, of course, discipline. It often enough happened that after some successful engagement they would break off the attack and go home . . . to drink tea and eat roast mutton.

After the suppression of the rebellion it was the turn of the Russian settlers to get some of their own back at the expense of the Kirghiz, to loot their *auls*, drive off their cattle and take away their property, but in doing this they made no discrimination between the rebels and the peaceful Kirghiz who had remained true to the Russian allegiance. All were indiscriminately robbed, plundered and killed, including many who had fought on the Russian side.

As a matter of fact, the Russian population obtained considerable advantage from the rising in the long-run, as great quantities of Kirghiz stock changed hands, and as a result of the operations a good many of the Russians acquired wealth. Those Kirghiz who had looted from the Russians at the beginning of the rising and slipped across the frontier into China with their booty were afterwards skinned clean by the Chinese officials.

In the village green of Samsonovka, in a small enclosure, are the graves of Russians killed in the rising, among them one of a young and beautiful girl and a student of the same name as myself. They had been out on a botanical expedition in the mountains when a band of Kirghiz appeared. The companions of the young people urged them to mount and gallop off as quickly as they could, but the girl was too slow picking up her things and her collections. The young student, like a gallant gentleman, refused to abandon her, and both were killed by the rebels.

With the introduction of Communism and compulsory labour for all citizens of the Soviet Republic, another misfortune overtook the Kirghiz. At the time of my journey into Semirechie the Soviet authorities issued a decree mobilising the Kirghiz for agricultural work, and the mobilised men, together with their horses, were distributed among the Russian peasants, subject to the penalty of death for refusal or desertion. By this decree the Soviet authorities definitely introduced slavery into Semirechie. What an instructive instance for those Socialists of all lands who contemplate a " dictatorship of the proletariat " !

When at the time of the rising Samsonovka was surrounded by Kirghiz on every side and the help awaited from Verny did not come, the position of the inhabitants became critical. The Kirghiz made numerous attacks, in a hurry to take the town before the arrival of the Russian troops, and very likely they would have succeeded but for the ingenious idea of a local schoolmaster.

One fine morning at the break of dawn the thunder of a gun in the mountains, echoing through the ravines, threw the besieging Kirghiz into a panic, and they retreated in a hurry, for it seemed clear to them that a powerful force was advancing to the rescue of the besieged town with heavy artillery, of which the Kirghiz were very much afraid. The sound of guns lasted a long time, although it did not inflict any damage on the retreating Kirghiz. Still, it made them raise the siege, leave the inhabitants in peace and withdraw hurriedly beyond the River Chu. The inhabitants of Samsonovka were just as surprised as the Kirghiz, and had not the faintest idea where the artillery came from. It turned out that a teacher in the local school, a Cossack settled in Semirechie, had very ingeniously fixed the trumpet of a gramophone on to the end of the barrel of a shot-gun, and with it made a good imitation of the report of a cannon.

After spending the night in Samsonovka I rode out the next morning with a couple of acquaintances over the mountains to the valley of the River Keben. Just before I mounted, a large grey dog, something like an Airedale terrier, caught sight of me some distance off and began wagging his tail cheerfully and galloped up to me. The extraordinary thing about it was that he laughed, he actually laughed, exposing a double row of perfect teeth with immense fangs. This was totally unexpected, and it was very odd, even uncanny, to see a dog smiling, almost laughing like a human being. It was not the ordinary drawing back of the lips to show the teeth, as most dogs will do, but a real human smile, a silent laugh. I had heard before that there are such dogs that can really smile, but had never believed it. This phenomenal dog was famous the whole country round.

Our route lay through low grass-covered hills, the valleys between being full of dense vegetation and in summer a mass of flowers, irrigated by a whole series of streams and springs of crystal clear water. There were neither trees nor shrubs, but the grass was splendid. Such grazing land as this could have well fed the thousands of herds of cattle and horses that have now disappeared.

In two places we rode through the ruins of houses of Europeans, the homes of bee-keepers killed by the Kirghiz. In the empty yards and among the ruins there were dozens and dozens of chukar (*Caccabis chukar*), the Himalayan partridge, that were perfectly tame.

In Semirechie excellent results have been obtained from apiculture. In the course of a summer hives have yielded as much as two hundred and forty pounds of excellent white honey, thick as butter, with the wonderful aroma that is a speciality of the country. All that remains of it now are pleasant memories.

As we were riding past a thicket of very high grass I heard a rustle as though some large animal were moving in it. I reined up, when a large covey of chukar ran out. One of my companions rode up at that moment, fired into the brown with his shot-gun and killed several. After the shot the noise in the grass continued, and just as my companion went to pick up his birds, out there stepped from the grass a fine big roebuck with a splendid head, and slowly walked up the flank of the hill. By the time I had dismounted, flung the reins to my companion and loaded my rifle, the roe was about a hundred and fifty paces away. I fired . . . and missed. I fired again . . . and missed again, while the roe quickly disappeared round the angle of a rock. I could not understand missing such an easy shot until afterwards I had occasion to test the rifle, when I found that it hit two and a half feet high and a foot and a half to the right. The old *berdianka* was worn out. So we did not have venison for dinner that night.

A little farther on, where we stopped to water the horses, we found the spring thronged with countless chukars. Evidently it was their regular watering-place. This partridge likes drinking the clear mountain springs and is fond of coming to water when the sun is fairly high and warm, and sometimes they will spend the whole of the heat of the day by a spring. Here there were chukar everywhere, on the sides of the ravines, among the rocks, squatting among the stones and on the grass, dusting themselves on the road, not taking any notice of the horses, sitting on the ground even between their feet ; wherever you looked there were nothing but chukar. My companion shot several for the pot, but they did not pay any attention to the noise of the shots. Never before have I seen such quantities of these birds in one place. It seemed even a pity to shoot them with a shot-gun ; a small bore rifle would have been a more suitable weapon. The chukar is not only easily domesticated but even becomes quite attached to human society ; a tame chukar likes to settle on its master's shoulder and caress his cheek with its head, crowing gently to itself. The bird seems to want to be domesticated by man. When it is not shot at, it will live quite close to human habitations and run about the farmyard and the garden. I have seen them reared from wild eggs under domestic fowl. These half-domesticated birds will go out to feed in their favourite ground among the rocks and return punctually to roost at home in the evening.

We stopped to rest in the valley of the Keben on the river bank between some clumps of shrubs and enormous granite boulders. The gravels of this river contain gold, and on the opposite bank we could see some ruins of some ancient brick buildings. The interesting thing about them was that the bricks were inscribed with letters in the alphabet of the long extinct Uigur language.

At nightfall, accompanied by a Kirghiz guide, we took our fur-coats and rugs and began to climb the mountains to the top of the crest to the zone of firs and pines. We rode for hours, always higher, sometimes by little streams, sometimes up the grassy slopes, zigzagging up the steepest places. It grew cooler and cooler, the air crisper and the breeze sharper, until we came to the forest and reached the crest of the ridge, where patches of snow showed up brightly in the night. Here, among the huge firs, we lit a good camp fire and quickly warmed ourselves, rolled up in our sheepskins and slept the sleep of the just. Early in the morning we began to look for roe—*illik*, as the Kirghiz call them. The locality was very beautiful. Far beneath us we could barely discern the valley and the river ; the forest-clad slopes dropped down sharply, with deep rocky defiles ; around we could see the tops of the distant chain of Tian Shan, with patches of snow among the rocks. Where we were, on the top of our mountains there grew immense firs, with smaller ones and junipers scattered among them to form impassable thickets. Above the forest zone rose the steep craggy rocks, dotted with snow pockets. On the alpine meadows grew a thick luxuriant turf.

As far as shooting is concerned I was not at all successful. My rifle was of no use, so my companion lent me his 8 mm. Mauser, a splendid weapon, but he had only two cartridges for it. There was, however, plenty of game. A huge, great black boar quite unconcernedly strolled past over the slope, but I could not get near him in time and he disappeared into the jungle. There were plenty of roe, but in choosing the best buck I missed altogether. It is a curious thing that the Asiatic roebuck (*Capreolus pygargus*), although a larger animal than his European cousin (*C. caprea*), when galloping through the long grass of these mountain meadows, does not look any bigger than a hare.

Being left with a single cartridge, I waited for a better chance in order to make certain of my last possible shot, and, as so often happens in such cases, in constantly putting off for the better, I let go many that were good, and at the end of the day was left with that same single unlucky cartridge. The European sportsman can hardly conceive what men had to go through in Soviet Russia when they risked their lives in order to keep a rifle and a few rounds. The proletariat, frightened for its own skin, was terrified of leaving even a harmless smoothbore in the hands of the *burjui* or of any intelligent person. We had to shoot with worn-out old rifles that were practically useless, if not actually dangerous. Not having a shot-gun, I had seriously entertained the idea of arming myself with a bow and arrows so as to get some birds for the pot.

While in this district I had the chance of seeing some interesting crevasses in the soil made by the earthquake of 1910, when the town of Verny was destroyed. In these few years these great rents had been half filled up with earth, but they were still quite deep and looked very much like military trenches dug in parallel rows up the slope of the mountains.

For a long time we went down a lateral valley by a narrow path down the steep mountain face, and stopped at the bottom by a brook in a thick clump of birch and currant bushes. The whole district was extraordinarily like the Southern Urals, and reminded me of the river valleys of the hilly district of Bashkiria. It was very pleasant resting here after our exertions and having some lunch before returning home. Back at Samsonovka, I took my carriage and horses and set off once more in the valley of the Shamei.

The Semirechie breed of horses is not handsome but has several good points. They have strong legs, good manners and remarkable endurance ; for the most part the breed is derived from the horses of the Kirghiz steppes. This district is very suitable for horse-breeding, and some small studs were started recently, raising half-breds from Kirghiz mares and English thoroughbred sires, which showed very good form on the race-course. Thoroughbreds, too, foaled in Semirechie and raised in the mountain pastures have turned out splendid horses, better than the Kirghiz, not only in both mettle and endurance but even in the powers of resistance to the accidents and strains of the road and shortage of food.

The drivers, on the other hand, are hopeless, without the faintest idea of how to handle the reins or look after their animals. For this reason carriages are very often overturned and the passengers commonly break an arm or leg. In fact, few people who have spent any time in Semirechie escape scot-free without having been capsized at least once. I had my share. My driver, a Kirghiz, simply did not drive at all ; the horses wandered about all over the road at their own sweet will, the driver contenting himself with pulling first one rein and then the other without any rhyme or reason whatever. At one place, when driving down by the side of a stream, he turned the cart so sharply that it capsized, and in a moment I was flung into the water with the overturned cart above me. I had the greatest difficulty in getting my head free from all the baggage and things that fell on top of me, and there I stuck, the river rushing by up to my chin, until some Kirghiz came running to the rescue and set me free. Meanwhile all my driver could do was to run helplessly to and fro on the bank exclaiming, " Oh, Allah ! Oh, Pirim."

The Dungans are very fond of horses and look after them very well ; they are, too, excellent whips. They train their horses to obey the word of command—" right ! " " left ! " " steady ! " " faster ! " and so on, scarcely using the reins at all. It is very interesting to watch a heavy waggon, loaded up to a great height, with a team of three, or even five, horses, being driven along a mountain road and directed entirely by the word of command of a Dungan perched up on top. Their waggons have no brakes, but yet they drive them downhill, often on a winding road, completely under the control of the horses.

The valley of the Shamei runs down a narrow ravine between vertical limestone cliffs ; the road winds along, sometimes rising, sometimes falling. Below dashes the torrent, so violent that it rolls over immense boulders, which crack together with a noise like great billiard balls. Presently the gorge opens out into a huge rounded valley like a circus, the upper part of which is covered by a pine forest full of wild pig and roedeer, while the river teems with trout. The Semirechie trout are rather small but very good eating. We succeeded in getting hold of a net which we used for casting, and by this means we would often get ten or a dozen at a time. Where the water is still and deep, just by some big stones, there is excellent fishing for them with rod and line ; a bucket could be filled with good trout in an hour.

In the mountains round there are plenty of ibex. The Kirghiz showed me eight pairs of horns from these fine goats

which had been enticed into the very *aul* the preceding
winter and easily killed. The ram is a powerful brute, and
can give a very good account of himself against a wolf.
He has an original method of defence. He does not butt
or prod with his horns with a horizontal stroke like the
common goat, but rears up on his hind-legs and drops with
the full weight of his body, which is considerable, hitting
with a slashing downward blow of his great, massive, knobby
horns, just like the stroke of a cavalryman's sabre. I once
kept a tame one with immense horns in my garden. Sometimes when playing with the dogs he hit them so hard that
I was obliged to chain him up for fear that in his clumsy
play he would maim, or perhaps even kill, some of my sporting
dogs. The ibex, however, has an unexpected enemy, which
will kill more of them even than leopards or wolves, and
that is nothing more nor less than the cowardly sneaking
jackal. When food is scarce in the winter, jackals join up
into large packs and hunt big game. They will hunt just
like a pack of hounds, and at that time even such creatures
as wolves, bears and leopards will give them a wide berth.
A heavy ibex, sinking deep into the snow, is quickly tired,
and soon falls a victim to the hungry pack. Driven by
terror, the ibex will sometimes seek refuge even with its
other bitter enemy, man, counting on his nobility and
sportsmanship, but seldom, I fear, with justification. The
previous winter, at a time of deep snow, a pack of jackals
hunted a herd of eight head of ibex. At last the terrified
goats in despair sought refuge in a Kirghiz *aul*. The jackals
did not dare follow them there and stopped their pursuit,
but the Kirghiz have no sentiment about them. For them
the terrified hunted animals were a heaven-sent supply of
meat. We must not judge the simple Kirghiz too severely.

The " sacred right of asylum " for the persecuted, as many Russian émigrés know to their cost, has become a mere empty formula even among some cultured nations.

Big-game shooting is still better in the adjoining valley of the Kegat. Like all the mountain valleys of this part of Semirechie, this one begins in the south among the peaks of the chain, and falls away down to the River Chu. The lower broader portion is filled with the fields and farms of Russian settlers. Higher up, the valley of the River Kegat turns into a rocky gorge, accessible only on horseback up to the rocks and moraines of the old glaciers, the whole covered with a fine pine and fir forest. This portion of the gorge is very picturesque and recalls the views of the Swiss Alps. The traveller can ride up this path right up to the alpine zone and snowfields without any particular difficulty, and up there the ibex has his home. Here they go about in herds of several dozen head. While we were riding up the lower portion of the valley we could see and admire a quantity of these handsome goats grazing on the elevated grassy slopes. Here, in these alpine heights, one can see a single old ram standing on some isolated crag, contemplating the world around in great dignity, with his great curved horns reaching back almost to his spine, or perhaps a whole herd of them, resting during the heat of the day in the shade of a rock or by a pocket of snow, the kids gambolling and frolicking while the older ones rest. Early in the morning and in the evening the ibex come down from the heights to graze in the meadows lower down. At this time they are not difficult to approach, or else one may lie in wait for them among the rocks near their favourite feeding-grounds. I was successful with them by waiting by the track where they come down to feed, sending some experienced Kirghiz hunters round along the ridge to drive down the animals when they were grazing or resting. It is a remarkable thing that the ibex-paths often go down absolutely vertical cliffs, and it is marvellous how they are able not only to walk but to gallop about among perpendicular crags, in doing which they sometimes undertake simply enormous leaps from one projecting rock to another, when they look more like a bird in flight than of a quadruped at full gallop. It is only when one comes to examine the body of an ibex that one can realise how splendidly adapted he is to life in the peaks and crags : the muscular development of the legs recalls that of an English hunter from the shires ; the heels are elastic and springy as though made of the finest rubber ; the hoofs as though of steel. A *tau tekke*, or ibex, is well worth shooting ; the meat, though apt to be a little tough, has a good flavour and makes first-class soup. The skin afford a handsome, strong and warm fur, with the remarkable characteristic that the more it is worn and the more the hair is rubbed, the more even and beautiful it becomes. As well as the typical *Capra sibirica*, we get a second form in the Tian Shan, distinguished by the form and curvature of the horns.

On arriving at the top of the valley of the ravine of the Kegat, you come out at the very top of the mountain range on to a huge, gently undulating plateau, covered with the steppe flora, at an altitude of from 7000 to 10,000 feet above the sea. The impression produced is very strange after passing through the alpine zone forest, when, instead of perpetual snow and glaciers, you come out on to a steppe. This is very characteristic of the Tian Shan range : difficult rocky gorges in the middle portion of the river valleys and a steppe plateau on top of the mountains.

Later on we shall see the explanation of this strange phenomenon.

Here there are quantities of wild sheep (*arkhar*, *Ovis karelini*), which go about in large flocks. They are not difficult to shoot, as it is easy to approach within range on horseback in the shelter of the hummocky ground, dismounting to stalk them only when quite close. Here, too, one may fairly commonly meet with that most beautiful creature the snow leopard or ounce (*Felis irbis*), and the lakes of turquoise blue are full of trout.

In winter in the valleys of this part of the Tian Shan the climate is like that of St Moritz or Davos and, in spite of the snow, the sun shines all day long ; the air is warm and there is no wind ; the summers are cool and rainless, the autumn dry and warm. With the extension of the railway to Pishpek, these wonderful valleys will be only one day's ride from the railway. Truly an ideal country for summer hours, shooting and winter sports.

FROM the Kegat I was obliged to go back to Ivanovka.
The road leads from the mouth of the valley down an even
slope facing north ; the slope seems barely noticeable when
you are driving down it, but steep enough when you look
up it from the River Chu. For a good long time you drive
along at the edge of a deep ravine, along the flank of which
there runs a good big irrigation canal. The line of the canal
forms an acute angle with the plane of the road, the result
of which is a curious optical illusion. It looks exactly as
though water in the canal is flowing uphill. The illusion is
so strong that men will quarrel about it. A similar effect is
produced in several places in Turkestan, and the belief is
widely spread among the Russians that the Sarts, who laid
out the canals, have the secret of making water flow uphill.
It is even difficult to persuade people to the contrary. " I
have seen it with my own eyes," they are sure to say, a
good instance of the doubtful value of the evidence of eye-
witnesses.

In Ivanovka the cheerful I found the universal drunken-
ness had led to the inevitable trouble. A prominent member
of the Communist party, in an access of frenzy, bit off the
president's nose. As usual, it was a case of *cherchez la
femme.* It appeared that the president had been paying
attentions too openly to the wife of the offended member,
and the Communist Party had not succeeded in stamping

180

out so vulgar and *burjui* a feeling as jealousy, even among
its own adherents. There was a general party meeting to
discuss the affair in the office of the Ispolkom.

I went to hear and see the fun. A large, filthy, evil-smelling
room, formerly the office of the local government, full of
smoke and soot, dimly illuminated by a small, smoky,
kerosene lamp, was packed with people. At one end, seated
at the table, which was covered with a red oil-cloth, sat
the ' presidium ' of the Party, and on the table, on a china
dish, was a bright-red object, the *corpus delicti*, the president's
nose !

From the detailed report of the ' presidium,' I learnt
that at first they tried to put the nose back in its proper
position in the hope that it would take root and grow, but
as by this morning they had found that this did not work,
they decided to salt it, as it was necessary to preserve it
as an exhibit for the decision of the plenary session of the
Party, which was to be held with open doors.

I did not wait to hear the discussion. The atmosphere
of the meeting was so thick that it was simply impossible
to breathe. The chief impression that I brought away was
astonishment at the sharpness and strength of the teeth of
the injured Communist. The nose had been bitten off cleanly,
as though sliced off with a sharp knife. But, after a whole
month's uninterrupted debauch on home-brewed water-
melon vodka, anything might happen.

Here in Ivanovka I met an interesting young Kirghiz, by
name Turdý, who was interested in archæology. He was
self-taught, knew Russian quite well and was very fairly
well-read. With the greatest keenness and at the cost of
much effort he had made quite an extensive collection of
the antiquities of the neighbourhood. He told me that he

had had an old Uigur manuscript on parchment seven feet long, but everything had been destroyed at the time of the fire, when his village, Keben, had been burnt down by the local Russian settlers in revenge for the Kirghiz rising. The only complete manuscript in the ancient language of the Uigurs known to exist was also found in Semirechie some years ago, and is now one of the most precious rarities of the Public Library in Petrograd.

On the road from Ivanovka, in the valley of the River Issygat, I passed the interesting ruins of some old town of unknown period. A tall imposing tower, visible for miles, rose out of the shallow valley of the foothills. The Kirghiz call it ' Buraná,' after a small stream that flows past the ruins, the Buraná-su. The architecture of the tower is admirable ; it is built of bricks covered with a pattern, the whole forming a design like a carpet. At a considerable height above the ground level there is a doorway with a corridor rising inside the tower. Formerly there was a stairway from the base to this doorway by which one could reach the entrance and climb up inside to the top of the tower, but the Russian settlers have taken away the stairs and are still going on breaking away the bricks at the base, which have the appearance of having been gnawed, and the day is not far distant when this remarkable monument of ancient architecture will collapse, destroyed by the hands of the real barbarians of the north.

Besides the tower there are also ruins of very large buildings, quite likely larger than the tower itself. They are now but a pile of rubbish, bricks and ashes. The burnt brick-work and numerous pieces of fused glass speak of a great fire which has destroyed some old palace, as only palaces and temples were built of brick in this country,

and in the temples there was nothing to burn and no glass-
ware. In two places in the neighbourhood there are old
large irrigation canals, now quite dry, and places which had
evidently been locks. All these are situated within the
walls of a fortress in the form of a quadrangle facing the
side of the light. These walls are now merely heaps of
earth, though still fairly high on the western side. The
eastern aspect of the fortress looks out on to the dry bed
of the Buraná-su, the waters of which have now been tapped
for irrigation purposes higher up. Along the banks of the
canal the so-called 'culture layer' is visible, in which I
found bones of men and animals, skulls, crockery, fragments
of glass and so on. Who was it who built this fortress, with
its tower and its palace ? Who lived here and when ? Who
destroyed what must have been one of the most splendid
buildings of Turkestan ? Neither written records nor tradition throw any light on the question. What an imposing
sight it must have been in its heyday, this tall and stately
tower, surrounded by verdant gardens, reflected on the
smooth surface of the water, in the midst of large and handsome buildings and palaces, against the background of the
green and grassy steppe, at the foot of those lofty mountains
crowned with perpetual snow. And now all around is desert
and dead. Robbed of its irrigation, the soil is parched and arid,
and the ruins provide a home only for scorpions innumerable.

The lower portion of the valley of the Issygat is un-
fertile ; it is covered with thick deposits of gravel and talus
washed down from the neighbouring heights, through which
a bubbling brook cuts its path. We decided to camp for the
night at the spot where the road crosses on a bridge to the
left bank of the River Tuyuk and comes out into a lateral
valley of the Issygat, at the head of which there is a hot

spring. The night was cold, and the next morning the ground was white with hoar-frost.

In this part of the valley I made an interesting observation, showing that the mountain-building process is still continuing, and that the range, the Alexandrovsky of the Russian cartographers, is still slowly rising. The brook does not flow in the centre of its valley, but cuts, as though with a knife, a small spur which runs down from the northern slope. The effect is that, as seen from the road, this spur looks as though it were entire. The stream, maintaining its constant level, is cutting its way slowly through the gradually rising ground. There are several other observations in this interesting valley which point to the uninterrupted elevation of these mountains.

The valley of the Issygat is bare ; it is all covered with immense boulders of granite and other crystalline rocks. The slopes of the mountains are covered with numerous patches of stunted juniper.

There is a small Russian settlement here, and when we stopped to buy some bread, my cart was surrounded by a crowd of inquisitive inhabitants bombarding me with questions : who was I ? where did I come from ? and where was I going ? One young fellow handed me a fistful of juniper berries and asked me what they were good for ? Weren't they good for medicine ? I remembered that juniper berries are used in the distillation of gin, but I did not tell him that, as I had no wish to increase this young Russian's capacity for brewing *samogonka*, of which there is quite enough in the country already. Still, it would have been useful for them to know how to make gin, as watermelons do not grow in this valley, so they have to make their vodka from corn.

Farther on, near the hot springs, the country is very picturesque. They gush out on the right slope of the gorge which, on the south, connects up with a lofty mountain, with a rocky jagged crest and pockets of snow. The springs are of varied contents and temperatures and are considered highly medicinal. There are some rather primitive baths and a few simple huts for people who come to bathe here. Just above the springs there is a thicket full of wild raspberries, and while I was having a feast a pair of roes walked out and strolled off quietly uphill among the rocks.

Clouds were circling high up around the peaks of the mountains, but lower down the sun was shining and the air dry, cool and invigorating. The Issygat, with its beautiful waters of a dark turquoise tint, bubbled down its bed, covering the huge boulders with foam. From here, up past the lofty mountains, the road to the elevated valley of the Sussamyr ran by dizzy corners overhanging fearful abysses. This valley is famous for its pastures, and in the summer the Kirghiz drive up their countless herds of cattle and horses. There is plenty of evidence that this valley is also rich in gold. Hearing of its wealth, the Bolsheviks sent some of their propagandists here to convert the nomad natives to the Gospel according to Karl Marx. The Kirghiz did not accord them a very hospitable reception; they asked them straightaway: "When is all this 'freedom' of yours going to stop and when shall we have the Ak Padscha (White Tsar) back again?" The Kirghiz do not take kindly to the doctrine of Communism.

Near one of the medicinal springs, on the face of the granite, there is an incised inscription in Tibetan; it is the sacred formula of the Buddhists, *Om mane padme hum*.

Long before the arrival here of our Orthodox conquerors, long before the introduction of Islam, when the human and humane teaching of Zarathustra, the gloomy faith of the Manichæans, Christianity and Buddhism all flourished peacefully here side by side, the hand of some Buddhist monk from distant Tibet cut into the living rock the sacred formula of his Creator who gave to mankind the healing springs in this remote and deserted valley of the Mountain of Heaven, Tian Shan.

Some years later, when Fate had taken me across the deserts of Central Asia past the towering heights of Kuen Lung and over the Karakorum into Western Tibet, and I went down the granite stairway from the cloud-capped peaks of Karaul-Davan, down to the fairy-like valley of Numbra, there, too, I saw such inscriptions, in great numbers, carved on the face of the rocks, from which hot healing springs gushed forth.

Chukar are abundant throughout the valley of the Issygat, and coveys of them are constantly to be seen ; the cock birds are fond of perching on prominent stones or edges of rocks to crow out their challenges, not paying attention even to the approach of my cart, which they let come so close that I could reach them with my hand. From the valley of the Issygat I drove straight into the main valley of the Chu to Pishpek, and the whole way chukar kept running along the road in front of my cart, just as though they were enjoying it.

Just at the point where we drove out from the mountains into a small ravine, there is a deposit of rock salt which could easily supply the greater part of Semirechie, but even such a simple job as the preparation of salt from brine is beyond the powers of the Communist ' competent administration,' with the result that there is a great dearth of salt in the country and the price is extremely high.

After that I had a look round the ravines to the west of Pishpek, by the streams Sukuluk, Ak Su, Kara Balta and so on. I found nature much the same as in the district already described, only there is no pine forest ; there is just as much game. Here, on the road from the village of Dunganka to the south, in the ravine of the Ak Su, to the west of the road, I happened to see some extremely interesting prehistoric remains. In a broad flat plain extending for several miles towards the foothills of the Alexandrovsky range there are several rows of immense *kurgans* or tumuli. Such *kurgans* are by no means rare in the Russian steppes ; singly, they are scattered all over Southern Russia, the Kirghiz steppes and the plains of Western Siberia, but they seldom occur in groups. Several of the South Russian *kurgans* have been excavated and yielded very considerable archæological treasures. Beneath these, deep down in the soil, there are chambers where repose the remains of Scythian kings and princes, their captains, wives, slaves, favourite chargers, weapons, clothing, domestic utensils and so on ; in fact, everything with which the departed was surrounded during lifetime. But never have I seen such a huge quantity of *kurgans* as here ; nowhere are they so numerous and so systematically arranged in straight rows as here. Besides the very big ones, there are also *kurgans* of ordinary size. This was clearly the necropolis of the Scythian kings of old, which must have grown for centuries. Cannot this be the ' Imperial Tombs of the Scythians ' of which, with all their terrible ritual, Herodotus writes so graphically ? If so, what a spot of extraordinary interest for the archæologist and for the historian !

During October and November I was busy on expeditions in the mountain valleys of the southern elevated portion of Tian Shan. Here in places there lies perpetual snow, and I had to bivouac on it and melt it down for my water supply. As an alternative I could cut big pieces of ice out of the mountain tarns. I suffered a great deal from the cold at these altitudes, as I had no warm furs, not even a cap, and my very modest salary did not permit me buying such luxuries. My tattered old military cloak was my only protection against the weather, and at night I was saved from being frozen to death only by a good big Kirghiz felt rug, in which I rolled myself to sleep.

Snow falls very irregularly in these mountain valleys. In some it accumulates in immense masses and makes all movement impossible, while others remain free from snow all the winter, such as the basin of Issyk Kul, where there is never any snow. The valley of Arpa is filled with snow, but that of Aksi, quite near, affords splendid winter grazing grounds, where cattle and sheep winter splendidly and even improve and put on fat. The southerly valleys running towards the Chinese frontier, such as the Tuyun, are quite dry both in summer and winter, and have hardly any precipitation. It was here that I saw a curious phenomenon. There were severe frosts at that time but no wind; the sky was clear, cloudless and transparent, of a deep dark-blue colour, and the atmosphere already considerably rarefied, for it was at an altitude of between nine and ten thousand feet. The air was saturated with electricity. The tails and manes of the horses fluffed up in an extraordinary manner, each hair standing out independently, giving the animals a strange and unusual appearance. The fox-fur trimming of the big Kirghiz caps crackled sharply when stroked. At night anything touched with a dry hand—leather, boots, hair, clothing—began to glitter and sparkle. Water poured from a bucket on to the ground fell like peas, in large frozen drops, just like hail. This last phenomenon was very odd to see, especially when these frozen drops fell on dry, dusty soil.

I spent most of the time on expeditions. During the warm weather I preferred spending the night on the open ground, by a brook or river, where there was good grazing for the horses; but with the arrival of winter I had no choice but to stop in the Russian villages, which was sheer misery. There are no inns in the country nor even post-houses; the nearest approach to them are the caravanserais, or, as they are locally called, caravans; these have not even an external resemblance to the real caravanserais of Kashgar and Bokhara. They consist of nothing else than an inexpressibly filthy yard, with a single dark room, often quite small, without windows or stoves, with an earth floor. At night this will be packed full of dirty people crawling with vermin. In these dens the air is always suffocating, the place black with soot and the stench indescribable. I could not stay a single minute in such a place, preferring to sleep in my carriage rolled up in my Kirghiz felt blanket, even when the temperature fell far below zero.

In addition to the other amenities of a night in a caravanserai there was the certainty of being honoured by a visit from a Red patrol to inspect documents. His arrival was announced by the sound of heavy footsteps, the rattle of arms and a deluge of violent swearing, not directed against anybody in particular but just for form's sake, so to speak, or to show off.

Semirechie is in fact notorious for its filth and the dirt

of its inhabitants. Even quite rich peasants lived in tiny, low, dirty hovels, with an earth floor and never by any chance ventilated. In the towns the houses often have no system of ventilation, and in winter the windows are shut and most carefully sealed. Why let any warmth out? On my rare visits to the town I stayed with a charming and refined family, consisting of the mother, her daughter, who was a young and good-looking girl, and an old aunt. They did not live right in the town itself but just outside.

At that time, of course, it was strictly forbidden to have domestic servants. The Soviet decrees laid down the principle of equality and the obligation of personal labour for everybody. On Saturdays all adult men and women were obliged to go and take part in the " public works for the edification of the town "—that is, cleaning the streets, sweeping the snow and so on. Of course, this produced no results. The streets remained impassable from mud; the bridges over the streams, made of huge stone slabs simply placed in position, were broken down by the water and formed something like cyclopean ruins.

As I was not registered on any of their Trade Unions nor official lists, I was in effect a ' free citizen,' and so did not report for these duties; but, on the other hand, I was not a ' toiler,' and therefore could not draw rations, nor buy anything in the Soviet shops, which were the only ones. There was nothing else, as everything had been nationalised and belonged to the people. Consequently I had to procure my food and other necessities of life as best I could. As I had been accustomed for a long time to this Robinson Crusoe sort of life on an uninhabited *burjui* island in the midst of an ocean of Communism, this did not bother me. Not only did I not die of hunger, but actually supplied my friends with sundry little luxuries, and was able to send some flour, butter and lard to my family in Tashkend.

Besides the scarcity of provisions there was a general shortage of everything. I did my best to help my friends, and as a result my occupation when in the town was extremely varied. I boiled soap for the ladies, made hairpins for them, brought wool from the mountains so that they could knit stockings and gloves; I managed to bring in, too, honey and butter, to say nothing of game and fish. I gave popular lectures on geology in the intimate family circle; I traded in the villages in *mata*, a kind of coarse cotton material from Kashgar; I drove carts and even grazed the pigs! The last job, as a matter of fact, was the most pleasant of all, as it took me out for walks with a very charming young lady. At that time all ladies of gentle birth and breeding were compelled to undertake the heaviest and dirtiest work possible: to wash the floors, split logs for firewood, tend the cattle, carry water, running the gauntlet all the time of the sneers and insults of the 'conscientious' proletarians of both sexes.

It was a positive disaster for girls and women if they had any talent for singing, dancing, or playing any musical instrument, or even if they were only good-looking. They were then exposed to the constant danger of being 'mobilised' to amuse and entertain the 'toiling masses' in the national theatres and Communist clubs. Plays, dancing soirées and masquerades were organised often, and frequented by the *élite* of Communist society, members of the Party in their leather jackets and dirty shirts, with revolvers on their belts, Red Army soldiers and the corresponding Communist ladies. Attending these gatherings where the proletariat was enjoying itself was by no means free from danger. Everyone ended inevitably in a 'verification of documents,' which meant a detailed search of every man and woman present except ' Party · Comrades,' when they took the opportunity of helping themselves to anything of value that might come in handy for the Socialist Government, such as field-glasses, silver coins and so on. What the audience was like may be imagined from the fact that once a Sart was searched and an axe found under his *halat*. This, of course, was confiscated, as there was a great shortage of useful tools, and axes had been proclaimed national property. The poor Sart was marched off to prison. For concealing valuable objects, such as gold coins or ornaments, one might have to pay with one's life.

Educated and intelligent people sat timidly in their own poverty-stricken quarters, carefully blinding the window to prevent any beam of light escaping into the street to betray the presence at home of the *burjui* reading or working ; that would be the signal for the invasion of a Red patrol and inevitable arrest.

There were neither books, nor newspapers, nor letters, nor telegrams. No news whatever from Russia and the outer world. The whisper was passed round . . . that General Yudenich had taken Petrograd . . . that General Denikin's army had reached Kursk . . . that the end of the Soviet power was nigh. . . .

A curious coincidence happened one Sunday morning. As we were sitting at breakfast my hostess asked me what kind of a dream I had had. I replied that I had dreamt that we had stopped a Soviet train full of Communist commissars, that we had searched all the waggons and found them full of money.

" What sort of money was it, paper or coin ? " asked my hostess.

" Paper money, good old imperial rouble notes," I answered.

" Then you'll get a letter with good news, and soon too, as dreams before a festival are fufilled before dinner," my hostess answered.

" I certainly hope so," I said, " as it is ages since I had any news from Turkestan."

A little later, as we were sitting down to our frugal meal, a cart drove up in which were sitting a couple of men in leather jackets and caps. These, of course, could be only Communists or members of the Che-Ka.

" They've come for me at last ! " was my inner thought. Before opening the door one of the ladies took me by the arm, led me into her own room, opened the window and said—

" If I call out loudly to the dog, jump out of the window and bolt for it." She went out and locked the door behind her.

Then came what seemed an interminable delay. I listened intently and could hear the men come into the room, their conversation, their laugh, and every moment expected to hear the signal. I peered out of the window on to the street, and decided that if I jumped out I must shut the window behind me.

Then they left. The door opened, and the younger woman called to me with joy in her voice—

" They've gone ; they were not Bolsheviks but two engineers we know ; they are on their way from Tashkend to Verny and brought us a huge parcel ; it must be for you, and your dream has come true ! "

Yes, so it had ! The big package contained warm clothing, a fur coat and cap, which I needed so desperately, and

several letters from my family. Still I lost faith in such
dreams, as often again I dreamt of money, but they never
again came true !

The news was bad : the death of Admiral Kolchak, which
threw the Bolsheviks into a frenzy of delight. To celebrate
the occasion they fired so fiercely out of the two old guns
in the market-place that the explosion shattered the windows
of a lot of houses near, at a time when more glass was
unobtainable.

We were very depressed. One by one fell to the ground
our hopes for the emancipation of our country from the gang
who held her in thrall.

One day, when out for a walk in the street near the house
where I was living, I saw a man I knew coming towards me,
an acquaintance from Tashkend. He was a very decent
fellow, the very reverse of a Bolshevik ; but still I did not
want to be recognised, as it did not suit me that my presence
here should become generally known. So I blew my nose
and hid my face in my handkerchief and crossed over to
the other side of the road. A day or two later I met him
again. This time it was useless to try to escape him. I
heard him call me quietly by name, so turned and greeted
him in a friendly way.

" How did you know me ? Don't my beard and costume
disguise me ? " I asked him.

" Of course, it is not easy to recognise you," he replied,
" but the first time I saw you I noticed the contrast between
your costume and your face, which struck me as strange,
so I looked closer and then recognised you by your eyes.
You must be careful, as a lot of people have arrived in
Pishpek from Tashkend to escape starvation and you might
easily be recognised."

I knew the danger very well, and my friends and hostesses were very worried about me when I was out in the town by myself ; but that was unavoidable.

In order to avoid such dangerous meetings I made a suitable excuse for going away, and said I was going shooting boar in the lower reaches of the Chu. This river dies away in the desert, forming a series of lakes and swamps full of reeds, the home of quantities of game of all sorts. A very cold winter had set in ; the frosts were heavy and the conditions favourable for such an expedition.

IN these reed-beds of the Chu there are deer and roe ; wild sheep come down in winter and boar are particularly plentiful ; tiger are still to be found, and the saigá (*Saiga tartarica*) antelope seeks refuge there from the blinding blizzards of the steppes. This is a most interesting animal, the last representative of an extensive group of antelopes with snouts which were numerous in the Miocene Period. The best known is the *Sivatherium*, a huge creature with a small trunk, found in the tertiary deposits of the Sewalik Hills in India.

The saigá has a short but quite distinct trunk, which is especially noticeable in the males. It is an inhabitant of the grassy plains, not a desert animal, and was extremely numerous on the steppes of Southern Russia as recently as the middle of the last century. After the Glacial Period it was an important object of the chase for the tribes of the Stone Age, and its range extended away westwards as far as the east coast of England. But now the saigá is on the verge of extinction, as it is mercilessly persecuted for the horns, which will fetch as much as four or five hundred gold roubles a pair, say, forty or fifty guineas ; they are sold in China, where they form an important ingredient in one of that country's mysterious medicines. They are like gazelle's horns but of the colour of translucent amber. The Russian Government has never taken any steps to protect this important and interesting animal, and with the inauguration of the 'liberty' presented to the Russian people by the comrades of Communism there has arisen a new form of sport—that is, shooting saigá hunters. They will track a lucky sportsman who is bringing home a valuable trophy in the form of a pair of saigá horns, lie in wait for him, put a bullet into him and help themselves to the booty, which can be turned into cash. The lone unpopulated steppe hides the traces of the crime.

I have kept saigás in captivity; they quickly become tame if caught young, and will breed in captivity. It would pay to breed them in the steppe, just as they do with marals for the same market. Maral breeding has become a profitable business in the wooded districts of the Altai, the horns being sold into China.

Apart from the sport, this expedition would be useful in giving me a good supply of fresh meat for my friends and myself. Meat had become very dear and difficult to obtain, and I missed it from my diet. By this time I had corrected my old *berdianka* by sawing off a few inches of the barrel and altering the sight; now the old thing shot very well, as I proved by testing it on bustard.

It was difficult to find a driver. Nobody wanted to go out into the hard frost and drive in winter so far as the reedy district. At length, by an order from the Soviet of Workmen, I got a young Russian named Fyodor, a Communist. I did not bother about that, as I had a very good method for knocking communistic nonsense out of his head once we were out in the desert. A hearty good-bye from my kind friends and hostesses, who implored me to avoid unnecessary risk and not be eaten by tigers, and I started on my hunting expedition.

The driver had not the faintest idea of how to handle the horses, letting them wander about the road at their own sweet will, contenting himself with tugging sometimes at one rein, sometimes at the other. He did not even think it necessary to hold the reins in his hand, but tied them to the hood of the cart above his head. It is not surprising that we got into difficulties before we were out of the town, and directly we were really outside we capsized. Luckily, I was able to jump out in time. After this, in spite of Fyodor's communistic objections, I insisted on him holding the reins in his hands all the time, and explained to him the elements of the art of driving. But to get anything into the thick head of a Russian mujik, who is absolutely convinced that he is endowed with all knowledge by nature from birth and is worth far more than any *barin*, is quite impossible without a stick.

When we came to the steep slope down to the bridge over the Chu, we were almost into the waves of the deep and turbulent stream. I was just in time to give him one that put a grain of sense into his communistic brain, and we had no more accidents for the rest of the journey.

We spent the night in a Russian village with an elderly and well-to-do peasant. Both he and his wife were delightful ; they gave me a tolerably clean room, while Fyodor took up his abode with them in the kitchen.

While I was drinking tea and having something to eat, a young man came to talk to me, son of my host, and, introducing himself as the Secretary of the Local Communist Committee, sat down to the table and asked me why I was sitting there alone having my tea without asking Fyodor to join me.

" Because he is the coachman," I answered calmly.

" But he is a man, the same as you are ; all men are equal."

" Not by any means," I objected.

" Science has proved it ! "

" Just the contrary. Science proves that men, like animals, are profoundly different from each other, and on this fact is based the development and progress of mankind," I said.

" But you are both citizens of one and the same State, equal in rights ; you both serve the same department, you both do the same thing," the young Communist persisted.

" Not at all," I objected. " Perhaps your Fyodor will undertake the hydrographical survey instead of me and draft a geological section."

" But he is doing the work entrusted to him ! "

" And he is doing it extremely badly. He has not the faintest idea how to do his job. I can drive better than he and look after the horses too. To-morrow I'll sit on the box and drive and let Fyodor look after my instruments and make the survey of the river."

' " But he has never learnt to do that," persisted the disciple of Karl Marx.

" Don't you think that twelve years out of my life given up to my education give me some superiority over a man who can scarcely read and write ? "

" All men have equal rights from birth to the good things of life and so everything ought to be shared equally among them," said the young man, repeating the hackneyed phrase by heart.

" To this I agree," I answered with a smile. " Fyodor's father has a couple of hundred acres of land, a farm, garden, four horses, three cows, sheep, pigs, poultry and so on.

Fyodor brought with him ten pounds of lard and lots of bread and butter, and none of it cost him anything. As all men are equal we receive the same pay, twelve hundred roubles a month. For my bread I paid six hundred roubles and for a couple of pounds of sausage I paid another six hundred roubles. What is left over, and how many days will this last me? I am quite ready to share Fyodor's property and his father's and divide it up equally among us; all my property is here," and I pointed to my scanty luggage.

The Communist was silent. He sat there a few minutes, and then got up and went out and never appeared again. Presently his old mother came in, having listened at the door to our debate. She brought me some eggs, some excellent *smetana*, or soured cream, and bread, and whispered—

"Don't you pay any attention to that young fool; don't be offended. He is all the time chumming up with the Bolsheviks and is quite dotty about it."

The next day when I was driving away she flatly refused to accept any money for her hospitality.

It snowed all night and the road was very heavy going; the wheels sank in so that our horses could hardly pull the cart.

Towards the second evening we had difficulty in reaching the next Russian village, where we had to leave the cart and take a sleigh. The room which they gave us for the night was so dirty and stifling that I preferred to sleep in the cart in the yard. My feet suffered terribly, as leather boots afford no protection against cold. I had to take them off. A blizzard was blowing, I was covered with snow, and my slippers were frozen so hard that I could not put them on till they thawed out and became soft.

In the sleigh we drove fast over the endless snow-covered plain towards the distant horizon with its leaden sky. The horses pulled well, the bells of the harness tinkling merrily. The sharp air caught one's breath and reminded me of my early years on the snowy plains of the Orenburg steppe, the storms and blizzards and those fearful nights out in the open, when you lose your way during a blizzard and have to spend the night under the snow.

It was late when we drove into the village of Voskresensky, the last on my road. Not far from the entry into the village, on the road, there stood out grimly against the moonlight three recent graves surrounded by a low fence, a reminder of the power of the Bolsheviks. The victims had not been shot for any particular offence, but merely *pour encourager les autres*, the deliberate policy of the Communists. The system of ruthless terror, to which alone Lenin owed his success, followed us even into this lonely and remote village on the boundless steppe.

In Voskresensky I was disappointed to find that it was impossible to drive any farther. The deep snow had blocked all roads on the steppe, and there was no food for the horses. My consolation was the news they gave me that I could shoot pheasants and hares here to my heart's content. It was a bitter disappointment to abandon my cherished idea of a shooting expedition into a district that was not only full of game but new to me, but I saw the impossibility of driving another two hundred versts into the steppe under present conditions.

" But what can I shoot pheasants with ? I haven't a shot-gun," I exclaimed.

" We'll find a good gun for you," was the answer.

After a short time they brought me an old .400 rifle sawn off so as to make a sort of long pistol. The rifling had been planed off. For cartridges they gave me a few of the old cartridge-cases, which could take only a tiny charge of shot. The powder was home-made and the wads were of bits of newspaper.

" But I couldn't kill anything with a gun like that ! " I exclaimed. " Why, it's only a toy ! "

" That's all right," they replied. " The birds are quite tame in our country ; we catch pheasants with our hands here."

And that was quite true. When there is a fall of soft deep snow the pheasants sink into it, begin to struggle and sink in deeper and deeper until they are exhausted, when they can be picked out with the hand. Early next morning they brought me a live bird caught in a neighbouring kitchen garden in this way.

Then began my very original ' pheasant stalking,' the way they often shoot blackcock in Russia and Siberia. A local sportsman drove a sleigh and pair quite close to the birds, which came out in the mornings and evenings to feed on some rising ground on the banks of the Chu that was free from snow, where they were able to pick up a little grain or seeds. They let the sleigh come quite close, so that I was able to shoot them with that absurd weapon.

At first the thing kept missing fire, and sometimes I had to shoot two, three and even four times before it would fire. Luckily, the pheasants were extremely patient, and strutted about and waited till I could get in a real shot. Sometimes the hit was so weak that the shot simply spattered the bird without doing any harm. The bird would shake itself and quietly walk off a little farther, though sometimes they would wait for a second shot. During sharp frost the feathers of pheasants become very hard, and there is a thick layer of silky down beneath where the shot is held up, so that the plumage is an effective armour against a weak charge. Sometimes the birds would try to hide in holes in the snow, but their long tails stuck out and betrayed them. The birds we killed were very fat and excellent eating.

In spite of the primitive weapon and all the absurdity of my outfit, in the course of three days' shooting I was able to get quite a good bag of pheasants, hares and duck. I killed a stoat, and with the help of my companion and his bag-net we caught more than two score fine fat carp. I bartered a pair of leather soles for ten pounds of butter, and so was able to return to Pishpek with a stock of provisions for myself and my friends. In that cold, of course, it kept perfectly well.

A few days after my return to the town, in a large meeting which my friends attended, intimation was made of the sentence pronounced by the Soviet Government on my friend, Colonel P. G. Korniloff, in Tashkend, and of his execution. Although worn out by torture and hardly able to stand upon his legs, he held his own like a hero, and replied with all the contempt of a man of noble character for the ruffians who were carrying out the tragi-comedy of the mock trial. His judges were all criminals who had been released from gaol by the revolution. In the account read out, the Bolsheviks expressed their regret that the " chief organiser of the rising in Turkestan, Nazároff, had succeeded in hiding himself, but the Soviet Government was taking all possible measures to trace him."

Common-sense made it necessary to hide at once to avoid the avenging sword of the Soviet Nemesis. There was only one way—to escape to Kashgar, to the territory of Chinese Turkestan. I had long since realised the eventual necessity

of such a step, and had collected all possible information
about the road, but now, in the height of winter, this was
closed to me. All the passes were full of snow. Besides,
the appearance of a stranger at such an unusual season
would attract attention and lead to immediate arrest. So
I had no other alternative but to spend all my time on
constant expeditions and avoid the town.

The tragedy of my position was that if I fell into the
clutches of the Bolsheviks, by that very fact I should involve
in a mortal trap not only those dear to me but the good
friends who had given me shelter, not knowing nor suspect-
ing whom they were harbouring, nor even that I was mas-
querading under a false name.

The snow thawed by day and froze again at night and the
roads were covered with puddles ; the sun gained strength
and warmth. There was something in the air, the feeling
of spring. The silvern peaks of the mountains stood up
sharply against the clear blue sky—the peaks behind which
lay the land where I hoped to find safety and rest. Often
had I gazed at that ridge. Thence there came flying from
the south flocks of swan, and often I used to hear their
melodious whistle like a blast on a silver trumpet. Huge
triangular gaggles of geese, flock after flock, that had
wintered in distant India, were now winging their way to
the lakes on the Kirghiz steppes. All this stirred the soul
and kept me awake at night, that penetrating *honk honk*
which brings delight to the sportsman's ear. Then there
poured, as though from a sack, dozens of all sorts of duck,
which covered not only the lakes and swamps but the fields
of melting snow, and even ventured into the villages themselves. Towards evening the main roads, where the snow
melted sooner than on the fields, were simply covered with

mallard, which refused to fly off till my carriage seemed to be on the verge of crushing them.

It turned warmer still at the lower levels. The snow disappeared almost everywhere, and green grass began to show itself on the steppe. Snipe and other waders appeared, and I had some first-class shooting, as I was able to secure an excellent hammerless double-barrelled gun. Little bustard appeared on the scene, too, and the greater bustard, and sand grouse (*Pterocles arenaria*) and various plover and other game birds. I shot a huge bustard with my rifle ; it weighed forty pounds and gave us a splendid feast for Easter.

At this time I was making preparations for an expedition to the north of Lake Balkash to a district little explored but very rich. It is enough to say here that the mountain range of Kan Tau passing to the west of Balkash has not yet been properly marked on the maps. Kan Tau means the Mine Mountain, and the range justifies its name from the abundance of useful minerals. There are a lot of ancient workings there of an unknown epoch. Now merely a few Kirghiz melt themselves down a little lead for bullets, but they also extract some silver.

There is an interesting natural deposit of saltpetre here, like the nitrate deposits of Chili, but on a potassium instead of a sodium base. It occurs among the sands. Under a covering of friable loose earth there is a layer of clay intersected with veinlets of this nitrate of potash. These deposits of natural saltpetre have nothing in common with those which occur frequently in Turkestan in the sites of old towns and settlements ; during the Great War I took an active part in the exploitation of these. There are similar natural deposits in other parts of Semirechie, as, for instance, at Belya Vody. Natural nitrates may one day form an important and profitable article of industry in this country.

Another source of wealth which generous Nature has lavished on Semirechie is 'sapropellite.' This is a very useful product which Nature not only prepared during past ages for the eventual use of mankind, but it is actually in process of formation before our very eyes. In appearance it is like ozokerite, from which it is distinguishable only by its behaviour under polarised light ; it is of organic origin. On distillation, sapropellite yields kerosene, benzine, paraffin, cerozine and derivatives of the benzole series, including up to 40 per cent of toluol, a product that is valuable in perfumery, but especially for military purposes. Immense quantities of this valuable material are lying covered with sand along the banks of the gulf of Ala Kul, which is part of the immense lake of Balkash, while still greater reserves are reposing on the bottom of this very extensive but shallow sheet of water. Sapropellite is a product of the metabolism of a water weed, *Botryorchis brauni*, which occurs in enormous quantities in the waters of Ala Kul, and every year produces and deposits this valuable product on the bottom of the lake. Sapropellite occurs in numerous lakes and inland seas in Russia and Europe, but nowhere in such immense quantities or of such excellent quality as here in Ala Kul. Bituminous shales, which are now an important object of industry in Europe, are nothing more nor less than deposits of sapropellite formed in remote geological ages. I know of only one attempt to exploit the sapropellite of Ala Kul. A Semirechie Cossack, by name Plotnikoff, put up some small works and made cart grease, but he was shot by the Bolsheviks as a *burjui* and ' exploiter of the toiling masses.'

At the risk of being wearisome with this catalogue of the wealth of Semirechie, a country where, after all, I did not spend a very long time, I must include one more natural product which might well play a very important part in the textile industry. This is a plant called *turka* or *kendyr* (*Apocynum venetum*), which grows in many parts of Turkestan in the river valleys, but is especially numerous in the lower reaches of the River Chu and in the Amu Dariá. It is a small shrub with pretty narrow leaves and clusters of small pink flowers. Its young shoots, cut in the spring, give a brilliant white thread, which makes up into a first-rate fabric exactly like silk. In the autumn the fibres turn brownish and thicker, but are still very useful. In Khiva they cut it in autumn and use the fibre for making nets and rope, which have the important quality of not rotting under water and not being spoilt by damp, however long they may be exposed to it. There is any quantity of *turka* growing wild, but it would not be difficult to cultivate it. All that is necessary is to clear the ground on a piece of suitable soil, remove other shrubs and plant it. It likes a poor marshy soil where nothing else will flourish. This shrub might do for Turkestan what jute has done for India. Russia abounds in all sorts of wealth, but her people are lazy. Hitherto she has been too occupied with world-wide social problems, and now, of course, she is quite incapable of cultivating and developing a new source of textiles.

The banks of Lake Balkash, the reed-beds, marshes and the grassy steppe around, and the patches of shrub and bush on the steppe, abound with all sorts of game, both feather and fur. In the reeds there are pheasants by the thousand, and in summer the water is simply covered with geese, swan, duck and every kind of wild-fowl. Quantities

of boar make their home, too, in the reed-beds, and themselves afford food for the tigers, which are quite numerous.
The Balkash tiger is famous for its thick fur. In the steppes
around there are herds of gazelle and saigá, and, what is
strange, among the shrubs of the undulating steppe there
are not only roe, but also deer, the big deer which the
Kirghiz call *maral*. Of course, this is quite distinct from the
Siberian maral, which is identical with the wapiti (*Cervus
canadensis*, v. *maral*). The deer of Russian and Chinese
Turkestan have been very little studied, and I have no
doubt that there are several sorts there not yet known to
science.

The district of Balkash is an interesting, richly endowed
but still wild, unspoilt corner of nature, not yet ruined by
the greed and destructiveness of man. After the Bolshevik
revolution there were plenty of people in Turkestan who
could not reconcile themselves with Socialism, and sought
refuge in the distant lone lands on the banks of Balkash.
Several took their families with them. They led the free and
independent life of hunters. Wild pigs supplied them with
first-class pork, while the waters of the lake provided
quantities of excellent fish, including big lake trout, and on
the juicy grasses of the steppe cattle quickly grew fat and
multiplied. The rich virgin soil yielded a fabulous harvest
of corn.

These sportsmen lived in separate homesteads. In the
winter they traded with the towns, supplying hams and
fish. In the midst of famine and unrestrained persecution
by the Bolshevik Terror this was the only spot in the whole
of our vast empire where men still might breathe the air of
freedom and live as they wished. They were extremely
hospitable and always delighted when anyone paid them a

visit. They even arranged among themselves turns in which to receive and how long each might entertain a guest. They invited me to come and make my home among them in this sportsman's paradise, where the hand of the Bolshevik had not yet reached.

But I preferred the more enterprising road to distant and unknown China, to go away once and for all from this hell of a 'workmen's and peasants' world,' from this enormous prison known as the Socialistic Soviet Republic.

When I was safe in Kashgar, in the end of 1920, a special 'punitive expedition' was sent by the Soviet Government to Balkash, which quickly wiped out the free and independent population of this wonderful spot. The entire population of the Balkash hunters, their wives and families, including even little children, were shot by the Bolsheviks.

Spring made progress. The fruit trees broke into blossom. Beneath my window there burst out the fragrant clusters of the *cheriómuha*.[1] This tree, the favourite of so many Russians, does not grow in Turkestan, and for many years I had not seen its flower, which recalled the memories of my distant birthplace, the Urals. Every day it was regularly visited by the red grosbeaks (*Carpodacus rubicilla*), and I could not tear my eyes away from the picture of the scarlet birds fluttering among the white clusters of flowers. Now all that, my birthplace and my own folk, all must be left behind for many a long day, perhaps for ever. I was going into exile. I was going to flee from my own land to a strange, wild, unknown country, there to seek refuge and repose.

For two whole weeks it had rained unceasingly, uninterrupted downpours punctuated by storms, hail and thunder. At length, after one final desperately violent

[1] The Birdcherry, *Prunus padus*.

storm, which caught me in the open and made me shelter myself and my horse under our rugs, to shield us from the violence of the hail, the sun broke through, the clouds rolled away and there set in a long fine spell of splendid cloudless weather.

Nature was now in her full beauty : the lower levels already covered with thick grass and all sorts of delightful flowers, chief among which I loved our Turkestan tulip (*Tulipa greigii*), with its broad leaves spotted like a leopard. Nowhere does this flower attain such beauty and size as in Semirechie, where its thick stalk reaches a length of over two feet and its dark red flower the size of a teacup.

The higher foothills were covered with a short, bright green, tender turf, through which were scattered on every side by the thousand another species, *Tulipa hesneriana*, golden-yellow, rose-pink, white, white and red, yellow and red, in every variety, all wonderfully fragrant. The air was crisp and invigorating, full of the wonderful fragrance of the flowers. Just the picture I remembered from the days of my childhood in the Orenburg steppes, where in spring just such tulips as this bedeck our grass.

Spring was well advanced. The roads were clear. The time had come to prepare for my long and dangerous journey.

Officially, I was going a long way into the mountains on a geological survey.

My friends arranged a farewell, picnic, during which we collected a mass of mushrooms and flowers of pheasant's eye (*Adonis vernalis*), which would be very welcome in the hospital, where there was a great shortage of medicines.

A great feeling of sadness gripped my heart at leaving, perhaps for ever, everything that was dear to me in life and my beloved Turkestan, where I had spent the best years of my life, studying Nature and her mineral wealth. Before me there awaited a wearisome wandering in a strange land, a lonesome, shelterless life, in poverty, without friends, in a strange and unfamiliar world. . . .

But before I could reach even that I had to slip out unobserved from the confines of the socialistic fatherland across a border now strictly patrolled by Red frontier guards. The Government of Workers and Peasants did not permit anyone to escape from the paradise they had built up on earth. To do so was possible only at the risk of one's life.

A FRIEND of mine arrived from Tashkend. He warned me
that the Soviet authorities had found out that I was somewhere in Semirechie, and that orders had been given to the
local Che-Ka to spare no effort to find me. For this reason
it was vital to get away from Pishpek as soon as possible.

To put their agents off the scent and to mask my tracks,
I managed to get official orders to start on an expedition to
the neighbourhood of Lake Balkash to prospect for useful
minerals, while as a matter of fact I set off in exactly the
opposite direction, to the south, making for Naryn on the
Chinese frontier near Kashgar.

I drove out of Pishpek on 18th May in a light cart drawn
by a troika of horses. I intended to ride one of these animals
from the frontier to Kashgar, and to send back the cart
with the remaining pair. This time my driver was a smart
young Kirghiz, Azamat Bek, a resourceful fellow of proved
trustworthiness. Formerly he had been extremely rich, but
now he was totally ruined, as after the rising of 1916 the
Russians had stolen all his property and stock, although both
he and his old father, who was killed, were loyal to the
Russians, and he himself had done a great deal to help those
who had suffered in the rising : he had saved from captivity
among the Kirghiz seventeen Russian women and girls whom
the rebels had taken off to Chinese territory. Azamat Bek
had not been let into the secret of my destination, and had

no idea where I was bound for really. He merely thought
that I was out on one of my usual expeditions into the
mountains.

Splendid weather set in, warm and bright. Everything
was green on every side, and the whole steppe was variegated
with the mass of flowers of all sorts. Very striking were
the dark blue bells of a splendid lily (*Ixiliridion tartarica*), a
plant that will grow anywhere, and is well worth introducing
to horticulture. Another charming spring flower here which
garden lovers ought to cultivate is a diminutive sort of iris
of a delightful violet colour, with a wonderful perfume ; it
could grow from the bulb in the tiniest of pots, and would
be a very suitable plant for indoors or as an alternative
for crocuses in the garden.

We spent the night at Tokmak, and the next morning
was a great Orthodox festival, Ascension. It was a lovely
sunny day, and the music of the great bells resounded
through the still morning air. I listened for the last time
to the voice of my native church calling me.

After the service the crowd of worshippers came tumbling
out of the church, men and women in brightly coloured
and variegated costumes and kerchiefs. Grouped along the
fence round the church, they formed a brilliant and somewhat original background for the military parade which
would shortly take place—a parade of the Red Army on
the model of the old days, when such a function was indispensable from an important church festival. The occasion
was the second anniversary of the existence of the Red
Proletarian Army. The pseudo-Bolsheviks of Tokmak had
stuck to their guns, combining a Communist display with
the old Russian church festival.

I took up my position on a large stone near the orators,

where I could see and hear very well. They spoke fiery words, both Russians and Mahommedans. They enlarged with eloquence on the theme of the necessity of the ' universal arming of the people ' for the support of the ' universal social revolution.' The former army of the Tsars had been created by the Imperialists for international bloodshed, for the protection of the interests of the capitalists and land-owners, but the present army, the Red Army, was organised for the protection of the ' toiling masses ' and the interests of the ' world-wide proletariat.' " Capital is already destroyed," they said, and the only task left was the union and arming of the ' international proletariat ' and the formation of an international Red Army, and then when this task was finally accomplished would dawn the day of universal happiness, of the brotherhood of nations, of peace throughout the world, the ' sacred empire of the toilers.' Machine-guns would be seen only in museums, while cannon would be converted into agricultural machinery.

As I listened it seemed to me, every now and then, that the orator spoke with his tongue in his cheek, hardly suppressing his smiles at his own words, at his audience, and at all that precious rubbish and ridiculous jargon which the Soviet authorities on high compelled him to learn and discourse upon in public. All this comedy was played by an excellent fellow, a former captain in the Tsar's army, who was in command of the parade.

Then, to the strains of the " Internationale," there marched past, in straggling order, a handful of Red soldiers, disgracefully turned out. After them came, in good order and shaping very well, the ' little soldiers,' Mahommedan children and boys—Kirghiz, Sarts and Tartars—singing the " Marseillaise " in their own language. In front marched a little girl with a red flag, and behind came the Red Cross detachment, children with stretchers and a 'doctor' in white overalls, and then little 'Sisters of Mercy' with red crescents on their breasts.

All this playing at soldiers was very amusing to see, only I felt sorry that these ripping little chaps should get into the clutches of the Bolsheviks, just as I was sorry for the orator who was compelled to talk such rubbish, which he himself must have hated and despised. I was sorry, too, for all these simple village crowd of rustics, who gazed with uncomprehending eyes at the Soviet parade and listened unmoved to all the Bolshevik nonsense.

Deeply engraved on my memory is this last picture of a Russian town, this last scene from the drama of life in Russia, in my fatherland, which I was now leaving . . . perhaps for ever. . . .

And I could not dismiss from my head one constantly recurring question : What *is* this immense Russian people, that a handful of ruffians with a thick stick can do what they want with it, even turn it into disciples of Karl Marx, into Communists ? Yet at the same time the natives of Turkestan, whom everyone used to look down upon as a rough and timid people, these same natives stubbornly cling to their rights, to their independence, to their traditions and age-long manner of life. In another corner of Turkestan, in Ferghaná, they are actually putting up a good stout fight against the Soviet authorities.

Even when several years had gone by and the silence of the tomb had fallen on Russia, and many among even the higher circles of Russian society had compromised with the Soviet Government and made their peace and reconciled themselves to Bolshevism and sold their conscience, still the despised *basmachi* of Ferghaná had risen again and again against the hated yoke, continually taking whole towns and villages and killing Communists. Neither Bolshevik gold, nor Budionny's cavalry, nor the lavish promises of the Soviets, not even a highly ornamental national autonomy, could quench the holy flame of hatred in the hearts of the Mahommedan *basmachi*.

In the afternoon we drove on. The gardens of Tokmak were a mass of apple, pear and cherry blossom. We came to a comparatively new settlement, Berdovka, which had a bad reputation in the district, as its inhabitants were ardent Bolsheviks. As we drove into the village we saw a large crowd in the street watching a horse gallop about the place, with the body of a boy of about twelve tied across the saddle. It appears that the little chap was drowned when bathing, and now they were employing this highly original method of restoring him to life and consciousness.

Between this settlement and the next, Bely Piket, where we spent the night, the whole country is a wilderness, though before the Kirghiz rising it was densely populated. All along the road were numbers of Kirghiz homesteads and farms, caravanserais, tea-houses and fruit gardens, and plantations with lofty poplars, willows and elms. There used to be an abundance of everything, and everything was very cheap. For instance, a pailful of fine apples could be bought for a penny, and a Kirghiz would be quite glad to give a sheep in exchange for fifteen pounds of rice. It was a great sheep-farming country, and hundreds of thousands of rams and ewes were driven from here into Turkestan and Ferghaná.

But now everything around had been destroyed; there were only a few wretched ruins to be seen, stumps of trees and desert all around. It is astonishing how quickly here in Central Asia all traces of settled life and civilisation disappear and turn into desert, especially when the destruction is carried out by such masters of the art, who first of all hack down all the trees and then destroy the irrigation.

The village of Bely Piket is famous for its poteen industry. No sooner have the shades of night fallen upon the crests of Tian Shan than the whole village begins to reek of the sickening smell of fusel oil as hundreds of home-made stills start work. I saw many ' factories ' of this flourishing branch of ' national industry.' They were all of extremely crude design. A large iron pot is placed over a small fire and covered with another, the joints caulked with clay ; the condenser is a gun-barrel stuck into a small hole in the upper pot, resting on a gutter with a constant stream of cold water assiduously fed from a jug by the distiller. From the end of the barrel there drips into a bottle waiting to receive it a thick evil-smelling fluid. In a night they can distil several bottlefuls. The whole plant can be dismantled in a moment, each part taking on the most innocent appearance, and all traces of the illicit industry hidden, except, of course, the atmosphere, which is saturated with fusel oil.

This kind of apparatus is, however, relatively complicated and costs a certain amount to construct. But in one village in Semirechie I saw one still that for sublime simplicity was simply a stroke of genius ; it had no condenser or any other apparatus, but consisted simply of ordinary kitchen utensils, a bucket, cups, dishes and so on, just the most innocent things of everyday life. It was the invention of Russian women, and I must admit that I was immensely struck by its ingenuity. It is surprising that the

Americans have not hit upon the idea ; Russian craft has quite beaten them here.

I had to drive through Samsonovka again, and there found the drunken debauch still in full swing ; groups of men were staggering about the streets and others were lying dead drunk on the ground. This time there was some Communist holiday or other, and men were holding forth long, inter-minable, disconnected speeches.

Farther on the road crossed the River Chu, entering the gorge of Buam, and the Russian part of Semirechie was left behind and, of course, the realm of *samogonka*, home-brew. Bolshevism and *samogonka* . . . Blood and Vodka . . . that is my dominant impression of this part of my unhappy country.

The imposing gorge of Buam is a lateral valley cut by the River Chu through the most northerly ridge of the Tian Shan, the Alexandrovsky. The entrance into the northern part of the gorge is grand. The road drops steeply to a fine wooden bridge perched boldly above the deep channel of the stream, and rises again on the far side. Imposing moun-tains guard the entrance. On the left, down in the depths of the cañon, we could see the Keben flowing into the Chu from the east. The waters of both rivers are of the colour of aquamarine, but when they mingle they boil up into a white foam, which tumbles and dashes at a fearful depth below, from which a dull thundering roar reached our ears.

Ages ago, probably some time during the Tertiary Epoch, the River Chu cut itself a way through the Alexandrovsky range, at that period not very lofty, acting as a drainage canal for the extensive mountain range, carrying away quantities of eroded material, which it deposited at the base of the foothills. The mountains of Tian Shan were gradually elevated, lifting with them the river gravels thus formed. The river grew old, as we say—that is, lost its violence and powers of erosion, becoming more and more quiet and consequently carrying much less solid matter with it. There was then a lull in the mountain-building process, and now the river was flowing over its own masses of conglomerates. Then again the process of elevation set in at a quite recent date, geologically speaking, and this movement still continues; the mountains are growing. Their lofty central portions began to attract greater precipitation, snow and ice; more water ran into the river, which thus became rejuvenated and once again began to erode, this time its own conglomerates which it had itself deposited, cutting through them like a knife, deepening its channel proportionately as the mountains through which it flows rise on either side.

Not far from the post of Djil Aryk, the Canal of the Winds, on the left side of the valley, high up a mountain composed of red sandstones and grey clays, probably of Jurassic age, there is a deposit of coal suitable for smiths but rather high in ash.

The gorge of Buam is barren, with neither shrubs nor trees; the flanks of the mountains are merely covered here and there with a little herbage, but yet it is picturesque. Rain falls here, but when you get through the gorge and come out into the extensive rounded valley of Kok Mainak, you at once notice the aridity of the climate with typical desert flora. The valley here is bordered with hills of a sort of mud-like loess, interbedded with pebbles washed out of the adjoining mountains. The ground is covered with quantities of pebbles out of these beds. Along the flanks of the mountains there are lacustrine deposits and shore terraces, clear proof that the lake of Issyk Kul at one time extended as far as the entrance of the Buam gorge.

On the dry soil here wire grass, known as *chiy* (*Lasiagrostis splendens*), grows in abundance. The stalk is straight, smooth and hard as wire ; it reaches a height of ten or twelve feet, but is not thicker than about quarter of an inch ; the cluster of inflorescence at the top is quite pretty, while at the base the long, very narrow, ribbon-like leaves make a thick bunch. *Chiy* grows in clumps and forms extensive thickets, which are full of pheasants and hares. This strange grass is characteristic of those parts of Central Asia where there is little rain but where the subsoil water is not very deep and the soil a sandy argillaceous clay. It is a curious thing that horses and cattle will eat the flowers and even the hard stalk willingly enough, but will not touch the leaves.

On the high clayey hills, just as though on artificial pedestals, there are clumps of another plant characteristic of Central Asia, *Nitraria stroberi*, with white stalks and small succulent leaves. In the summer it yields black berries with a sweetish, rather salt taste, which are edible though not particularly nice. This is a most widely spread desert plant ; it occurs everywhere from the Turgai steppes through all Central Asia. I saw it in Tibet and in the plains of India. And the extraordinary thing is that it grows also in the deserts of Australia. The roots branch out to a remarkable degree and work their way down very deep into the soil ; after a time the sand covers the whole plant, which then grows through it to the top of the hillock, until the wind again heaps up the sand and clayey dust which accumulates at the foot of the hillock. Like this, the plant keeps creeping up to the top of the hill, until finally the hill gets a very curious aspect of a labyrinth of hummocks with bunches of these plants on top. It grows just as well on a hard clay soil and among stones.

The sides of the mountains here are dry and absolutely bare. All the moisture of the atmosphere, which this country receives exclusively from the west—that is, from the Atlantic —is precipitated on the peaks of the more westerly heights, and there is none left for the valley of Kok Mainak and Issyk Kul. This phenomenon is common enough in the mountainous regions of hot countries. This is the explanation of the curious fact that alongside peaks in eternal snow and glaciers there are arid regions of real desert.

Along the banks of the streams here there are small thickets of buckthorn (*Hippophoe rhamnoides*) and small-leaved willow. It was very cold and a penetrating wind was blowing. Spring was only just beginning here, and the leaves of the plants starting to unfold. A few small sandpipers were flying up and down the sandy banks of the rivers, piping shrilly, and in the thickets cock pheasants were crowing loudly.

In Kok Mainak wild sheep (*Ovis karelini*) and ibex come down from the mountains in the early morning to water in the Chu.

We spent the night in a tumble-down old post-house, and next morning continued on the road, which now turned, following the Chu towards the east, in a broad and level valley in which the river now flows, covered with shifting sands or gravels and clay. Vegetation was now thicker; in places there were green fields and dense thickets of *chiy*. These are full of life, and it was interesting to drive past them. We saw a herd of wild pig making its way through the bushes on the far side of the river; pheasants strutted about the road in a brazen manner, and in the field hares went on grazing quite unconcerned by my approach. The hare of Semirechie is a bold and entertaining fellow, quite different in character from his timid European brother, although decidedly smaller. Chukar were running about the stony sides of the hills, and there were a few coveys of the common partridge, a species closely related to, though actually distinct from, the common European bird.

We reached the lake of Issyk Kul fairly early. Although our road went past at some distance, I could not resist driving up close to have a look at this famous and interesting sheet of water, with which are entwined the names of so many myths and legends. Although the surrounding country is absolutely bare and barren, the view of the lake is extremely fine.

The whole panorama is clothed in a bluish tint, like a picture by a skilful artist, with soft and mellow outlines. Beyond the lake, away to the south, I could see the blue chain of mountains with its white peaks; on the east the face of the waters passes insensibly into the blue and misty distance, fading away into the horizon. It is all covered in a pale, greyish-blue haze, and the whole scene recalls those views on Danish pottery. Even the great flocks of glistening white swans and thousands of duck floating near the banks did not clash with the general tone of the picture.

The lake extends away about a hundred and twenty-five miles towards the east. Not a glimpse of a sail, not a wisp of smoke, for there were no boats to ruffle its surface. The water, which is brackish, does not freeze in winter, hence its name, which in Djagatai Turkish means the warm lake; it communicates its warmth to the surrounding valley, which is enclosed by mountains, thus giving it a mild winter. The shores are flat and covered with shingle, but drop away rapidly a short distance out, so that quite deep water occurs fairly close to the banks. When the evening breeze from the east sprang up, the water became rough and the crests of the waves broke on the shore, the backwash rattling the shingle ; this, and the white foam, made me think I stood on the coast of a sea.

It has long been known that on the southern banks of the lake ruins of some old buildings can be discerned at a considerable depth, and after storms, bricks are often thrown up on to the banks and fragments of pottery and so on. These have given rise to many legends and inspired General Chaikovsky to write a most entertaining book, ' Turkestan and its River, from the Bible and Herodotus.' This is an awful warning of the danger in trusting to the ' testimony of history,' which may lead one to the most fantastic conclusions, and shows how simply and easily these wonderful theories are overthrown by the slightest touch of the natural scientific method.

General Chaikovsky, basing his arguments on the stories of Herodotus and the evidence of biblical history, discusses the remote prehistoric past of Turkestan in general, and of Issyk Kul in particular. According to him, the centre of life in ancient Turkestan once upon a time was a great river emptying into the Caspian Sea, while the Amu Dariá and Syr Dariá flowed into it as tributaries. This river flowed out of the basin of Issyk Kul, and was composed of a whole series of streams which came down from the mountains and abundantly watered what is now an entirely desert part of our country, giving rise to life and plenty. Many ' peoples of the earth ' lived in those days in this highly favoured land in peace and happiness.

Suddenly there befell a fearful catastrophe. A most violent earthquake rent the mountains ; the outlet of the river of Turkestan was plugged up, and the depression of Issyk Kul, the valley in the midst of the mountains, became a lake, as the Bible testifies. Deprived of their irrigation, the prosperous valleys of Turkestan were converted into sandy deserts, the rivers Amu Dariá and Syr Dariá lost themselves in the sands, forming the Sea of Aral ; " the peoples of the earth " went from this ruined and desolate land, leaving behind numerous remains of their buildings and of their most ancient civilisation. It is worth considering for a moment how far the history of the valley of Issyk Kul based on ancient literature agrees with the facts as shown by nature and geological observation.

At first glance it is quite obvious that the age of the lake is incomparably greater than any historical or prehistoric antiquity of man, that in the past geological epoch it was even much greater than it now is, extending even, as we have seen, to the Buam gorge, and that not so very long ago the River Chu flowed into the lake, while another river flowed out ; then the Chu, by the deposition of masses of its own sediments, cut itself off from the lake and flowed past it, joining up with the stream that comes out of the lake, thus forming the present River Chu as we know it. Deprived of this influx, the water of the lake became brackish. We may still observe traces of the stream out of the lake into the Chu, and about twenty years ago it was still in existence, and it often happened that some of the water of the lake discharged into the river.

As a matter of fact, there is a whole series of legends, traditions and fantasies, even among European peoples, about the mysterious and little-known regions of Central

Asia. Everything that is incomprehensible, everything that is enigmatical and mysterious, from the origin of our 'Aryan' ancestors to the Mahatmas invented by my gifted compatriot Madame Blavatsky, everything is traced to the deserts of Central Asia and the inaccessible region of lofty mountains. Legends about Central Asia are being founded even to-day, not only by partly educated people but by authors of many talents, though ill-informed on matters geographical, who describe their own fantastic theories, and among them sometimes are even scientific men.

For instance, in many so-called 'scientific' works there are allusions to the existence at a relatively modern period of an inland sea in the interior of Asia, Han Hai,[1] with which Chinese imagination has filled the elevated valleys of the present Kashgaria and the deserts of Takla Makan. I have read an article by a German historian who attributed the 'universal flood' to the eruption of the waters of Han Hai through the Tian Shan into the valleys of Turkestan, Siberia and the Caspian depression. And I have actually listened with amusement to a lecture by a well-known Russian botanist who attributed the glacial moraines and lacustrine muds which he had observed in the Tian Shan to the action of the mythical Han Hai of the Chinese.

The origin of all these suppositions that the valleys of Central Asia were recently the bottom of a sea is to be found, of course, in the shifting sands and the salt marshes among the Central Asian deserts, which, in the eyes of the inhabi-

[1] Some Russian geologists use the name 'Han Hai' for a series of tertiary sediments in the Tian Shan and desert of Gobi, but, of course, without implying the remotest connection with the mythical inland sea, which, according to the Chinese, existed until recent times in Central Asia. In scientific works it would be better to drop this term altogether, together with the similar expression 'antediluvian.'

tants, incontestably point to the recent existence here of
ocean depths. We may remark that the bottom of this
mythical Han Hai is at present at the same altitude as
the Rigi Kulm in Switzerland—that is, at 4500 feet above
the sea—and that this region, not only at the very dawn
of history and beginnings of antiquity but throughout the
preceding geological period and the greater part of the
Tertiary Epoch, consisted of arid desert.

Another widespread but fallacious belief about Central
Asia is that it is drying up, that this process is continuing
at the present day and that this desiccation was the cause
of the destruction of her ancient civilisations. In order to
investigate this theory, which is not based on any real
scientific data, the Americans equipped and sent to Turkestan the well-known scientific expedition of Pumpelli, which
made immense contributions to our knowledge of the
country.

At the present day, as L. Berg's observations on the level
of the Sea of Aral have shown, Turkestan is not only not
drying up but, on the contrary, the amount of precipitation
is actually increasing. Towns and civilisations here were
blotted out through the destruction of their irrigation
system. It would be quite enough, for instance, to cut the
canals of Bos Su and Zakh for the whole of the flourishing
district of Tashkend to be converted into a sun-baked desert
in the course of a few years, like the numerous other once
prosperous ruined cities lying in what is to-day an unpopulated desert.

' Historical data,' in fact, are very unsubstantial things ;
with them, if you want to, you can prove anything you
like and draw any conclusions you want. You can lay the

foundations of the doctrine of Karl Marx or the alternate desiccation and refilling of the Sea of Aral within historic times, as does Elisée Réclus on the strength of the writings of Sultan Babur. But directly you apply the facts and methods of the exact sciences, these wonderful theories come tumbling to the dust.

ALL the post-houses along this road were in ruins, a result
of the Kirghiz rising ; the one nearest to Issyk Kul, Kute-
maldy, was the scene of a very gallent defence by a handful
of Russians against an immense horde of Kirghiz, who attacked from all sides. We stopped the night here. The
place was kept by a single caretaker, a genial Kirghiz who
turned out to be a friend of Azamat Bek.   He had once been
a water-carrier in Pishpek.   He complained that a comrade
of Azamat Bek had enticed his only wife away from him.

"The next time we come here," said Azamat, consoling
the unfortunate husband, "we will bring your wife back to
you."

"*Khop djaksi*," "Splendid !" cried this Menelaus of
Pishpek, and to show his gratitude he charged us only one
hundred roubles for food for the horses instead of two.

After passing through the gorge of Ortakui, the road
comes out on to the broad level plain of Kachkorka, rich in
pasture-land and formerly crowded with wandering Kirghiz
with their flocks and herds. Now Kachkorka, the centre of
the cattle trade, is almost entirely in ruins ; all trees and
orchards have been felled. On the two sides of the village
there are numerous *mazary*—that is to say, tombs—like
regular mausolea, of varying and original architecture, some
recalling motives in the Moorish style. It is in fact a veritable
necropolis. Most of them are built merely of sun-dried
bricks or even merely of lumps of clay, and so they quickly

fall into ruin. Nowhere else in Turkestan are these tombs so numerous or in such big groups as here in the valleys of Tian Shan, to which they give a very peculiar and character-istic appearance.

Just at the entrance into the village there stands what the Russians call a ' stone woman.' That is a crude statue of a man, rudely carved out of stone. These statues are not rare in Semirechie, and formerly were very common in the steppes of Southern Russia, in the Orenburg district and in Siberia. They are the tombstones of the remote ancestors of the Kirghiz, the Scythians and Massagetæ. In their folded arms they carry a cup or goblet, which is interesting because until quite recently a cup was the in-separable and inevitable companion of every Kirghiz, just as it is to-day among the Tibetans, and they had a leather holster of original design attached to their belt or saddle in which to carry the cup. The Kirghiz word for such a cup is *kisé*, which seems to me to resemble the Greek word $\sigma\kappa\acute{\nu}\phi\sigma\varsigma$, which in turn is very close to the ancient name of the people, Scythian. It is curious that the Sarts call a cup *pialé*, from the Greek $\phi\iota\acute{\alpha}\lambda\eta$.[1]

[1] The connection between the Turki *kisé* and the Greek $\sigma\kappa\acute{\nu}\phi\sigma\varsigma$ does not seem very close, but the resemblance of the latter to the name Scythian, Scythos, is certainly suggestive, when we remember that the author tells us that the goblet is almost emblematic of the nomad of the steppes. The Greek letter θ is foreign to the Turki languages. It is interesting to quote the opinion of so eminent an authority as Professor Ernest Gardner, whom I consulted on the point. He writes : " It is a curious coincidence that Horace, Odes, lxxvii, begins, ' Natis in usum laetitiae scyphis Pugnare Thracum est,' and this is said to be an imitation of Anacreon's $\mu\eta\kappa\acute{\epsilon}\theta$' $o\acute{\nu}\tau\omega$ $\Sigma\kappa\nu\theta\iota\kappa\grave{\eta}\nu$ $\pi\acute{\sigma}\sigma\iota\nu$ $\pi\alpha\rho$ $o\acute{\iota}\nu\omega$ $\mu\epsilon\lambda\alpha\tau\hat{\omega}\mu\epsilon\nu$. The introduction of Thracians seems to suggest an allusion to Scythians. But the resemblance may be purely imaginary." In a later letter Professor Gardner suggests that another old Greek word for cup, $\kappa\acute{\nu}\alpha\theta\sigma\varsigma$, would be nearer to Scythian than $\sigma\kappa\acute{\nu}\phi\sigma\varsigma$, and adds, " How about ' cup ' and ' scoop ' ? "—M.B.

The village of Kachkorka has a clayey soil and is covered with grass and *chiy*. The foothills of the mountains surrounding the valley are formed on enormous masses of shingle, gravels and pebble beds washed down from the mountains out of the gorges, which form huge 'cones of deposition' with very steep sloping sides at the mouth of the valleys.

The valley of Kachkorka and other valleys of this part of the Tian Shan—Djungal, Naryn, Arpa, Chatyr Kul and so on—run in a direct east by west. They form a series of immense steps, like a huge stair rising up to the top of the crest. They are arranged one higher than the other towards the south ; and so the traveller, hardly noticing the rise in altitude, keeps passing into a colder locality until he would think that he is not making his way towards the hot sunny south but to the chilly north, until at length he comes into the regular arctic district of Chatyr Kul and Turgart, from which points there is a gentle uninterrupted rapid slope down by meridional valleys to the hot plain of Kashgar. The rise is so gentle in this part of the range that we did not notice it, and my cart bowled cheerfully along just as though on a level ground, although we had risen several thousand feet above the valley of Pishpek.

After the post-station of Kum Bel (Sandy Ridge) the road leaves the valley of Kachkorka and enters the wild gorge of Djuban Aryk, shut in by almost vertical cliffs of granite and syenite, which are replaced farther on by limestones and schists. The road is well laid out and follows the capricious windings of the torrent. In the gorge itself the mountains are rocky, wild and completely bare, but the road and the gorge are very fine. Huge rocks, under the action of alternate heat and frost, split off and crash down into the river, where the violent current at once starts wearing them down, grinding and crushing and hammering, converting them into sand, gravels and boulders, carrying all this broken-up material far down its bed to deposit in the valleys. Here indeed is the laboratory of nature, and seldom can one see so clearly in full action before one's eyes the break-up of rocks and mountains and the removal of the product of their ruin by water.

There is no vegetation here to conceal the process of attrition, to mask the outlines and retard the work. It goes on rapidly and clearly, under the very eyes of the observer.

Near the post-station of Sary Bulak the gorge widens, the sides slope back more gently and here and there a scrap of herbage or weed appears. At one spot here I saw a sheep browsing on a spot of grass. At first sight I took it for a stray member from the flock of some Kirghiz, but when it stood up and I distinctly saw its outline against the sky, its great size, long legs, magnificent horns curved back in a spiral, showed me that I was looking at a splendid ram of the wild sheep of Tian Shan (*Ovis karelini*, Sev.), a rare and highly prized game. There can be few other places in the world where one may come across a wild sheep peacefully grazing by the side of a post-road.

I at once stopped the horses, slipped out of the cart, steadied my aim and fired. To my delight the ram fell, but a moment later sprang up again, and in a couple of great bounds quickly hid itself behind the rocks. A second bullet failed to bring it down. When we reached Sary Bulak, where we stopped for the night, I sent a couple of Kirghiz to look for the wounded ram. Late that night they came back, bringing the body with them. The bullet had penetrated his lungs, and he had not gone far. The bullet of an old rifle like my *berdianka* is not very fatal for big game, especially for such strong animals as sheep, which can carry a lot of lead. There are lots of these *arkhars* in this district and also plenty of snow leopard. The broad part of the valley of Sary Bulak is covered with *chiy* and littered in places with immense boulders, and at the mouth of one ravine on the left of the road there is a huge moraine of an ancient glacier. At an altitude of over seven thousand feet it was cold and cloudy, and here and there beyond the adjoining crest we could see the lofty peaks covered with snow.

From here the rise to the pass of Dolon begins, the only mountain ridge between the valley of the Chu and of the Naryn, which we had to cross. It is the watershed between the Chu and the Naryn, which is a tributary of the Syr Dariá. It is perhaps the most difficult pass between Semi-rechie and Kashgar, although not, relatively speaking, very high. It is, moreover, the only serious obstacle to a railway into the heart of Central Asia. But the carriage road is well laid out and offers no difficulties.

From the post-station there is a fairly stiff rise up heights of limestone and clay shales, intersected by quartz veins. Then the road drops to a small depression covered with last year's grass. Here for the first time we met with the alpine rock dove ; it is of a light-grey colour, with a white rump and a broad white band across the tail. These pigeons always occur in big flocks ; they have a very swift flight, and are always fat and tender.

As I was examining the quartz veins to see if I could find any interesting minerals in them, I disturbed a stoat, which ran off a few yards and then sat down on a stone and looked at me with an expression of alarm and reproach when I knocked off bits of quartz with my geological hammer. Probably it had a nest with young somewhere among the rocks.

Alpine choughs (*Pyrrhocorax alpinus*) appeared too, in pairs, and their melodious whistle enliven these grim mountains and showed that we had really reached the alpine zone. Then the road began mounting by zigzags to the crest. The higher we went, the softer became the outline of the mountains, the fewer the bare rocks and stones, while the surface was covered with herbage and last year's grass ; the top of the ridge has the appearance of an undulating steppe. Here and there, on top of the hills, patches of snow were still lying. The altitude of the pass is about ten thousand feet. Farther on the road drops gradually down a small valley into a narrow rocky gorge, becomes stonier and stonier, while cliffs of schists form a jagged edge to the crest ; thick veins of porphyrite appear, and then the road enters a belt of cherty shales which replace the conglomerates. On the sides of the mountains at first there appear extensive dark-green patches of juniper, then small firs, and then a dense forest of firs entirely covering the sides of the gorge, which becomes very picturesque ; at the bottom a greenish-grey torrent roars. In the patches of shrub studding the banks I caught glimpses of the redstarts flicking their bright red tails as they frisked among the shrubs, with stonechats, Indian pratincoles and some kind of mountain finches. This is the gorge of Kara Ungur, the Black Hole.

Although we arrived here very early, only half-past two, we decided to bivouac and give the horses a rest after the heavy pull up the hill, to catch a few fish and do a bit of shooting, as we were told there were plenty of roe here. I got some tackle from the man in charge of the post-station, and we quickly caught enough quite good trout for dinner, and while that was being prepared I went off with the man as guide to try to shoot a roe. Unfortunately it came on to rain, which spoilt it all, and we never saw a single animal, although we could hear them in the forest, making a noise something between a man's cough and a dog's bark.

This was a picturesque and attractive place and full of game. Farther up the mountains in the forest there are wapiti, and flocks of wild sheep graze on the plateaux above the gorges, and ibex too, the latter in herds often numbering up to fifty head. They are very easy to shoot here, as the guns can ride everywhere, and it is easy to arrange to drive them with the help of some Kirghiz. The whole region of Naryn is very interesting for a zoologist, as there is a great abundance and variety of animal life. Apart from the game already mentioned, there occurs here the red alpine wolf— a very rare kind. Unfortunately I was not able to arrange to get any shooting at these rare types of game; it was too dangerous for me to linger on the road, and, too, I had to husband my modest financial resources very strictly, for I had very little left.

At this post I smelted a little piece of ore that I had found, and produced a button of tin. I had found the ore quite by chance a day or two previously in a thick vein of tinstone running through the granite. This was very interesting when we remember that this was the first discovery of tinstone in Central Asia, although certain signs had long since led me to expect its presence. In Russia tin occurs only in one place, in the Trans-Baikal region, and there in insignificant quantities. This discovery in Semirechie would have been very useful if my unfortunate country had had anything resembling a respectable Government.

This was the second chance discovery of useful minerals during my enforced explorations. The first was a gold placer in a small valley on the banks of a stream. In this sand there are also gemstones, including sapphires, and I found a couple of pieces of excellent topaz, which I brought away with me. A trial washing of this sand in a pan of a sample taken off the top showed that the place is quite rich in gold. What a rich country it is, where a man fleeing for his life can casually stumble upon valuable deposits of ores and other minerals! In the district in question one commonly comes across veins of excellent asbestos; sometimes the natives use it for making gloves and scarfs as a sort of curiosity. In one of the valleys near the Chinese frontier there is a substantial deposit of cinnabar; I saw a very fine crystal from there.

From Kara Ungur we drove off early the next morning. There had been a sharp frost during the night, and the ground was thickly covered with hoar. There were hardly any signs of spring up here. The firs had not yet turned to their bright spring tint but kept their sombre winter colour; the shrubs had hardly begun to bud and the grass only just begun to show, but here and there were a few low-growing tulips, with their leaves curiously undulating at the edges. The views in the gorge are very fine of the rocks, forest, enormous isolated firs and the turquoise blue of the stream. Not far from the end of the gorge on the left bank in the face of a huge cliff there is a very large cave. In places the limestone is of a yellow colour. The gorge terminates in a really narrow gateway, formed by splendid picturesque cliffs, which almost look as though made by hand; through this the view opens out into a broad expanse of steppe, through which winds the river with its mouth covered with thickets of *chiy*. Numerous Kirghiz *mazary* dotted here and there in groups give a strange and curious appearance to the scene.

Here we stopped to rest at the post-station On Archa (The Ten Junipers), where we did some fishing while the horses were having their feed. The postmaster, a young Tartar who had been very well off before the revolution, gave us a net, and in half an hour we had caught several good-sized *marinki*, a fish that is very good eating, but the roe and a black membrane inside are extremely poisonous, and so in cooking them it is necessary to take the greatest precautions that not one scrap of either remain, or the consequences may be quite serious. The genus is *Schizothorax*, of which there are several species in the lakes and rivers of Central Asia.

When we left for Naryn, the postmaster and his brother set off for the head waters of the On Archa to shoot wapiti, of which there are plenty in these mountains. They were good fellows, and so I was very sorry, though hardly surprised, to hear afterwards that they were shot by the Bolsheviks.

After about twelve or thirteen miles over an undulating plateau the road drops down a steep slope into the valley of the Naryn, where there is a fine view of the little town of the same name, picturesque as a pretty toy, far below in a dead flat valley at about 7000 feet, surrounded by high tiers of mountains on the north and south.

The bottom of the valley consists of a compact conglomerate; the river is very deep but not broad, and has cut a channel with vertical sides as though dug out by hand;

they are so level that the river is hardly noticeable until you come on to it suddenly when driving down the valley.

The town of Naryn, before the war and the revolution, was famous for its trade in wild animals, which was started here by a man named Nezhivoff, who was known as the Russian Hagenbeck. He exported from here to Germany whole caravans of animals every year. The business was a big one, and he was a rich man. He built himself a fine house surrounded by all sorts of cages. When I last saw the place the cages were empty except one, in which there was a splendid ounce or snow leopard (*Felis irbis*). Nezhivoff contemplated trying to renew his business in spite of the Bolsheviks, but it was not to be. Before the end of the year, five months later, he with all his family, including his little twelve-year-old boy who showed me the ounce, even the animal itself, were shot by the Bolsheviks, who sent a 'punitive expedition' to wipe out this nest of *burjui*. Of the whole European population of Naryn, the only two who escaped this fate were very old men.

But at the time of my visit the unfortunate town little suspected the grim fate in store for it. Life went on quietly enough much as in the old days, and the Soviet officials were Bolsheviks in name only, and even the Che-Ka itself was quite gentle, thanks to the presence of Kirghiz and Sarts, who restrained the fiery zeal of the Communists sent from headquarters.

It is a curious thing that practically everywhere in Turkestan the native Moslems—that is, the Kirghiz and Sarts—showed far more humanity, justice and mercy towards the victims of Communism than the Russians, and especially than the Letts, Jews and other foreigners from European Russia, although it was only the outcasts of native society

237

and the dregs of the Mahommedan population who entered the Soviet service. When people speak of the cruelty of the Mongolian races a decided reservation should be made, or, at all events, the Turki peoples should be excepted. This fact was long since realised by the older settled Russian population in the country, although so contradictory to the received opinion. Together with this illusion must go another, that of the Great Bloodless Russian Revolution, and of the fable, started goodness knows by whom, of the gentle, good-natured humanity of the Russian peasant.

All the Communism of Naryn consisted in the ' nationalisation ' of a considerable quantity of cows at the expense of the Kirghiz, and their distribution among the natives of the town who had none, for the princely sum of three roubles per cow, at that time equivalent to threepence. Families with children received two or even three cows. But the Kirghiz are good sorts and did not bear any malice for this ' nationalisation,' and on the day of my arrival at Naryn the whole adult population, with the commissars at their head, had gone off at the invitation of a rich Kirghiz in his *aul* some twenty-five miles distant, where he was giving a party in commemoration of a relative of his who had been hung four years previously for taking part in the rising. One of the chief attractions was a race meeting for very substantial prizes. The first was a hundred camels, the second a hundred three-year-old horses, and the third a quarter of a million Soviet roubles. Neither did the generous host forget to supply twenty buckets of poteen for his Christian guests !

The road from Naryn plunges at once into a gorge, following its stony bottom for a considerable distance along a small stream, with here and there a native mill on the banks.

These are of one and the same very primitive design throughout Central Asia and Tibet : the blades are set obliquely on a long wooden spindle and the water runs in on a wooden gutter, the whole forming an embryo turbine. On the upper end there is fastened a small and usually very uneven stone. Nothing could be simpler.

Then the road makes a sharp turn to the west into a small valley winding along grass-clad clay hills, and then once more it rises to a lofty plateau, covered with handsome, great yellow poppies with huge flowers, branched stalk and thick succulent leaves. Among the mountains the smiling meadows stood out covered with a low-growing, dark-green, velvety rush known as *bitego*, probably a species of *Carex*, which became famous at this time for its nutritious qualities, making it a valuable feed for horses, cattle and sheep. These grow fat on it very rapidly and recover condition lost through bad times, and horses are as strong and become as fit and enduring on it as on good oats. These fields of *bitego* are the best grazing land in the Tian Shan and Pamir. Even when dry, in winter, it is valuable to fatten sheep, and half-starved animals quickly recover on it.

Along the roadside we found quantities of an excellent kind of mushroom, and very good eating it was. It grows in groups under a thin crust of earth, which cracks slightly as they push their way up ; the umbrella is tucked in and the gills are pink. I picked a whole bucketful of them. Stewed in cream they made a dish fit for a king.

The road then drops by long gentle slopes for several miles to the valley of At Bashi, the Horse's Head, over a very gently sloping plain covered with *chiy*. On the south there rises a steep, lofty, dark-blue ridge with its peaks covered with snow. Down below the sun was warm and the air balmy, with a gentle breeze, but higher up dark clouds were gathering and the sky threatening.

The valley of At Bashi itself is delightful. From the village of that name towards the east, looking up-stream, it is all covered with forest and dense shrubby thickets. The folk produce a good impression : they consist of Sarts and Kirghiz, the few houses of European construction being occupied by Customs and other officials and a few petty traders.

Through the whole of the Autonomous Socialistic Soviet Republic of Turkestan this was now the one and only spot where the bazaar was open and one could freely buy a pair of boots, of pretty poor quality, it is true, but still one was thankful to heaven for the mercy ; and one could buy fur caps, *mata*, a coarse local textile, oats, mutton, bread and so on. Consequently the inhabitants of the " freest country in the world " concentrate here from all parts of Semirechie to lay in stocks of these necessities.

On leaving the township we had to ford the rapid and fairly deep River At Bashi, a fairly risky proceeding, as a short time previously a cart had been capsized and a woman drowned with her two children. Beyond the river, to the left of the road, there is a lofty massive hill crowned with a *mazar* and a mosque ; the way up is by a steep and wearisome path, up which at the cost of great fatigue toil the Faithful desirous of performing an act of sanctity. It is a fine mountain, visible from a great distance from every side, and enhances the beauty of this charming valley.

About six miles beyond the village of At Bashi we stopped at a large farm, the property of a Kirghiz *kazi* or judge who was formerly very rich, but now totally ruined by the Bolsheviks and despoiled of everything. They had deprived him of his post, but he still retained great influence and prestige with the natives.

Near here the At Bashi is fed by the stream Kara Kain (the Black Birch) from the west, and the At Bashi, making a sharp bend to the north, cuts through an almost inaccessible gorge and falls into the Naryn.

Here, with the help of the judge, I hired the services of a Kirghiz with a camel to carry food for our horses, as the plateau of Chatyr Kul and Turgart, I had heard, were still covered with snow, so that there was no grazing at all.

The sight of the judge's farm was depressing. It was laid out in the Russian manner and thoroughly well equipped by this rich Kirghiz, who so confidingly gave up his own nomadism for the settled life of a farmer in full confidence in the stability of Russian civilisation. And now it was laid waste. In the doorway, alone and mournful, sat its owner ; all that was left him was life itself. This is, however, another instance of the milder nature of the natives of this part of Asia. If this had happened in Central Russia the mujiks would certainly have burnt the whole place to the ground, and the owner would have inevitably been murdered. In this remote corner of the vast Russian Empire there had not been true Bolsheviks, real Communists acting in the name of the doctrine of Karl Marx, ' nationalising ' the property of others. The men who had robbed the rich Kirghiz were simply Russians, who adroitly profited by the alluring slogan thrown by Lenin to the mob, " Help yourselves ! " Sometimes they were cynical enough to admit openly that they had no communistic feelings whatever, but were simply taking the opportunity. " Our chance has come," they said. " Why waste it ? " and " Let's make hay while the sun shines. We don't know how long it'll last, and then we shall be left out in the cold again."

As a matter of fact, Lenin and his myrmidons never did convert the Russian mujiks and labourers to the delights of the doctrine of Socialism ; he simply gave them a very convenient excuse and longed-for opportunity to unbridle their native instincts of plunder, their hatred of civilisation and that love of destruction for its own sake so highly developed in the masses of the Russian people, which has given vent to these passions at all times and places when the restraining hand of the educated classes has failed to curb them.

The farm was surrounded by meadows and paddocks of tender fresh grass, while down below on the marshy soil there was a mass of white and lilac primulas. When I was strolling about there just before sunset the sky clouded over, a cuckoo repeated her monotonous song in the garden, high-piping sandpipers whistled in the marsh, peewits flapped their wings over me, uttering their plaintive cry.

I felt very sad. Even in this uttermost corner, in this smiling alpine valley, were felt the eddies of the crash and ruin of the Russian Empire. . . .

The valley of the River Kara Kain, through which our road ran, is really only a continuation of the At Bashi, but that runs in the opposite direction, towards the west, gradually rising to the pass of Ak Biit and continuing farther to the pass of Yassin in the mountain range of Ferghaná, the natural and easy road from Naryn into that province. The lower portion is covered with first-class pasture-land and numerous irrigation canals, now abandoned and dried up, sure evidence that once upon a time it was thickly inhabited by an agricultural population.

We still had a little over forty miles to the frontier post at Ak Biit. About seven miles beyond the place where we spent the night, on the left of the road, are the ruins of an ancient Chinese town, crumbling walls, old watch towers and so on. In places all traces of the road disappeared. In one such spot our cart and horses stuck in the marshy ground. We pulled and pulled in vain. Then we unloaded everything and dragged it back to firm ground. To do this we had to make ropes fast to the rear axle and make the horses drag it backwards. We were entertained at the time by numbers of a very beautiful little wagtail (*Rudites iranica*, Zar.), which were running and flying about over the swamp. This delightful little bird has the head, neck, breast of a brilliant golden yellow, while the back is of a velvety black and the wings grey with white bands. Against the bright green background of the fields, still covered with short fresh turf and speckled with golden tulips, these little gems were extraordinarily effective, and it seemed just as though they had been specially designed to fit in with the background, and I could not tear my eyes away from the charming picture.

It was late in the evening when we stopped to spend the night in an isolated Kirghiz *yurtá* or hut. The owner, a fine old fellow, was uncommonly polite and attentive to us. I slept out in the open, and when I went into the hut in the morning to warm myself a bit at the fire I was witness of a touching, if barbarous, scene of wifely devotion. Our host's son was deep in the sleep of the just, in the usual Kirghiz way, quite naked under his blanket. Meanwhile his affectionate and devoted wife profited by the opportunity to clean his shirt of the vermin swarming in it. She performed this operation in a manner that was effective as

243

it seemed to me original. She systematically took every fold and seam in the shirt and passed it between her glistening white teeth, nibbling rapidly. The sound of the continuous juicy cracking could be heard clearly. This strange scene reminded me of the words of Herodotus, " the Scythians who eat lice. . . ." How accurately he described the habits of these same Kirghiz tribes two-and-twenty centuries ago ! This little incident shows how increased knowledge of the world is confusing the pedants who accuse the Father of History of credulity and exaggeration.

Nearer to Ak Biit vegetation almost entirely disappears ; all that is left is here and there a small clump of stunted alpine plants. The post-station of Ak Biit is situated at the mouth of a small valley leading up to the pass and to the lofty plateau of Arpa. Here there is a detachment of frontier guards of the Red Army, patrolling the entry and exit from ' Sovdepia.'

I purposely delayed my arrival a day so as to pass this dangerous point on Trinity Sunday, when most of the Red patrols would have gone into the village of At Bashi to celebrate in the usual way, and the few who remained at their posts would, of course, be drunk too.

My calculations were brilliantly justified. At the post there was left only a Tartar and a Kirghiz, both illiterate. I showed them my imposing ' mandate,' specially drawn up for the occasion, instructing me to buy *mata* at the nearest possible place in Chinese territory, by order of the Soviet of National Economy at Tokmak ; at the same time I soothed their hearts by giving them half a bottle of real, undiluted, genuine, old vodka and three pounds of raisins, which were very much appreciated owing to the impossibility of getting sugar in the district. The Red guards grinned appreciatively, wished me a pleasant journey and success in my mission, asking me to come hurrying back and to bring their wives and children some nice brightly coloured *mata* to make frocks of.

" Our women-folk are almost going about naked ! " they exclaimed.

CHAPTER XVII. DESOLATION.

A FEELING of intense relief, of real joy and freedom, came over me when this last post of Soviet Russia was left behind and my cart continued its road up to the lofty plateaux of Arpa and Chatyr Kul. Snow lay about the place in patches still, and in it I saw the tracks of wild sheep, foxes and wolves.

In the valley of Arpa, which looks like a real steppe in the Orenburg district, the thawing snow gave rise to rivulets all over the place. We stopped to bivouac at the entrance to the valley of Kara Su (Black Water), at the foot of some rocky hills. The next morning I was aroused by the ringing cries of ruddy sheldrake (*Casarca rutila*), a flock of which was busy among the stones on top of the hill, behaving just like chukar. These duck nest in holes in absolutely waterless spots, and obviously they had found a suitable site up here. I have found their nests even in fresh Kirghiz graves, and as they often feed on carrion, joining in with vultures and crows, it is better to cut them out of the list of edible game, especially as the meat is tough and stringy.

The road kept mounting. High up on the right above the hills there rose a column of cloud, just as though out of the crater of some volcano, black and threatening. This was the steam rising from the Lake of Chatyr Kul (the Lake of the Tent). From the hills there opens out an extensive panorama over a vast plain, surrounded on all sides by not lofty

246

but very rugged mountains with jagged peaks. Only a very small portion of the huge area of this basin is occupied by the lake itself, which is about fourteen miles long by about five or six broad. Here we were on the top of the central ridge of the Tian Shan, at an altitude of eleven or twelve thousand feet, yet to my astonishment, instead of glaciers, crags and cliffs, with which one associates such altitudes, here was a level valley covered with snow and hills which would hardly be called mountains; the scene, in fact, rather recalled the polar regions of the far north. The ice on the lake was only just beginning to melt, which increased the illusion. Driving over this arctic valley was a misery. The whole area round the lake was covered with a deep, friable, thawing crust, beneath which was water, with streams, often quite deep, running in every direction, it seemed, with water, snow and ice mixed together. Our poor horses one moment were sinking in soft snow, another into the water, struggling, plunging and floundering. Then we had to unharness them and drag the cart out with ropes. In places where the snow had gone they stuck in a wet clayey soil like treacle. Azamat Bek and I went on foot all the time, both wet through up to the waist and worn out by the effort. The tired horses had great difficulty in pulling even the empty cart, and I feared that we should end by spending the night in the open in the middle of this awful expanse of cold slush.

At one place, where we spent a whole hour tugging at the horses and the cart, a common sparrow, the ordinary domestic sparrow of Turkestan (*Passer indicus*), flew up and kept fluttering round us, just as though it recognised its old friends and hosts, human beings, in that desolate wilderness. This was remarkable, as sparrows do not live at these altitudes, their place being taken among the Kirghiz huts by some kind of finch, perhaps the brambling. I suppose the poor bird had flown up here from At Bashi, lost its way among the mountains and now, seeing us, flew up in delight to find humans again. When we succeeded in driving off, I flung it a handful of barley.

On the banks of the lake we were met by a flock of handsome and interesting geese (*Anser indicus*), which examined us with considerable curiosity, flying round us twice, wondering, no doubt, what was this extraordinary phenomenon which had invaded their sanctuary, for they had probably never before seen a cart with a troika of horses.

It was already nearly dark when we got through to the pass of Turgart, where there were a few tumble-down huts inhabited by a couple of Kirghiz families about a quarter of a mile apart. The word 'pass' hardly seemed appropriate. There is no sign of elevation here, and the cart bowled along easily without any suggestion of rising ground.

We stopped at the first, and here, in this stifling, dirty, dark hut, we had to spend the night, dry ourselves and our clothes and have something to eat. A storm arose and a gale howled the whole night through, with a blizzard of whirling snow as dry as sand. The altitude was a good twelve thousand feet, and the slightest exertion made me feel the rarefaction of the air. Next morning we left the cart behind and, mounting our horses, rode on towards Chinese territory. There was snow all round us. About seven or eight miles farther uphill the road leads to a steep descent about a thousand feet down into a valley. At one time it had been in very good condition, but now it was badly washed away, and although a light cart might have got down all right, it would have been very difficult to bring it back again. However, carriages from Kashgar and Chinese *mapas* manage to climb up sometimes and find their way through to At Bashi.

Down below the snow was already gone and the air noticeably warmer. The descent led to the beginning of a broad level valley, where was the Chinese Customs Station. There was not, however, any Chinaman there, but only a few Sarts and Kirghiz.

On the slopes of the mountains, alongside the road, on every side there were quantities of marmots, of a greyish-brown colour with black tails. They were running about in pairs or singly, squatting in various positions at the entrance to their burrows, sometimes right in the road itself, and trustingly let us come within a few paces of them, when they stared at us with obvious curiosity.

It seemed almost as though the very animals felt themselves more free and independent in this land where there was no Bolshevism. The marmot, as is well known, hibernates over the winter, and now, awakening from their long sleep, they were unusually busy and active. They are amusing little creatures with one feature that is exceedingly rare among animals—that is, they can literally cry, shedding real tears.

Once I happened to see one caught by a couple of dogs far from its hole. Not knowing where to turn, the wretched creature pressed its back against a stone, sat up on its hindquarters and, clenching its little fore-paws, wiped away the tears that were running down its little muzzle. All its movements and its attitude were so human that it looked just like a little terrified child. I drove off the dogs, which as a matter of fact were not hurting it at all but only barking at the little thing and frightening it, and the comical little creature hopped off to its burrow. It was a female, and no doubt had its babies.

Unfortunately human greed and the caprice of fashion has reached even this harmless little creature in its remote and desolate haunts. The constantly increasing demand for furs and the perfection in the art of dyeing them, for which marmot skins are very suitable, and converting their very ordinary pelt into a luxurious fur coat, has led to the merciless persecution of this interesting little animal. In some parts of Russia, for instance in the Turgai steppe, the country was alive with them once, but now they have been exterminated, and in the most brutal and barbarous manner imaginable. The hunters poured water down their burrows. This drove the marmots to the surface, where they were caught, but the helpless young were drowned in their holes. The fashionable ladies of Europe and America, who wear furs of unnatural colour made up from the skins of marmot, should think how many hot and bitter tears these poor little creatures have shed on their account in the depths of the mountains of Tian Shan ! [1]

The country round the Chinese post is typical of a mountain valley. It is the source of the River Tuyuk, which flows by a gentle slope down to the valley of Kashgar, cutting through the last crest of the Tian Shan chain at the fort of Chokmak. Of all the roads leading to Kashgar, or in general from the civilised world into Central Asia, this is the best, most convenient, shortest, easiest, cheapest, and it would not be difficult to improve it into a good carriage

[1] The European marmot is *Arctomys marmotta*, and occurs in the Alps. Farther east it is replaced by the baibac (*A. bobac*). It is known in the fur trade by the Mongolian name *tarbagan*.

road, so as to connect up the railway systems of Europe with the very heart of Central Asia.

We spent the night at the Chinese post, and in the morning I explained to Azamat Bek that I was going through to Kashgar and should not return to Semirechie. I gave him a written certificate to the effect that he had acted as driver with a cart and two horses and sent back by me to Tokmak owing to "want of food for the animals." I gave him a handsome present, including my high shooting-boots, which threw him into an ecstasy of delight, as at that time the citizens of the most advanced and freest country in the world were for the most part going about almost barefoot.

I watched Azamat out of sight, and when he had gone and I was left alone without a companion, I could not shake off a terrible fit of depression. I had now cut the last thread that connected me with the land of my fathers, and I was left utterly alone in a remote and strange land, a very strange land, among strange and unknown people. Hard it was to imagine what was in store for me and what trials fate still held for me to go through. But the thought of freedom and my escape from Soviet slavery consoled me, afforded me complete consolation, and a great calm settled upon me.

I took a mounted Kirghiz as guide and pushed on to the Chinese post of Kizil Kurgan, the Red Fort, where there was a police post to patrol the entrance into Chinese territory.

Farther southwards, on the sides of the valley of the Tuyuk, the mountains become higher and higher. At places they open out and form a broad plain, at others they almost meet at the banks of the stream. The country is desolate and almost lifeless, with neither grass, shrubs nor trees, only bare cliffs, screes, gravel and sand in the bed of the river which our path followed. The river itself is but a rivulet winding among great masses of shingle.

The whole region is of extraordinary interest to the geologist. To the traveller in Central Asia who comes here from Russian Turkestan, the first thing that strikes him are the traces of violent volcanic action in the Tertiary Period in connection with the elevation of these mountain masses. The mountains themselves are composed of red ferruginous sandstones of cretaceous or tertiary age. Great thicknesses of these beds have been crumpled in various ways and folded, in places standing vertically. Obviously they have been subject to intense mountain-building strains. These sedimentary deposits in their turn have been cut by intrusions of basaltic lava, in some places forming immense sheets of considerable thickness and extent. Weathering out in tiers, the basalt in places assumes the appearance of a sedimentary deposit, and in others is stained red by oxides of iron. Nowhere in Russian Turkestan, Semirechie, the Pamirs, Bokhara or the Transcaspian region are there such remains of volcanic activity.

The existence of active volcanoes in Central Asia has been believed in for a long time, but the origin of this belief was eventually proved to be underground fires of beds of coal, giving out smoke and steam and also sulphur, sal ammoniac and similar products. There is such a fire of this sort now still burning near the town of Kuchara in the eastern part of Chinese Turkestan, where, according to the belief of the Chinese and natives, there dwells in the fire an incombustible animal, according to some a dragon, to others a rat of gigantic dimensions which they call ' Salamander.'

The famous traveller and geologist, Stoliczka, the first European to visit the valley of the Tuyuk, in the 'seventies, described in detail the remains of an ancient crater, ' somma,' with slags and scoriæ, seen by him in one place in the valley of the Tuyuk. I have twice ridden through this valley, but could never find any trace of an old crater, although intrusions of basalt into the sandstones and great beds of lava here and in other parts of this locality are very numerous. The origin of all phenomena seen by me, the relief of the mountains, exposures and so on, is due solely to erosion. This accounts for the indication on old maps and books on geography of ' extinct volcanoes ' near the lake of Chatyr Kul. But, of course, this volcanic activity is to be referred to the remote past of the Tertiary Epoch, and has nothing in common with contemporary volcanoes. Farther on we shall see that in the central portion of the plain of Kashgar, on the northern edge of the desert of Takla Makan, there are remains of an enormous volcano, also of tertiary age.

We rode fast, hurrying to reach Kizil Kurgan before dark for the crossing of the River Suyuk, which flows past the actual fortress. In the evening the water is substantially increased by the snow melted during the day, and the ford is impossible.

We rode twenty-eight miles without stopping, and towards dusk came to the broad and rapid River Suyuk. Although this river is much bigger than the Tuyuk, it takes that latter's name after the confluence and flows into the Kashgar plain, where all its waters are absorbed by irrigation canals.

On the near side of the river there stood a small blockhouse or fort built of red stone, surrounded on all sides by lofty sheer cliffs and crags, mostly reddish in colour. Beyond the fort I could see the usual Kirghiz necropolis so characteristic of the valleys of Tian Shan, the *mazary*, also usually of red stone or clay. The place is appropriately named, as all around red is the dominating tint, although, thank God, politically the country was ' White,' for there was no Bolshevism here.

The general atmosphere, however, was gloomy, and produced a mournful impression of wilderness and lifelessness. There was neither grass nor shrub, nor yet anything green whatever ; all around was bare stone or gravel.

On the roof of the fort there stood a tall Chinaman in a long black cloak, who looked with incredulous eyes at the sight of a Russian arriving from the north, from the fearful land of Bolshevism and Communism.

A Kirghiz policeman rode out to meet us across the river, showing us the best and safest ford.

" Who are you, and why have you come here ? " asked the Chinese official, who spoke quite good Russian, when I dismounted and greeted him. " I cannot let you go any farther ; for that I must ask permission of the Tao Yin, the Governor, of Kashgar," he continued when I explained why I had thus come to China. " But first of all let's go and have some tea," he added kindly, " and then we will see what we can do."

The little yard within the fort and the two modest rooms which afforded a home to this Chinaman struck me by their cleanness and neatness, while the Kirghiz policeman and Chinese servant astonished me by their discipline and respectful manners, two things which had long since been forgotten in Russia.

By the front door there were some official notices in Chinese, stuck to a board on the wall, intelligible, of course, only to the commandant of the fort ; but on both sides of the door were eloquent emblems of Chinese justice, perfectly comprehensible to all : two long, fairly broad, thin lathes with handles. Hundreds and thousands of strokes with these might be generously delivered upon the citizens of the Chinese Republic at the discretion of authority.

Glass after glass of tea I drank, real fragrant Chinese tea, sweet with sugar, such as I had not drunk for many a long day; the long and rapid ride and the rarefied air had given me a desperate thirst.

The white-washed walls of the room were hung with Chinese newspapers from Shanghai with advertisements and notices in English, which gladdened my eyes, as proof that I had reached the confines of the civilised world, that, God be praised! I was now in a *burjui* country and that I had really extricated myself from that oppressive, murky, hermetically sealed crypt, the Land of Communism.

The walls of the front room were covered with military rifles, the muzzles and locks carefully wrapped in blue rags. There hung, too, cartridge-cases and skins of fox and wolf, and on the floor were a couple of quite good bear-skins. The commandant of the fort, according to the Chinese custom, supplemented his salary by dealing in furs and skins and also, as I learnt afterwards, in opium.

We sat late that night, each busy with his own correspondence, by the dim light of my last and only candle. I wrote a petition to the Tao Yin requesting permission to enter his territory, and also a letter to the Russian and to the English Consuls, while the Chinaman carefully painted his hieroglyphics with a brush, giving a report of my arrival, a description of my person and a request for permission to let me through to Kashgar. The messenger we had to send through on my horse, as the policeman's horse had been sent a long way away owing to shortage of food; and if my horse had stopped there, there was nothing at all to feed him with. I gave the messenger some money and sternly told him to feed and take care of the animal on the road.

The next morning the river had swollen and it looked impossible to ford it, so that the messenger was not able to leave till the following day. All that time the poor animal was left without any food except the bread that I gave it.

The time spent here at Kizil Kurgan was anxious and hungry. It was the very worst season of the year. All winter stocks had been consumed and no fresh grass had yet appeared, and the Kirghiz' animals had been sent far away to the south. It was impossible to bring provisions and fodder up from At Bashi as they used to in the old days, though a few Kirghiz had tried to do so at the cost of their lives. We were short of food, too, for ourselves. The Chinaman's entire dinner consisted of boiled rice and a few special Chinese preserves, so that a ham from one of the pigs I used to pasture in Pishpek, which I had succeeded in bringing so far as a reserve, came in very welcome, and was the *pièce de résistance* of our scanty menu. How grateful I felt then to my kind hostesses at Pishpek who had provided me with this excellent provision for my journey !

The surroundings were depressing and gloomy. The place was lifeless. The wild forbidding mountains around consisted of massive beds of red sandstone reposing on alternating beds of grey, massive, ferruginous and white grits, mingled with quartzites. The beds were sharply folded, thrust and contorted, the bedding in places vertical, the peaks assuming fantastic jagged outlines. Below, on a few patches there stood up like huge bristles the hard dry stalks of the wire grass, *chiy*, the tops grazed off by cattle. High up on the tops of the rocky crests I could just distinguish spots of stunted *archa* (*Juniperus pseudo-sabina*) ; that is all.

The weather fitted in with the gloomy atmosphere of Kizil Kurgan. The clouds were lowering, and at times there blew a cold penetrating wind, which howled mournfully around the fort.

It was a hundred and twenty-five miles to Kashgar, and I had to drag out eight long, desperately dull, weary days on this deserted threshold of the inhabited world, waiting for the reply of the Chinese Governor. The commandant of the fort held out little hope of a favourable answer. It sounded very odd when he spoke Russian, as Chinese pronounce their R's like an L, and instead of Sh say S, so that in their lips our melodious Muscovite sounds like the lisping of a child.

" Why don't you go back to Taskend ? " he asked me, " now evelyting sould be all light now."

" What is all right there ? "

" Now thel' is no mo' wa' ; now evelyting is Bolsevik, evelyting is quiet . . . and dey won't let you tlough into Kasgal. Ou' China is neutlal . . ." thus assured me this naïve son of the Heavenly Republic.

My heart sank and my very soul seemed desolate. In alarm, I pondered over the problem of my movements if I were to receive a refusal to pass through to Kashgar.

There was nothing to read. I whiled away the time in walks in the neighbourhood examining the rocks ; I tried to crush and wash a conglomerate which contained a lot of quartz in the hope of finding gold. I sat and yarned with the Kirghiz policemen. They told me that they were not taught to shoot, and weapons were not given them.

" When it is necessary the officer will show us how to load a gun and shoot with it," said these highly original soldiers.

In their turn they asked me a whole lot of curious questions. Was I not a priest ? Could I lift up with one hand . . . a horse ? " We think you must be a very strong man," they said, " you look like a *batyria* " (meaning *bogatyr*, the semi-mythical heroes of Russian tradition). " Could you kill an ibex with your rifle if he were standing on the top of that cliff ? " and they pointed to a rock that was at least a mile away.

These strange gendarmes had no official uniform ; they were dressed just like any other Kirghiz, only, when on duty, they put on a blue canvas sleeveless jacket, with a large white circle on the back on which were some Chinese hieroglyphics ; this converted them into official employees, but it can hardly be claimed that these jackets gave them a smart military appearance.

Animal life was very scarce here. Apart from a few alpine choughs and rock doves, all the bird life I saw consisted of a few alpine larks (*Otocorys alpestris*) and some chats (*Saxicola*).

Somewhere in the neighbourhood the Kirghiz get a lead ore, which they smelt and sell the lead to the Chinese officer at the fort, who in turn issues it to Kirghiz hunters to bring him sheep and ibex. But at the moment even these wild creatures were so thin from scarcity of food that they were hardly edible.

I looked with envious eyes when these gendarmes drew their pay. This was actually in a silver currency, Their salary was ten *sar* a month—that is, about £6, 10s. In our Soviet money this represented about eighty thousand roubles, or more than an engineer's salary for two years. The exchange value of Soviet money was terribly low : for a thousand Soviet roubles a citizen of the " most advanced and freest State in the world " would here receive two miserable little Chinese copper coins !

At length, after a long and weary wait, the messenger arrived, bringing me the cheerful reply from the Tao Yin in the form of a categorical refusal to admit me into Chinese territory, which was neutral, and the friendly advice to return ' home ' to my ' fatherland ' !

The brain of the Chinaman is constructed on a totally different design from that of the rest of mankind, and the laws of logic and the ordinary feelings of humanity are utterly foreign to him.

My letter to the British Consul was returned to me opened. Evidently they had read it and considered it superfluous to deliver it to its address, and the letter to the Russian Consul was returned sealed, with the observation that there was no longer any Russian Consul in Kashgar. By a special order the Tao Yin gave a stern reprimand to the commandant of the fortress of Kizil Kurgan for admitting a Russian to Chinese territory, and gave him orders to send me back with an armed escort to the Russian frontier, with special instructions to disarm me and confiscate my rifle, about which evidently the commandant had not failed to report to his superior.

To this last demand I replied resolutely that I would not give up my rifle to any man, and that if they attempted to take it by force I would resist and open fire.

" All light ! " assented the commandant gently, and did not insist.

It was a sorry journey back to my ' fatherland.' The

rascal of a Kirghiz who had ridden my horse to Kashgar had tired it out, as I quickly found out. Some rickety old crocks had been sent up for the commandant and for the gendarmes who formed my escort, and which could hardly put one leg before another. There was only one decent one, a fine Karabair from Ferghaná—that is, a special breed of horses in Turkestan derived from a cross between Arab sires and Kirghiz mares. It had been formerly the charger of a *mingbashi*, a functionary in charge of several villages, and, although dreadfully thin, still stepped out vigorously. Blood will tell, even up in these grim mountain deserts.

I remembered the tale of a Russian smuggler engaged in the contraband opium trade from Kashgar, whom I consulted about the secrets of the road.

" For these trips," he had told me, " we take the strongest horses we can get, with the greatest powers of endurance, as we have to ride great distances over mountain deserts without any feed, and at the end of the trip the beasts are reduced to skeletons, and so starved that they chew each other's manes and tails."

A cold and penetrating wind blew all the time and a dry cutting snow whirled round us, stinging the faces and eyes. Heavy-laden clouds covered the sky, and seemed to overwhelm everything. The north, where we were now riding, seemed murky and especially menacing. I was miserable and depressed indeed, for all hope of rescue was gone, and ahead I could see only the inevitable result, falling into the clutches of the Soviet authorities, torture and death, and the grief of those near and dear to me.

What could I do ? How could I escape such a fate ? My brain worked at high pressure on this problem, but I could think of no way out. Where could I go, and what could I do in this cold, lifeless, mountain desert ? It was a desert, too, where the rarefied air made every movement an effort, and a man becomes flabby and weak as though in an advanced stage of anæmia.

About half-way, when my companions stopped to give the horses a blow, I felt my poor beast totter, and I barely had time to slip from the saddle before it collapsed. The poor brute was utterly done and could not carry me another yard. So I went on foot, leading him by the reins.

My escort went on ahead, in a hurry to reach a human habitation and shelter from the blinding snow. I was left behind alone with my wretched horse, who dragged more and more, getting slower and slower, keeping back even my slow pace. At last it tottered and again collapsed on the ground. I could see that its end had come. Its eyes rolled, and tears streamed from them. I took out my last remaining rolls of native bread and gave them to the horse, but the poor brute was not even capable of chewing them, for they were as hard now as stone, so I broke them between two stones and fed him with the crumbs. Then I tried to find a few dried wisps of grass, which the creature took greedily. It was dying of starvation and exhaustion. I crumbled up my last remaining bits of bread and gave them to it. Then one of the Kirghiz rode back, bringing me another horse. I told him to look after my animal and see if he could not bring it through to the *aul* after a little rest.

But even on this new horse I was not able to ride far ; its pace grew slower and slower, and before long I had to dismount again and go on foot, leading this one, too, by the rein. The blizzard, hurricane and snow grew worse, the horse kept me back, the thin air, wind and cold stopped my breathing. At times the snowstorm raged so fiercely and was so blinding that I was afraid I should lose the path and spend the night in the open, which certainly meant freezing to death.

It was quite dark when I struggled up to the Customs House post, worn out, dead beat and famished. I had not eaten anything since the morning, and was in fact a complete wreck, both moral and physical.

Late that night the Kirghiz arrived, bringing my saddle, and told me that the horse was dead. And next morning, when I went out of the hut, he pointed out some dogs, appeared from heaven knows where, trotting off in the direction from which we had come.

" All the dogs in the countryside are now off to the carcase. They know very well where there is any carrion lying," he commented.

Now how could they know that ? It was a good ten miles to the place where I had left the horse.

A lot more snow fell during the night and it was very cold, although it was now the 9th of June. To all intents and purposes we were in the polar regions with an arctic climate. The escort conducted me to the Russian frontier and, to my great relief, left me there, as the Chinese officer and the Kirghiz gendarmes decided that it was better not to go through to Ak Biit, which was about another fifty miles, and the road round the lake Chatyr Kul was difficult and dangerous. This saved me from being handed over to the Red Frontier Guards.

I was left at Turgart, and found shelter in the poverty-stricken tent of an old Kirghiz with his family, nearly half a mile from the one where I had spent the night on my way up from At Bashi.

CHAPTER XVIII. DESPAIR.

MY situation was now about as hopeless as it could be ; neither horse nor other means of transport of getting away anywhere, and, to crown my misfortunes, my financial resources had almost come to an end. I could, in fact, not see any way out of my desperate situation. The great altitude, which makes movement an effort and always has a lowering effect upon the nervous system, also acted upon me, and I was reduced to the depths of melancholy and gloom.

External conditions, too, seemed as though they had been specially designed to drive a man into despair. In the morning the sun would occasionally show his face for a brief moment and there would be a respite from the snow, but in the afternoon the storm would begin again and the blizzard rage the whole night long. The horizon was all the time covered with lowering leaden clouds. Below, from the basin of Chatyr Kul, as though out of an enormous crater, there arose a column of black evil-looking clouds, which crept over towards us and enveloped us in a blanket of hurricane and snow, till my very soul seemed blotted out in blackness and despair.

The hovel, with crevices in the walls and a leaky door, gave no protection against the weather. Fuel there was hardly any, and when the fire was lit it filled the air with a biting, suffocating smoke. Everything was dirty and poverty-stricken. The old Kirghiz, owner of the hovel, was a very decent and obviously sincere fellow, who gave me the best hospitality in his power. Seeing my hopeless situation, he consoled me by saying that sometimes smugglers came this way, who could get me through secretly past the Red frontier patrols and deposit me in the valley of At Bashi, where I could easily hide in the dense forest.

" And then perhaps you'll be able to find someone who will be able to smuggle you into Kashgar, past both Red and Chinese patrols. There are secret paths where they smuggle opium, through Kara Teke Davan (Black Goat Pass), through Urta Su and the country of the Sary-Bagishi. Only take care and don't trust these, as they are terrible brigands, and often enough kill and rob travellers. Of course you'll have to ride by night and hide by day in the gullies," he told me, doing his best to comfort me ; " but whatever happens, do not despair," added the good old soul, " *khudai ga salamys !* " (" Let us trust in Allah ").

This was all very well, but there was little hope in it. It was all a matter of chance, on which I could count but little. It seemed to me that only a miracle could extricate me from my desperate position.

Poor old man ! He, too, had his trials ; he was very unhappy in his domestic life, as I became an involuntary witness. His family consisted of his first wife, already an old woman, a son of about twenty, and a second much younger wife, who was barely fifteen years old. The old woman was obviously a hysterical, cantankerous, old hag. She spent the whole time abusing her husband, often enough hitting him with the nearest thing handy, and was liable to outbursts of real frenzy which only her son could calm down.

But on one occasion she drove even him out of his self-

control, and he hit her with all his might, which quieted
the raging virago at once. The old man bore her outbursts
patiently and stoically. Her special malice was directed
against the new wife, who was hardly more than a child,
a timid, shrinking, down-trodden creature. They shouted
at her, beat her and gave her all the hardest jobs to do.
If the blizzard was raging and the cold intense, the old
woman would send her to fetch water, and when the wretched
girl, half-frozen, struggled to the door of the hovel with a
bucketful, she would pack her off again to fetch firewood,
which meant somehow or other digging up roots of old
clumps of grass, a few bits of thorny shrub and so on. The
poor girl's bed was only fit for a dog. She used to creep into
a corner by the door and roll herself up in a few miserable
rags. If she stretched out so much as her frozen fingers
to thaw them by the fire, it brought on an outburst of fury
and rage from the old harridan.

Late one evening, when a particularly cold and penetrating
wind was blowing and all had turned in to sleep, the old
witch took it into her head to make a specially savage
attack upon the girl and tried to drive her out of the hut,
throwing at her any missile that came handy, tearing her
ragged shirt from her body, shrieking and yelling curses at
her husband and his young wife. Like a whipped dog or
a terrified little animal, the girl sat huddled and shuddering
in her corner, sobbing quietly. But when the old woman
in an access of maniacal fury flung herself upon her terrified
victim, her son could bear it no longer, but gave his mother
a blow that sent her reeling across the hut; she fell to the
floor and lay there in silence. The night and next morning
were passed in peace.

Once, when there was nobody else in the hut, I offered

the wretched girl a roll and a handful of raisins. Fearfully looking round, shy and cautious as a wild animal, she timidly crept up to me, snatched the proffered handful and darted out of the hut to hide herself somewhere among the stones and eat her little treat in peace bit by bit, just like the half-wild dogs that skulk round the houses of the Sarts.

These scenes of home life of the inhabitants of Turgart, in their primitive setting, reminded me vividly of the fairy stories of our childhood, of Cinderella and her wicked step-mother, Old Mother Red Nose. The only difference was that in the fairy stories the people were not crawling with vermin and did not emit such a sickening stench as these too realistic mountaineers, and the nursery stories always end up so happily, but this poor little Cinderella in real life might wait for her prince till the crack of doom. She would probably end her days of sorrow through cold and starvation.

These depressing surroundings, my own desperate position, the cold and the shortage of food very constantly made me turn my thoughts back to Pishpek, now so far away, to my kind hostesses, where I had lived so comfortably, where nature was so luxuriant and generous, where now, after a delightful spring, the land was in the full blaze of summer. The contrast with these arctic deserts, with their blizzards and the primitive folk, among whom I was grateful to find any sort of shelter, was startling. Life must have been like this in Europe during the great Ice Age, and this re-semblance, as we shall see, was not merely apparent. Here I learnt with my own eyes that in truth the striving of man-kind towards the heights has its limits, and very well defined they are too. Owing to the fierce cold and unproductive deserts, the only life that is possible is that of primitive man.

To sit in that hovel all day was out of the question, so

I profited by every lull in the hurricane to go for a stroll in the neighbourhood. I amused myself by examining the rocks, and found in the small hills among the sandstones a bed of clay shale and two seams of coal.

Whenever the sun broke through the clouds the view over Chatyr Kul was imposing, though wild and gloomy ; the play of shadows and the cloud effects were strange and fantastic. One day from somewhere behind the mountains there rose up towards us a great black threatening cloud which burst into hail and thunder.

The days passed, each one lessening my hope of ever succeeding in escaping from this dreadful place.

At last, one evening, through a whirring blizzard we heard the crunch of feet in the snow. My host went out and brought in a couple of Kirghiz smugglers, followed a moment later by two more. They had five camels with them, laden with goods from Kashgar. They willingly consented to take me with them over the frontier to the forest of At Bashi. So the next afternoon, to my inexpressible delight, I rode away at last from that abode of misfortune.

The usual storm was in full swing, covering us with thick wet snow, which prevented us from seeing the road. Only at one place could I discern that we were riding over a beautiful grey marble veined with white up a gentle rise.

Then we dropped down to the lake and rode round it on the eastern side. The banks are low and very swampy and the ground extremely sticky, so we had to make wide detours to avoid getting bogged. My companions told me that it happened fairly often here that travellers lost their path in the blizzards and perished in the bogs, men, horses and cattle.

We cut the stream that used to let out the water of Chatyr

Kul into the valley of Ak Sai and then forms the upper reaches of the Tushkan Daria (Hare River), a tributary of the great river of the deserts of Central Asia, the Tarim, which loses itself in the mysterious swamps of Lob Nor. At present Chatyr Kul has no outflow.

Towards evening we came to the foothills of the mountains on the northern bank of the lake, and bivouacked in a hut built of stones at the entrance to the gorge of Tash Ravat.

The next morning was fine and clear with a sharp frost. The sun was shining brightly, throwing a deep-blue light on to the thawing parts of the lake, and a flock of wild geese flew along the shore. Evidently spring was beginning here. Far away towards the north, in the lower reaches of the Chu, this phase had passed at the beginning of March, but up here spring was three months later. The warm period in these localities is very short. Green grass makes its appearance in July, when the Kirghiz drive up their flocks for a brief spell; in the end of August the frost begins again, and in September the lake is once more covered with ice.

The road goes on some four miles or so through a gorge with limestones and shales, while in the lower part there are granite boulders, often of considerable dimensions. I saw horns of wild sheep lying here and there on the ground, evidently the remains of wolves' dinners.

In spite of the cold and the fact that the country was still under snow, I was tormented by thirst. This was curious. I had often suffered from this in the mountains, although in a general way I am not particularly sensitive to thirst, and as a rule bear it without difficulty in the dry hot deserts of Turkestan ; but here, up in this alpine country among the snows, I was really tormented by it.

The rise to the pass of Tash Ravat is quite steep, but not

at all dangerous nor particularly difficult. The whole pass with the surrounding heights was covered with perpetual snow. The River Tash Ravat makes its way down into the ravine by a long and steep descent along the flanks, as it were, of a gigantic funnel formed by the sides of the mountains. Above the pass the sky was of a deep dark-blue colour, almost black, while the remote horizon was light blue—a very odd effect. Lower down the gorge green grass made its appearance, increasing as we went lower. It was strange that the northern side, contrary to the usual rule, here was warmer than the southern and the spring more advanced.

Lower down the gorge widens into a valley. Farther on still we rode out into a broad plain surrounded with mountains on every side and covered with bright green grass.

At the foot of the mountains, on the far side of the river, which was already tolerably broad, stood the imposing ruin of some ancient castle. It had a lofty and spacious gateway, through which I could detect a series of small courtyards. On the north side of the building was a huge round tower with windows. It was built of a peculiar kind of brick which looked almost like concrete. The whole thing was grown over with grass and shrubs, and on an arch near the tower was a good-sized tree. Evidently many a century had passed over this strange construction, but time could not prevail against those solidly built arches and walls, the surface of which now looked like an integral part of the mountain cliffs themselves. Within the walls of the building there were forty or more cells, dark and gloomy, filled with the dust of centuries. Who built this strange fortress, and when, and why? It is unlike any other building, ancient or modern, in all Turkestan.

Why was so much effort and art spent in this remote spot
among the desert mountains, so far from the habitations of
men and the main routes of communication ? Who required
these massive walls and arches, when all around there has
never been, nor is there to-day, anything else than the tents
and huts of the nomads ? What is preserved under the
arches of its immense tower ? Such questions as these kept
revolving in my head at the sight of this imposing relic of
the architecture of the remote past.

" This, *taxir*, is Tash-uy,"[1] my Kirghiz friends explained
to me, " but who built it and when we do not know ; it
was not built by Mahommedans. This is a bad place, and
we are afraid of spending the night here."

The broad plain with the mountains all round as a setting
for this remarkable ruin formed a wonderful picture, quite
unlike anything else in Turkestan. The site had been most
skilfully chosen. For some reasons I am inclined to think
that this must have been an ancient Buddhist monastery
of the ' Gondwana ' period, but neither in style nor character does it resemble the modern monasteries of Tibet and
China. I could detect the embryos of the Moorish style.

Here we turned off from the main valley to the left and
struck uphill without any path, then dropped into a dry
gorge and stopped there, waiting for darkness. By night
we went right over the hill and made our way down by a
game track to At Bashi.

When it was light we found ourselves on the bank of the
River Kara Kain, and rested at a Kirghiz farm, after having
successfully passed through all the risks attached to a
journey over the frontier. Once again I was in the territory
of the Soviet Socialistic Republic, under the Dictatorship

[1] Stone House.

of the Proletariat, and therefore once more had to keep my eyes exceedingly wide open and exercise the greatest caution.

The river flows here between high and steep banks of a friable conglomerate. On the left bank there is a series of four irrigation canals, constructed one above the other with consummate skill, supplying water to the valleys lower down-stream.

Down here it was now quite hot and the sun had plenty of power. The sides of the hills were dotted with quantities of a low-growing violet iris, with here and there a white one. Golden sheldrake (*Casarca rutila*) were strutting about the velvety-green water meadows, and where the grass was still short the horses' feet flushed *karabauri* or sand-grouse (*Pterocles arenarius*). Small hawks like kestrels were hovering in the air, spying the ground for prey, while among the shrubs and bushes near the stream I caught the flash of the brilliant fiery tail and white head of some kind of redstart (*Phœnicurus* sp.), while flocks of jackdaws (*Colæus monedula collaris*) took the place of the alpine choughs. There was life on every side, and all nature was filled with the air of spring, a sharp contrast to the murky cold world which we had left only the previous evening.

It was an enormous relief, and I felt my breast expand. I could hardly believe that only one day's travel separated me from the mountain valleys, where blizzards were still raging and nature still plunged in her winter sleep.

We made a wide detour round the hills to avoid the township of At Bashi, and came into dense thickets on the banks of the river. We then forded its wonderfully bright and clear water, over the mosaic of pebbles on the bottom, came out into a forest of big trees and quickly reached the wooden hut of the forester. He was one of our Whites, a former Cossack officer, a first-rate horseman and *djigit*, or trick-rider. Here, in the guise of a forester, he was hiding from the Che-Ka. It is sad to think that this fine fellow, gallant officer and keen patriot, was shot by the Bolsheviks not long after, together with his wife and little child.

In this interesting locality I spent a whole month. The livelong day I wandered about the forest, coming back to the forester's hut only for the night. My food consisted of bread, milk, butter and fish. The cows grazing in the fat grass of the water meadows gave us milk in abundance, and the sparkling waters of the stream that ran through the forest were full of trout ; all we had to do was to build a little weir of faggots and branches across the stream, and in the morning there would be a dozen or more fine trout in it.

The exuberance of the vegetation in the At Bashi valley is due to the humidity of the district. The altitude of the locality and presence of numerous snow-peaks in the At Bashi ridge lead to the condensation of the moisture carried by the atmospheric currents coming from the west—that is to say, from the Atlantic. These currents hardly deposit any moisture at all on the hot deserts of Western Turkestan and the burning valley of Ferghaná, but precipitate their humidity over this cool and elevated valley.

The forest consists of deciduous trees, and looks like a park with grand old timber dotted about, and groups of shrubs and spinneys on the banks of the streams and broad green meadows of tender grass full of flowers. This forest extends about ten miles eastwards as far as the spring of Bogushty, where it passes into mountain fir forest. There are enormous poplars, often covered with galls and growths, willows, briars, berberis, hawthorn and small-leaved willows. Often the shrubs and trees are covered from top to bottom with clematis. In the meadows there are iris, orchis, geraniums, primulas, and whole fields covered with large and delicate forget - me - nots. The banks of the river itself are thickly edged with buckthorn (*Hippothoe rhamnoides*) and tamarisk, the latter of an unfamiliar kind : the flowers, in the form of short, white, thick bunches, grow directly out of the stem, instead of those pretty, pink, feathery bunches at the end of light stalks, which give such a graceful air to the familiar bush.

But woe to the quadruped that ventures into these thickets on the banks of the stream. From all the twigs and branches there rain upon the unwary intruder hundreds and thousands of thin small ticks which insinuate themselves into its body and drink its blood until they swell up into big fat lumps like gooseberries. It is difficult even for a man to get rid of these disgusting parasites if he is rash or ignorant enough to go even a few yards into these thickets. The only creatures which disregard them are the hares which swarm in these localities. In the forest itself and on the banks of the open streams which flow through it these ticks do not occur.

On the southern side of the valley a ridge of mountains rises steeply, with its valleys and gorges covered with green, the peaks tipped with the white of perpetual snow. They are usually decked with fleecy white clouds, while the dells are often filled with thick mist, all of which gives a wonderful play of light and shade. The mountains appear at one moment clad in deep blue, at another in a violet light, yet another and their flanks are bright with green, glistening under the rays of the sun. Often enough violent thunderstorms play about the peaks with a deluge which, frequently enough, reaches our valley. Westwards the view melts away in the immense massive ranges behind the jagged peaks of which the sun goes down.

With all these beauties and the fresh charm of the forest, the pure and clear mountain air, through which the scenery stands out in detail, the fresh healthy climate, bracing without being cold and balmy without being hot, sunny and bright, the exuberant vegetation and wealth of animal life, all combine to make the valley of At Bashi one of the most delightful corners of Turkestan. The altitude is considerable, about nine thousand feet above sea level.

It is not to be wondered at that I used to wander about the forest for hours together, or that at times I would sit on the banks of the brooks and drink in the beauties of nature. The water of these streams and burns comes bubbling out of springs and does not contain any deposits. It is extraordinarily pure and clear, so that the stones and pebbles on the bottom glisten as though they were polished by hand, and the weeds and the speckled silvery trout are as visible as though they were out of the water. Over the surface there hang the red bells of the kendyr (*Apocynum venetum*), which form a pretty feathery border to the banks. A young butcher bird sits on a branch over my head, waiting for its mother to bring its breakfast, while a pair of speckled woodpeckers are at work industriously on the trunk of an old poplar ; scarlet grosbeaks flit about among the low-growing willows, while every now and then a dipper (*Cinclus kashmirensis*) darts down the stream like an arrow. Here one may catch a glimpse of a bird that is rare in Turkestan, *Trochalopteron lineatum*. Grey herons sit upon the trees, while in the forest can be heard the deep cooing of the wild pigeons and the monotonous voice of the cuckoo. Formerly pheasants were numerous here, but the cold and snowy

winter of 1918-1919 killed them off. The bird population of
the valley of At Bashi is rich and varied, and it is a most
interesting spot for an ornithologist.

Roedeer are abundant, but the commonest of all animals
here is the hare. They are to be seen everywhere, as bold
as brass, hardly paying any attention to humans. One
evening just before sunset, standing on one spot, I counted
no less than fourteen. The hare of Semirechie, although
considerably smaller than its European cousin, is much
bolder and could never be accused of timidity. It often
comes right into the town gardens. A friend of mine in
Pishpek once shot at one from his verandah and missed,
but this did not bother the hare at all; it came back again
the next evening, found its way into the fowl-house and
frightened the chickens out of their sleep. The common
hare of Turkestan is *Lepus lemani*, but this Semirechie hare
is different; it is of a bluish rather than of a reddish-grey
colour, and has a broad black stripe on the tail.

Jackdaws and magpies are exceedingly numerous here;
the latter are very bold and impudent. If any poor brute
of an animal has a sore on its back, as horses very often have,
a flock of these birds will settle on it and peck away at the
wound persistently. Often enough horses sent up to the
pastures here to graze are pecked to death like this, as they
cannot get away from their tormentors. It would hardly
be thought possible that magpies could peck to death so
big an animal as a horse, but it is a fact, and cases are
well known to the natives of the mountain valleys of
Semirechie.

Foxes are numerous here too, and occasionally a silver
variety is met with, but the skin, though very beautiful, is
said to be too delicate to be valuable.

In the evenings I used to love to listen to the chirruping note of the quail and the croaking of the landrail, sounds which recalled the evenings in the fields and meadows of my native Russia, quite foreign to the other parts of Turkestan. There the quail is only a migrant and its voice is heard only in cages in the bazaars, and the corncrake is quite unknown. There is, however, a noticeable difference between the voice of these birds in Russia and here in Semirechie.

The valley of At Bashi, like all the mountains of the Tian Shan and Alai, is inhabited by the mountain Kirghiz or Kara Kirghiz, who actually call themselves 'Kirghiz,' in distinction to those on the steppes of Turkestan, Siberia and the Orenburg country, who call themselves Kazák. In the old days they were known as Kirghiz-Kaisaki.

The language of the mountain Kirghiz is somewhat different from that of those of the steppe, and decidedly so from the Sart dialect, and at first I found it a little difficult to understand until I became used to it. These Kara Kirghiz are the descendants of the Saci of antiquity, who played an important part in the Persian armies of the Emperor Darius in his invasion of Greece. And to this day the most numerous clan of the Kara Kirghiz are called Sayaki. In antiquity they formed the population of the mountain districts of Turkestan which formed a part of the extensive Persian Empire. It is interesting to note that the various clans of the Kara Kirghiz can be distinguished by the characteristic head-dresses of the women, which are often enormous and extremely complicated in design.

It is perfectly astonishing how rapidly the Kirghiz transmit messages. Without either post or telegraph, these nomads have some means of despatching and receiving news which interests them, which they can even get through more rapidly than the telegraph itself. One evening, for instance, the forester told me that the 'Kirghiz telegraph,' *uzun kulak*, the ' long ear,' as they themselves call it, had brought the news that a mutiny had broken out among the garrison at Verny, the chief town of Semirechie. " We do not know exactly what is going on there now," the Kirghiz said, " but we pray to Allah to help the rebels."

For several days in succession we now had uninterrupted rain, punctuated with thunderstorms, followed by a spell of bright, fine, sunny weather, which enlivened the whole forest. In the fields the blue flax flowered and the Issyk Kul root (*Aconitum napellus*). This very poisonous plant has a bad reputation. It is enough to sit for but a short time near its handsome dark-blue flowers to get a bad headache. The root, dried and pounded into a powder, is a fearful poison, which contains a considerable quantity of aconite, an alkaloid so poisonous that a dose of 0.004 grams of the nitrate is instantly fatal to a strong man. Not a few natives of Turkestan, Russian as well as Moslem, have been despatched to the other world by means of this plant administered by a treacherous hand. It has the advantage that the cause of death cannot be discovered, but apart from this, the women of Semirechie have worked out an original method of packing off an unwanted husband or undesired friend to the other side before his natural time without giving rise to any suspicions at all. To do this they make an infusion of the root, and in it soak a shirt belonging to the victim whom they propose to despatch from this sinful world, dry it, iron it and give it to him to put on after his bath, when the pores of the skin are open. The venom is absorbed into the blood, the victim sickens and in a couple of months, or three at the outside, gives up the ghost in the most natural manner in the world.

It is a remarkable fact that here in Semirechie this plant develops a quite special virulence. If raised from the seed in another locality, as for instance in Tashkend, it almost entirely loses its poisonous character and remains a merely ornamental flower, which is by no means rare in the gardens of Western Europe.

Another poisonous flower that grows here is the hellebore (*Helleborus niger*). It may be known by its big handsome flowers like a wild rose. An infusion of its roots is used here for destroying dogs. Why this particular drug should be specially used for removing the friend of man is not known. There are two other very poisonous plants here which I was not able to identify. One has a flower like a large, dark-blue, single bell ; mere sniffing it is enough to bring on sickness and vertigo. The other has a small white flower on a slender stalk growing out of a big root ; it often is a frequent cause of sickness or death among horses and cattle that eat it with other grass when grazing. As an offset against these dangerous herbs, there are no snakes in the valley of At Bashi, nor lizards, though toads are common enough.

In the ravines of these mountains and in the valley of Ak Sai on the other side there is plenty of big game and first-rate shooting. Ibex roam about in herds running to a thousand head ; wild sheep are very common and also bears. These live in the caves which are so numerous in the limestones of these ranges. Some of these caverns are very extensive, dividing inside into numerous galleries and chambers. These ' cave ' bears attain an immense size, but are not famous either for their fierceness or for their courage.

The Kirghiz, armed with a candle and their matchlocks (*multuks*), boldly walk into these underground dens to shoot them. On going into the dark cave the hunter advances carefully, peering into all the nooks and dark corners. When he catches sight of the animal's eyes glistening in the candle-light, he walks right up to the astonished creature, which as a rule remains motionless and stares at the phenomenon of a light in his gloomy lair. The man then puts the candle down on the ground, sits down beside it, rests the heavy barrel of his rifle on a special prop, quietly and unhurriedly takes aim at the bear between the eyes, and fires. They do not often miss, but even if they do the result is by no means necessarily fatal, as these bears are very timid and extraordinarily quiet. Of course, the man must keep cool and not lose his presence of mind when undertaking a day's shooting of this sort, especially as the loading of the primitive native rifle is a complicated business which takes several minutes, for the patience even of so phlegmatic a creature as these bears has some limit.

These bears are very common in the caves of the valleys on this side of the Pamirs. I have never been lucky enough actually to come into contact with one and have not been able to secure a skull, and have seen only their skins, which, I have noticed, are huge. It would be very interesting to find out whether this is our common Central Asiatic *Ursus leuconyx* or some other species, perhaps a direct descendant of the cave bears with which primitive man of Western Europe carried on so stubborn a contest for the control of subterranean dwellings.

A GOVERNMENT INSPECTOR turned up one day in At Bashi representing the Workmen's and Peasants' Government, a certain Venediktoff. He forced the rich Kirghiz who had not yet been completely despoiled by the Bolsheviks to pay him a 'contribution' of several million roubles and a hundred sheep. The precious Venediktoff, however, was not a Bolshevik, nor even a " sympathiser with Communism." " I've got to live too," he admitted openly and cynically. " I must make hay while the sun shines as long as this freedom lasts. What does it matter that I was only a shoemaker under the old régime ? I shall be a shoemaker again before long, when all this has come to an end. . . . Meanwhile I'm out for a good time." That is what he said himself, this disciple of Lenin's great slogan, " Help yourselves." He said it to my friend the forester, whom he had come to see to ask where the Kirghiz had wandered off with their flocks.

It was by no means easy to find a Kirghiz guide who would face the risk of taking me through to Kashgar secretly, past both Russian and Chinese frontier guards, especially as I had hardly any money left.

Suddenly there was a heavy fall of snow on the mountains and all the passes were stopped except that of Ak Biit, where the Red Army patrols were now reinforced. The frontier guards all along the line were strengthened and fresh detachments of Red troops kept arriving.

At the beginning of July the snow in the passes began to thaw, and I found an experienced and resourceful Kirghiz, named Tursum Bai, who had been through to Kashgar several times with opium smugglers, so that he knew the road well and was up to all the tricks for dodging the frontier guards of both countries. As the price for getting me safely through into Kashgar I promised him my last remaining valuable, my gold watch, then worth about two hundred thousand roubles.

In the meanwhile I had heard from one of my friends in Naryn the alarming news that the local Ispolkom had received an inquiry from Verny as to the whereabouts, somewhere in the district, of the " organiser of the rebel bands in Ferghaná," believed to be hiding somewhere in the district, with instructions to take the most active steps to find this enemy of the Workmen's and Peasants' Government. Fortunately by that time I had everything ready for my departure.

Unceasing rains set in, and on the third day, when the River At Bashi was swollen and turned into a broad foaming torrent, a turbulent mass of turbid brown water and bubbling dirty froth nearly three-quarters of a mile wide in places, so that fording stopped, when all the burns and brooks came crashing down the gorges, Tursum Bai came and told me that this was the most favourable moment for our journey.

" Everybody will be stopping at home now," he said, " and the Red soldiers will be resting and drinking. Allah will help us to ford the river, and no one will see us on the road."

We started. It was dusk and we were at once hidden in the thickets on the banks, through which we rode a considerable distance looking for a suitable place to ford. It was raining hard and a thick mist hung over the valley.

It was by no means without hesitation that our horses stepped into the torrent, which was coming down in waves. A cold foaming mass of water and dirt gripped us. In places the water was not higher than the horses' knees, but the force of the current piled it up on the up-stream side of us like behind a dam, and it reached my knees. There were moments when the stream actually lifted my horse, although she was on the bottom. Then I was in up to the waist, and around me saw nothing but a brown whirling mass of foaming waves. The rain was coming down in floods. It was hopeless to try to guide the horse, and I let her have her head, so that she followed the other leading in front.

When at length we reached the opposite bank, it looked as though it were streaming past us and that our horses were standing still, a common illusion when fording a broad and rapid river. Under these circumstances it is best to do as I did and give the horse her head, only holding her well in hand in case she were to stumble. A good well-trained horse knows how to deal with a situation like that better than a man, and if your animal is not a good one, it is better to stay at home.

The far bank was steep and high, so that we had to ride quite a long way down-stream before we could find a place where we could get out on to dry land. A ford like that, of course, is quite dangerous. If the horse slips and comes down, the current will carry it away and the rider is pretty sure to be killed; but when you are escaping from a big danger, it never enters your head to bother about lesser ones.

We rode all night, and the rain never stopped. As it was quite dark it was only by the sound of the hoofs that I could tell whether we were riding on hard ground, on grass or through a marsh. The dawn found us in a lonely ravine near some tumble-down Kirghiz huts, where we found shelter to dry ourselves and have some food and sleep before tackling another night's ride.

Early in the morning after, when we were riding into a rocky defile to spend the day, we saw in the far distance the figures of two Russians on horseback, evidently patrols from the post of Ak Biit. To avoid them we had to ride a long way on the rocky bed of the defile to mask our tracks and penetrate as deeply as possible into the mountain gorges.

One day, when we were sitting under the shade of a huge rock on a patch of soft sand, three ravens flew into the ravine and perched on a stone not far from us.

" Shoot one of those ravens for me," asked Tursum Bai.

" Why ? The shot might give us away, and, besides, what do you want a raven for ? " I asked.

" If you eat a raven's eye, your eyesight gets so keen that you can see as far as Mecca," replied Tursum Bai, perfectly serious.

I smiled and shook my head. There was no need to increase the astonishing keenness of his vision. He could see better with the naked eye than I with a Zeiss field-glass, and he seemed to be able to see perfectly well in the dark.

The next night was the critical one for us, as we had to pass by the mountain round the frontier post of Ak Biit, where the Red patrols might ride out to look for smugglers, even at night. But my guide was a very experienced and resourceful smuggler, a real ' mountain wolf,' as we say ;

and in spite of the darkness he picked his way so cleverly that we were riding either on soft sand or grass, so that the sound of the hoofs against stone would not betray us. We worked our way by the tops of the mountains above the post itself, and far below us could see the fires of the guard-houses and hear the distant barking of dogs.

In the morning, the tension relieved by the comforting knowledge of danger past, we rested on a green alpine meadow, enlivened by masses of white and pink marguerites. We were at ease in our hearts, and a flock of choughs circling round our heads seemed to be giving us welcome with their cheerful whistling.

Thus for the third time I successfully crossed the Soviet frontier, and this time I felt sure that I was leaving the confines of wild ' Sovdepia ' for the last time and bidding farewell definitely to the Empire of Communism.

Presently some Kirghiz rode up on enormous shaggy great yaks and gave us some first-rate *kumys*.

Then we rode on quietly to a big *aul*, sprawling over the lofty valley of Arpa, where some relatives of Tursum Bai lived, to change our horses for fresh ones. The rest of the road lay through the unpopulated, dry and stony mountains of Chinese territory, and we required fresh, strong, well-fed animals, or else we might have to continue our journey on foot, as had already happened to me.

In the *aul* we were absolutely safe. The Kirghiz detested the Bolsheviks and would never have betrayed us. Here it was cold, and they were all wearing furs ; a biting northerly wind was blowing. We made our quarters in a big *yurtá* belonging to a respected old greybeard and his family. An ibex kid was tied up in a cage inside. The Kirghiz often catch them and tame them. The young ibex cannot follow their dam for some days after birth, and in the case of danger they 'freeze,' squatting down tightly among the stones or in a hole, and lie motionless so that they are very difficult to see. It is very different with the wild sheep : within a couple of hours of their appearance in the world the lambs are too nimble to be caught. When they want to catch one of these, the Kirghiz stalk a flock and look out for a ewe about to drop her lamb ; they lie in wait and seize it directly it is born. Domestic sheep and goats suckle them, and the young creatures quickly become accustomed to their foster mothers and to people. A full-grown ibex will 'freeze' in the same way if he has no other means of escape, lying squeezed down to the ground just like a hare. When hunted with dogs they will sometimes jump up on to a rock and stand there calmly without paying any further attention to the man with the rifle, who can then get quite close.

In the Pamirs the Kirghiz and Tadjiks have a special breed of hound for hunting ibex and wild sheep, which has a quite good nose and can hunt by scent. They are very useful in following up wounded beasts, especially sheep, which can carry a great deal of lead, and even when wounded in the belly can get away fast and far. These hounds are highly esteemed in the Pamirs, and, in contrast to the usual custom among Mahommedans, the local hunters keep them in their tents, feed them well and make a fuss of them.

The Kirghiz with whom we stopped was very well off. Around the walls of his *yurtá* there were rows of boxes in leather covers embroidered in various patterns, while heaps of rugs and cushions lay piled about, and the walls were hung with embroidered rugs.

After some tea our host asked me, " Where is the Ak Padsha now, the White Tsar Nikolai ? "

" He and all his family, the Tsaritsa, their daughters and son, have been killed by the Bolsheviks," I answered.

The old man gave a deep sigh, his head dropped a moment and then he asked me—

" And you, are you of white or black bones ? *Nikolai vakht adamlar-ma syz ?* Are you one of the men of the régime of Nikolai ? "

" Yes, of course," I replied. " I detest and despise the Bolsheviks."

The old man took me by the hand and pressed it firmly. I felt his hand tremble in mine. He began to blink and a tear rolled down his cheek, while the rest of the family sobbed, the women groaning aloud, and then there was silence in the tent.

I was deeply touched by the scene. On this remote frontier of the Russian Empire, in the depths of the mountain fastnesses, a family of nomad herdsmen was weeping for the tragic death of their White Pasha, as the Tsar was known throughout Central Asia.

The scene in the *yurtá* and all the furniture and decorations reminded me of years gone by, of my young days in the Orenburg steppe. It was just the same as with the Kirghiz in my country, and there was nothing to show whether I was at an altitude of some ten thousand feet above the sea in the mountains of Tian Shan, or sitting on the banks of the Ural in the tent of some old Kirghiz who had known me from childhood. Even the surrounding locality was not unlike the hilly steppes of the Orenburg country, and the weather, too, reminded me of the beginning of April at home.

Over an immense area in Asia where the wandering Kirghiz have scattered, their manner of life and their peculiar culture, developed through millenia of existence in the free open steppe, is the same, identical in space and identical, too, in time. These nomads were free to move about the plains at their own sweet will, as though upon an open sea, and there was nothing to prevent the Kirghiz of the Tian Shan from wandering away to steppes of Siberia, of the Ural or the Volga, except, of course, nowadays the Bolshevik Government.

This freedom and the mobility of the nomads of the steppe has evolved their own peculiar culture, character and manner of life, and has played a very important part in the history of Asia, which has not yet been properly appreciated by historians nor sufficiently studied. It has reacted profoundly on the fate of Russia, and even Western Europe has by no means escaped its influence. The burning sands of Egypt, the valleys of Mesopotamia and of Palestine (the myriad horsemen of Gog and Magog), and of India and the valleys of Russia and of Central Europe and even Châlons, the Catalaunian plains of France, Hellas, too, and Rome, all have seen the forbears of our Kirghiz of to-day, though under various names—as Scythians or Massagetæ, Huns, Polovtsi, Kipchaks, Kumans, Pechenegs, Alans, Tartars and so on. On every side their invasions have left their mark, not only destructive, for sometimes they have altered the course of historical development and affected the blood, language, character, manners and customs of the people with whom they have come into contact. Just as the Normans in their day made use of their mobility upon the seas to spread their influence and culture throughout the West, so these nomads of the steppes of Asia have done the same in the East. The broad belt of grassy plains across the old continent, which has given rise to the peculiar type of nomad Turki and his inseparable comrade, the horse of the steppe, has had enormous influence on the destinies of the settled nations and of civilisation itself.

All distant invasions and the ' migration of peoples ' have been possible owing to one single factor, hitherto ignored by historians, and that is the horse of the steppes. This animal is endowed with most valuable qualities of supporting fatigue and of endless endurance and the power of keeping up prolonged hard work on green food only, on mere grazing, of which other races of horse are quite incapable, being dependent on corn. These outstanding qualities of the steppe horse were fully appreciated and widely used by the great military leaders of Asia, conquerors, Jenghiz Khan, Tamerlane and the others,[1] which explains the secret of their success.

The limits of attainment and conquest of the countless hordes of Asia depended not upon the powers of resistance of the subject peoples nor upon their armies, but were defined by the moist meadow grazing, by the cold damp of the north and by the tropical heat of the valleys of India, which were fatal to the horse of the Kirghiz.

Now once again our road lay to the lake of Chatyr Kul and the pass of Turgart. Although the country round was green and dotted in places with iris and tulips, when we started a light dry snow was falling and whirling round us in the strong wind. This did not stop till the afternoon, when, after passing a small hill, we dropped down into the

[1] See Ivanoff, ' On the Art of War of the Mongol-Tartars ' (in Russian), a little known but extremely interesting work. Also two papers by me, " The Scythians Past and Present " (' Edinburgh Review,' July 1929, pp. 108-122), and " The Sons of Gog " (' English Review,' March 1930).

basin of Chatyr Kul. Here the snow had disappeared and the lake had almost entirely thawed, but there was hardly any green to be seen except a little miserable grass, all dried up, a relic of the previous season. The neighbourhood of the lake is marshy, and has exactly the appearance of the arctic tundra. On the banks there were piles of dried water-weeds, thrown up by the waves, and a huge quantity of guano, showing that the flocks of geese on the autumn migration rested here. A few sandpipers of some sort were flying about the swamps, probably come here to nest.

The polar character of the locality was very striking at this season. Why is it that here, at an altitude of from ten to twelve thousand feet, we do not find the alpine conditions that are usual at such heights, but a regular arctic tundra, where only reindeer are wanting to complete the picture ? Instead of them we find yaks, and they have a marked resemblance to another arctic beast, the musk ox. The explanation lies in the fact that this part of Tian Shan consists of elevated valleys rising one above the other like a staircase, and of relatively low crests separating them. These are not formed by the folding of the earth's crust, as are, for instance, the Alps and the Caucasus. It is what the geologists call a peneplain being re-elevated—that is to say, a plain, formed after the removal by erosion and complete destruction of ancient mountain masses, now being elevated again. Consequently it is being eroded in its turn, and one day will form a real mountain country ; meanwhile it has only the character of valleys in an extensive elevated plain, through which pass not very high ridges. Structurally it is not a real mountain plateau as is, for instance, the greater part of Tibet.

Elevated thus into the altitude of rarefied air and cold

atmospheric currents, this region is exposed to the same climatic conditions as the extreme north, whence the resemblance to polar districts. Properly speaking, it is now in a Glacial Period, and it is only the scarcity of moisture which prevents the formation of immense glaciers or of a solid ice-cap ; but there is no doubt that at a recent geological period, post-Pliocene, glaciers here attained immense proportions, as is shown by the numerous huge moraines and extensive deposits of glacial material in the river valleys. And this increase and reduction of the glaciers has been repeated several times. Whether this alternation is due to the periodic increase of precipitation in this region, or to a periodic elevation and depression of the locality, is difficult to say, but everything clearly points to the cause of glacial periods in different parts of the earth being due to just such an elevation of the region in question to a great altitude into the zone of cold and rarefied air. I warmly recommend all who are seriously interested in the problem of glaciation to pay a visit to this region, where there is scope for extremely interesting and important observations in dynamic geology.

We spent the night at Turgart in the same hut where I slept on my first visit there. The gale blew all night, driving a fine dry snow. The morning was bright and sunny but very cold. A brook running down from Turgart was covered with a film of ice.

Here we left the road and turned due east. We rode a long time on the tops of hills, avoiding the ravines and gullies, coming down to a broad, elevated, hummocky plain which extended far away towards the east, where we could see a steep headland, the extremity of a small ridge and the pass of Terek. Then we began to go down the upper part of the valley of the River Kashka Su.

The valley gradually drops and broadens, and we came into an absolutely dry river-bed. The high banks of red sandstone were vertical, like those of an artificial canal. The bottom consisted of a fine sand, firm and even, just as though it had been rolled, and on it standing out conspicuously were numerous flat, broad, round leaves of wild rhubarb. On the flat banks there was a little grass here and there and patches of some kind of yellow, mauve and blue alpine flowers, low-growing, in thick bunches firmly pressed together, as though afraid to raise their heads and huddled together for warmth, a form of vegetable association well known to all alpinists.

The bed of the stream became broader and broader, and soon came out into a broad open plain, where flowed the River Chokmak Tash (The Firestone). Here we stopped on top of a sandy hill to have something to eat and decide upon the direction. Two roads were open to us: one down by the Chokmak Tash and over Kara Teke, the Black Goat Pass, where there is a large Chinese post which it was impossible to get round; the other through the country of the Sary Bagishi, who have a very bad reputation, and through the pass of Urta Su, where there is no post, but where we might be exposed to an attack by the Sary Bagishi, who might rob and kill us. Both these roads come out into the valley of the Urta Su in a narrow gorge which we could not avoid, where there is always a post of Chinese soldiers guarding the road day and night. The chief of the post, Abdulla Bek, was well known for his severity and cruelty.

So now, like the hero in the old Russian fable, there lay two roads open to us, both equally dangerous and equally likely to lead to disaster. We could choose which we liked. I was for the second alternative, trusting to my rifle and a good stock of ammunition ; but Tursum Bai was for the first, confident in his cunning and ability to get through anywhere by night.

After a long discussion I agreed with him, relying on his experience, and we started down the river to the pass of Kara Teke.

The farther we went, the narrower and deeper the ravine grew and then passed into a rocky gorge, and we rode along the actual river-bed, sometimes sandy, sometimes stony. The walls of the gorge were formed by a massive series of shales of various kinds, clay or calcareous, strongly contorted and dislocated in various directions, with red and grey tertiary sandstones resting on them unconformably. The gorge became very rocky, and we had to ride first on one side and then on the other. At one place, on the right bank, on a very high mountain I could see beds of sandstone cut by streams of basalt lava. Obviously all this region must have been the theatre of violent volcanic activity either during the Tertiary Period or later.

About two or three miles farther down, before reaching the Chinese post, we stopped to bivouac in a small bay in the valley, where there was a little grazing for our horses and the isolated *yurtá* of a Kirghiz, who received us in a very friendly way.

" Load your rifle to be on the safe side," whispered Tursum Bai to me, " and keep it near you. These people are not to be trusted, and I will not go to sleep."

My guide cross-examined our host in detail and at great length about the road and the best way to avoid the Chinese post.

" You can't avoid the post at all," said the Kirghiz.
" The walls of the gorge are vertical and the path is very
narrow ; besides that, at the top of the pass there is always a
special patrol. But if you want to get through without being
noticed," he went on, " I advise you to turn back, and
about a couple of versts along you will see a narrow little
gorge on the right ; ride into it and it will bring you out at
a pass which is very steep and exhausting, but you can get
through all right, and then you can find your way to a small
stream which will bring you out into the valley of the Urta
Su. This pass is quite unknown to the Chinese and is not
guarded at all."

Tursum Bai kept up his questioning a long time to find out
all about this path, and then at last he said in a decided tone
of voice—

" If the Chinese won't let Russians through to Kashgar,
it isn't worth while going there ; better go back to At
Bashi."

I saw what his idea was and pretended to agree with
him, but afterwards, when we were riding along, I asked
him why he was so diplomatic in dealing with the old man,
as he seemed quite well disposed to us.

" You can't trust the people round here," he replied.
" He tried to persuade us to go by a roundabout way, and
then, as soon as we were well on the road, he'd go and report
us to the Chinese post, so as to curry favour with them,
and then they'd catch us on the Urta Su."

In the morning when we rode back on the way we had
come, the owner of the *yurtá* came with us quite a long way,
trying to persuade us all the time to go up the secret path
he had told us about. This made me quite sure that Tursum
Bai was right in his suspicions, so I said in a most decided

voice that I refused to take the risk and would go back to At Bashi. I thanked the man for his hospitality, said good-bye and started off at a trot. Tursum Bai followed.

We did not turn off into the gorge the old man had told us about but rode on, and only stopped when we had got well past a bend in the road, in a bay in the cliffs, where we waited a considerable time to see whether or not we were being followed. My cautious guide watched long and attentively, and it was only when we felt quite sure that the road was clear that we started back and rode up the narrow gulch, which rose steeply towards the pass. Then it widened out slightly, and there was a little vegetation, some grass and a few shrubs; then again bare crystalline schist, cliffs and screes, and banks of dirty snow.

The pass was very steep, and we had to zigzag up the loose gravel screes, which slipped and gave way under the horses' feet. We had to keep stopping to give the animals a blow. The poor brutes were gasping heavily, their flanks heaving, and I could feel the heart-beats beneath the saddle. At the top of the pass there was a thick bed of dirty snow mixed with stones and dust.

It was a strange view from the top ; there was an enormous, apparently endless, expanse away to the south. The crags dropped steeply, almost vertically, it seemed ; and there far below us at the feet of our mountains there extended a sea of narrow, rocky, absolutely bare, barren crests, with hardly discernible ravines between them, without a single sign of life or green thing. Everywhere a stony desert, a wilderness of rocks and crags.

Far, far away, at the very edge of the horizon itself, at the end of this sea of rocks, I could just detect a plain with a thick cloud of dusty haze overhanging it. Above, it was all illuminated with the brilliant burning light of the south. I guessed that that was the plain of Kashgar, the longed-for goal of my persistent efforts, the land of promise for me, an unhappy persecuted refugee! But between us there still remained two days, or rather two nights, of toilsome road.

To the south-west, above the dusty blanket which covered the plain, there arose a light conical mass, white like a clean cloud, raised high above the earth. This was, as I learnt afterwards, Kungur, the highest point of the Pamirs, a giant of 25,146 feet, beside which Mont Blanc, with its 15,784 feet, and our Caucasian Elburz, with its 18,573 feet, are but hills.

I learnt afterwards that at the very time when I first saw the plain of Kashgar, overjoyed at the sight of the goal of my wanderings, a detachment of Red guards arrived hot on my heels at Turgart. Obviously the Che-Ka had got on to my tracks, but too late! I was by then across the frontier and well away in a spot where even the lords of the land could not see me. Luck, bordering on a miracle, accompanied me all the time of my escape from the Bolsheviks.

The way down was very steep ; we had even to dismount and lead our horses, which was not easy. The rocks consist of shales folded in various ways. Here and there was a patch of fresh green grass that had found a foothold among the stones, with some white or mauve primulas. In a nullah we found a small patch of green grass and a delightful spring of fresh clear water, where we stopped to rest, have something to eat, give the horses a feed and wait for the evening, so as to ride farther down the gorge under the cover of darkness.

The night was extremely dark, and I could not even see

my horse's ears. I made no attempt to guide him, but simply held him up in case he stumbled. I could hear that some of the time we were riding on stones, at others on loose gravel which rattled and rolled under the hoofs, sometimes on soft sand between some great big clumps. Sometimes we went downhill very steeply, as though at the edge of a precipice, as when a stone was dislodged by a horse's hoof I could hear the noise for a long time, as though it were falling down a precipice ; at another time we were climbing a steep cliff, at another again going down almost vertically, so much so that I had to balance myself in the saddle so as not to upset the horse's equilibrium, when we might disappear together down the abyss.

In this way we avoided a camp of Kirghiz, no longer our folk but Chinese subjects, from which we could hear the furious barking of dogs which had evidently heard us ; but as Kirghiz dogs usually bark all night long uninterruptedly, which is credited to them as the chief function of a watch-dog, nobody paid any attention to us.

On these steep descents everything depended on the strength of the horse's legs ; all the rider has to do is to sit in the saddle and leave the rest to the animal, keeping on the alert, however, not to come down with the horse and all.

This was the first time my guide had been by this road, but, thanks to his lynx eyes, he was able to pick his way perfectly well. And this was the man who wanted to eat a raven's eye to improve his sight !

We kept getting lower and lower until at length we found ourselves riding along the level gravelly bed of a brook, avoiding the big boulders and constantly crossing and recrossing the stream.

It became oppressive and very hot ; there was not a

suggestion of a breeze, and the air was reflected from the rocks as though out of an oven. That evening I had eaten the last remains of my ham, and now was tormented by thirst. Besides that, I was much too warmly dressed for this locality. After all, it was well on in July, the hottest season in the Kashgaria. And that same morning I had been quite cold even in my thick clothes up there near the perpetual snow. I wanted to drink desperately ; my throat and mouth were parched, and inside I felt on fire. Although our horses' feet were often in water, I resisted the temptation, as I knew well how dangerous it is to drink water from an unknown source.

At length it grew a little lighter. I could distinguish the outlines of the mountains against the sky, and on the right the shadows of some immense poplars.

" This is the gorge of Urta Su," said Tursum Bai. " This is where the road comes out through Urta Bel and the Terek pass. I know this road well. Now let's ride on a bit faster so as to get past Abdullah before daylight."

Then the gorge narrowed again, and it was dark once more.

A few minutes later Tursum Bai said—

" We are just coming to the most dangerous bit of all ; it is very narrow with vertical walls ; we can't get round ; the Chinese sentry is on duty day and night. Still, we'll get through all right. Inshallah."

Soon on our right we could see the dark mass of some wall, and on the left a camel snorted and stepped aside ; evidently it had been standing in the path. A pack of dogs flung itself at us out of the darkness, barking savagely, and the voice of a Chinaman called out something, probably " Who goes there ? "

I froze.

At that very moment another pack of dogs appeared out of the darkness and furiously attacked the first; there was a perfect pandemonium, and the Chinese guard shouted out something again, this time in a different voice, probably swearing at the dogs. The din effectively masked our steps and . . . God be praised! the danger was behind us!

CHAPTER XX.   AT LAST!

WHEN it was light we rode out on to a broad desert. On both sides there were rows of small hills. By daylight I could see that the water in the river was full of dirt, and in spite of my raging thirst, I should have to hold out longer, until we came to a brook where, though muddy, it was fresh and cold. Here Tursum Bai filled his *tursuk*, a leather bottle made of smoked skins, in which he had a few drops of sour milk. We then turned towards the east, between the rows of hills, where we chose a suitable secluded spot to stop and rest.

The hills around were bare and stony ; they consisted of grey and red clay shales, often covered with a fine grey sand. In the stream beds and depressions there was a little xerophytic vegetation, typical of dry, hot deserts. It was strange and peculiar, and at once showed what sort of a climate we had come to. Each plant, shrub or bit of herb was growing separately, a long way from each other ; there was no thick carpet ; the sandy soil was far too poor in nutritive material and moisture to support a dense vegetation. There were clumps of *Ephedra*, a shrub that was a mass of sharp thorns, a tall, brilliant, green rush and, most effective of all, little clumps of desert bindweed, covered with pretty, sweet-smelling, pink flowers, just as though they had been planted artificially on their long, thin, pliant, green stalks, hard as wire, with the little leaves hardly noticeable. Each shrub was an entire bouquet a couple of feet in diameter, looking very handsome against the glistening background of yellow sand. Below by the brook there were gigantic bushes of briar or wild rose with creeping branches, studded with nasty barbed thorns, white flowers and tiny hard leaves. These desert plants protect themselves by thorns and spines against being eaten by wild animals where food is so scarce.

The sun came out in a cloudless sky and at once began to burn pitilessly. I lay under an *Ephedra*, and by throwing my overcoat over it fixed up a little bit of shade. The horses were tied together and covered with anything handy to protect them against the burning rays. They had to stand about till the evening without food, and then they got only half a handful of barley each. We had to pass the livelong day in this burning furnace. Luckily, and quite unexpectedly, a cloud suddenly came out from behind the mountains, accompanied by a peal of thunder and a few big isolated drops of rain and then a heavy hail. This was an unexpected stroke of luck ; for the air was at once cooled down, and for the rest of the day a gentle breeze fanned us pleasantly. The deserts of Kashgar welcomed me with a smile. The drops of rain were really thawed hailstones, as it is probably only in this form that moisture can reach the heated air near the ground ; in the form of raindrops they would be evaporated in the air, as I have often been able to observe in deserts.

We did not suffer from thirst. The water shaken up with sour milk in the leather bottles quenched the thirst splendidly. The Kirghiz always use this drink when on the road. It has the further advantage that lactic acid helps to make bad water harmless. This was widely employed at the time of our campaigns in the deserts during the conquest of Turkestan by the Russians. A special product made from sheep's milk, called *krut*, containing a high proportion of lactic acid, was issued to troops going into the steppe country. Thanks to this *krut*, the plains of Central Asia, which had so evil a reputation previously, where entire expeditions had perished, lost their sting and became an open road for the passage of armies.

The dark night had already set in, the last before Kashgar, as Tursum Bai told me, when we left our shelter and set out by an obscure path well away from the Terek, the Kirghiz *auls* and the frontier posts. Once more I had occasion to be astonished at the extraordinarily keen sight of my companion. I could not see either his back or his horse, although I was following close behind him, yet he picked out his way unhesitatingly, and if he missed it he picked it up again quickly and rode on quite confidently. After a time we came out on to a broad path, and here we moved pretty fast. It was probably about midnight when my horse suddenly stopped, and although I could not see anything at all, I heard a conversation between my guide and some other Kirghiz.

" You can't ride this way ; you'll bump right into a Chinese patrol ; the place between the river and the fort is very narrow, and the soldiers will stop you. Ride through the *kapchigai*, the gully, and look out for the *mazar* shrine, where there is a soldier on guard, a Kirghiz," said an unknown voice.

We turned sharply to one side, and I could distinguish the smell of camels and the breathing of horses as we rode by. I cannot understand how my guide found the trail now we were riding not only off the path, but even without any tracks to follow, straight ahead in an unknown locality, choosing the way somehow or other. But he rode on confidently, and only once asked me to strike a match to have a look where we were. It turned out that our horses were up against an absolutely perpendicular cliff which blocked our road. About ten paces farther on the rocks parted to form a narrow, hardly perceptible, pathway. This was the *kapchigai*. Another time, when in the gulch, he again asked me for a match to have a look at the tracks on the ground, as he thought that we were off the trail.

A long spell of wakeful nights and the impossibility of sleeping properly in the daytime had tired me out. I was desperately sleepy. Every now and then I began to dream and thought I was falling out of the saddle. Sometimes I awoke with a shudder, wondering when and how I had dropped off, and how long I had been dozing. The impossibility of seeing where we were going made me sleepier than ever. In vain I tried to occupy my mind with some sort of meditation, thinking over old memories, to concentrate my thoughts on to some object and banish sleep. But it was no good. At length it began to grow light, and I could just pick out surrounding objects and felt a little easier.

Presently we rode into a grove of withered trees near an old *mazar*. Suddenly Tursum Bai turned sharply back, leant forward in the saddle, and, signing to me with his finger on his lips, quickly slipped down a narrow little gully at the side. We soon rode away from the dangerous place. It seems that we had almost ridden right on to the very patrol against whom the Kirghiz had warned us.

About a mile farther on Tursum Bai stopped his horse and exclaimed—

" Now praise be to Allah ! we have passed all the guards ; now the road to Kashgar is open."

And he broke out into a cheerful song, the first time that he had struck up since we had been on the way, and we rode on in a happy frame of mind. I was enormously relieved ; my acute anxieties were over. This time at last I should reach Kashgar all right.

We now rode out on to a broad, flat, gravelly plain, completely dry and covered almost entirely by desert plants, such as the camel grass (*Alhagi camelorum*), and here we moved a herd of gazelle, which disappeared from sight in a moment.

To our left, in the east, on the horizon, there rose some separate, very lofty, steep mountains of peculiar outline. These were the heights at the mouth of the Terek. The plain rose regularly towards the south, and we imperceptibly came on to an absolutely barren expanse, consisting of beds of grey and yellowish sandstone interbedded with marls. The structure of these sandstones, their appearance, the form of weathering under the action of the desert winds, all reminded me closely of just such a series in the province of Ferghaná on the banks of the Syr Dariá, near the village of Naukat, where in years gone by I had found a very interesting deposit of native copper, which yielded a high quality of chemically pure metal. The likeness of the beds and localities was very striking and increased by the thin cover of pebbles on the tops of the hills in both, the scarcity of vegetation, which consisted, such as there was, of the prickly glassworts (*Salsola*) and the abundance in both localities of a curious little lizard (*Phrynocephalus*). It seemed to me that I was once more riding near my own mines along the familiar banks of the Syr Dariá, and my eye instinctively sought on the banks an exposure of the bright green oxidised

copper.[1] And as a matter of fact, as I learned afterwards,
in these sandy hills, too, there is an excellent copper ore.
Near the village of Kandjigan the Chinese Government
worked these ores and minted copper currency from them.

Then there followed beds of conglomerate, which form a
fairly high, steep, strongly eroded cliff, through which the
path goes into a deep extremely narrow gully, véry twisty,
for several miles, with steep almost perpendicular walls. I
rode into my promised land through this strange almost
subterranean corridor. In places there were lateral gullies
in which I could see fantastic outlines of arches, caverns,
grottoes, columns and so on, forms of what is known as the
vertical desert erosion.

At last this dark and gloomy defile came to an end abruptly,
and before my eyes there was unfolded, brilliantly illuminated in the southern sun, the picture of an oasis and . . . I
thought I was back in Ferghaná ! Everything down to the
smallest detail was exactly the same as in Ferghaná, which I
knew so well. The fields of *djugará* or sorgo, of cotton, rice,
tall slender poplars, *djidy* trees, the so-called Babylonian
willow (*Eleagnus hortensis*), apricot and peach trees, willows,
even the wild plants on the dry clay soil, were the same,
the same low shrubs of dark-green tamarisk with their
feathery tufts of pink flowers at the ends, the same tall
rushes and thorns.

We rode into the gateway of a new caravanserai that
stood a little way off the road, probably a den for smugglers,
where a well-deserved rest awaited us in the clean and

[1] This series was named by the English geologists, Stoliczka and Hunt-
ington, the Artysh Beds. A Russian geologist, Professor Bogdanovich,
refers them to the Pliocene. In view of the absence of fossils both here
and on the Syr Dariá and the lithological similarity of both, it would, I
think, be right to give them the same designation, the Artysh Series.

roomy *chai-khané* or tea-room. It was the seventh day
since we had ridden out of At Bashi, and the last stage
since the previous evening we had ridden fourteen hours
without dismounting, so we deserved our rest. The rooms
were excellent. The walls were hung in panels with a
material with a pretty blue pattern, with pleasing porcelain
cups and dishes of various colours in niches. Everything
bore the seal of cleanliness and order, even distinction, a
very striking contrast to the evil-smelling dens that are
called rest-houses in Semirechie.

I did not feel exhausted by the long ride, but desperately
wanted to drink, and was very sleepy, and so, after countless
glasses of tea, I slept like a top, with the blessed slumber
of a man relieved from acute anxiety in the knowledge of
achievement.

We awoke about two in the morning, drank some more
tea and started off again. It was light by the time we had
ridden through the oasis and come into just such another
mountain road as we had passed yesterday, and once more
we rode through a narrow corridor like that one of yesterday,
but even longer, more winding and apparently interminable.

At last it brought us out into the plain of Kashgar, all
glowing in morning sunlight, a mass of green gardens and
fields through which lay our road. It was bordered with
shady willows and elms, and along both sides were rows
of native farms, orchards, little shops and cemeteries with
the old-fashioned *mazary*, bordered with walls of open brick-
work. Uninterrupted fields of clover extended for miles,
of *djugará*, sorgo, wheat, which they had already begun to
reap, tall slim poplars and big apricot trees, studded with
beautiful golden fruit. Here I saw an unfamiliar bird, the
large Kashgar dove, handsome in a livery of light lilac with

a velvety black ring round the neck. This elegant bird is confined to the villages and gardens, where it shares with the little Turkestan dove (*Peristera cambayensis*), recently introduced into Kashgar from Ferghaná, the honour of being an inseparable feature of every yard and garden.

Where the road came out into an open space there was a magnificent view of the Pamirs. They rose directly out of the plain, it seemed vertically, rearing their grey mass of mountains to an enormous height ; high up in the heavens, above the level of the clouds, towered the glistening snow peaks of the crest. It forcibly called to my mind the words of Lermontoff [1] on Mount Kazbek, which I might attempt to paraphrase and translate—

> "Among them, towering o'er the cloud
> By head and shoulders, splendid, great
> Kungur, the Pamir's monarch proud,
> Arrayed in all his robes of state."

This panorama is, in effect, far grander and more imposing even than the view of the giant of the Caucasus, Kazbek, which is, both relatively and actually, much lower than Kungur. Few are the places on this earth where one can see a mountain rising over twenty thousand feet straight out of the surrounding plain and visible as one entire mountain from base to peak. Such a wonderful picture can be seen in Kashgar, though not very often, it is true. It is only in spring and summer, and then only sometimes in the early morning hours, that these mountains may be seen in all their majesty and splendid beauty. The rest

---

[1] M. L. Lermontoff (1814-1841), the poet of the Caucasus, was, as his name implies, of Scottish descent. He was a striking instance of precocious genius ; killed in a duel at the age of twenty-seven, he left an established reputation as one of Russia's greatest poets.

of the time they are concealed by the curtain of dusty haze which almost perpetually floats over the arid plain of Kashgar. One can live for months on end in the place and not suspect the presence of these monsters. Still more seldom, in fact extremely rarely, are there days when it is possible to distinguish in the far distant south the frozen peaks of Kuen Lung itself, scarcely distinguishable from the clouds.

Here around me I could see on every side the calm and peaceful work of men and the abundant fruits of the soil. What a contrast with the ' bright empire of the toiling masses ' which I had left behind me ! The faces of passers-by here did not wear that look of nervousness and oppression which we see on everyone on the other side of the Tian Shan. People were cheerful and had pleasant smiles, although under the Chinese Government this country is by no means a care-free Arcadia. I was now in European costume, and on every hand they kept asking where had we come from and offering us fruit, rolls and drinks of cold water. There were no Chinese to be seen ; the population consisted of Sarts, just as at home in Turkestan.

As we went on, the road became more and more lively as traffic increased. We kept meeting men riding asses, horses, laden carts and camels. There were plenty of women who wore *parandjas* of variegated colours, far more pleasing to look at than the sombre monotony of our women-folk. The black *chimbet*, too, was here replaced by a light veil in various colours, and many women did not conceal their faces at all, and we passed some made-up coquettes who looked up at us mischievously.

In the shade of massive trees merchants exposed their wares—fruits, bread, fresh water in high earthen jars that might have come out of some museum for classical antiquities.

Thicker and thicker became the traffic on the road. Shops were more frequent and traders more numerous, the trees closer together ; and then suddenly there glistened a strip of water, a broad and rather muddy river, a long wooden bridge over it, a massed throng of people, donkeys, the local cabs, with a tent extending forward over the horse, the sound of bells, all the hum and chatter of the bazaar ; then there appeared the great city gates in the massive, broad, embattlemented walls . . . and I was in Kashgar !

I did not ride into the town. We turned to the right and rode along past the walls, which had high towers at the corners and were crumbling badly in places, past another, smaller, bazaar and reined up before a European house surrounded by a shady garden, with a Russian notice : ' Russo-Asiatic Bank.'

.   .   .   .

Half an hour later I was sitting on the verandah enjoying breakfast. The snow-white table-cloth, the irreproachable service, the glistening silver, the flowers in vases, the comfortable furniture, the almond cakes, biscuits, sugar, American and English newspapers, everything transported me into a world of civilisation and culture.

It was a strange and unaccustomed feeling. I had the sensation of perfect bliss. It seemed that I had awakened out of a long, long sleep full of fearful dreams and nightmares. I had returned to my old life, to the normal course of ideas. The old familiar past had returned to me, the dear old past which I had thought gone for ever, destroyed by the savages who had ruined my country. The wild life, every kind of privation, hunger and thirst, persecution, all this was already a thing of the past. That murky tomb, that huge asylum of madmen which to-day represents my unhappy fatherland, was now left behind, thank God! far beyond the snowy peaks of Tian Shan. Once again I was in a world of decent normal people.

Five minutes after my arrival an orderly from the Tao Yin presented himself at the Consulate to inquire who and by what means had someone arrived in Kashgar out of Soviet Russia. Half an hour later I called upon the Russian Consul, and within an hour I was receiving a young, very polite official, speaking quite good Russian, who was sent by the Tao Yin. He congratulated me on my safe arrival in Kashgar, inquired about my health and hoped I felt at home in my new surroundings.

" I do not know," I replied, " I do not yet know whether I am still in this sinful world, or whether, rising higher and higher in the mountains, I have arrived without noticing it in the old paradise of the *burjui*, in heaven ! "

This answer pleased the Chinaman immensely, and he took it as a compliment to Chinese culture and the loving care of the administration for the good of the country.

The Chinese are extremely fond of flattery and politeness, and their idea of good form calls for the nicest and most complimentary expressions in conversation, however extravagant. The young official had heard of my speciality, and asked me, in the name of the Tao Yin, whether I would undertake to help the Chinese administration in the study and exploitation of the mineral resources of the country.

In accordance with Chinese etiquette, the day of my visit to the Tao Yin was fixed in advance.

Everything seemed smiling, but, as we shall see, events turned out to be the very opposite.

Having done with formalities, I now paid a very necessary visit to the barber, followed up with a magnificent hot bath, and then was relieved to see in the mirror, not the hairy physiognomy of an inhabitant of savage ' Sovdepia,' but the respectable face of a civilised man. I was myself again, and could once more appear under my real name. As to the unfortunate surveyor Novikoff, who had been sent on duty simultaneously in opposite directions to Balkash and to Naryn, did the Soviet authorities notice his disappearance from the scene ? The administration in Verny, capital of Semirechie, received official reports from Naryn that the surveyor Novikoff was drowned, together with his horse, fording the River Chu when in flood. The Bolsheviks never found out that the unfortunate surveyor who died in the execution of his duty and their unrelenting enemy whom the Che-Ka was pursuing so actively were one and the same man.

I was received with open arms by the European colony in Kashgar. They were not very numerous, consisting chiefly of Russians who had arrived here before the revolution. The old Russian Consulate was still in existence, and the Russo-Asiatic Bank, the director of which, V. V. Bogushevsky, showed me the most generous hospitality. The British Consul, too, Colonel Etherton, showed me the greatest kindness.

The beautiful gardens of the British Consulate, laid out in the European manner, and the handsome building of the Consulate itself, would have done honour to any place, let alone such a remote hole as Kashgar. For the rest of the European community the British Consulate served as a " window into Europe." Through its wireless we received Reuter's telegrams, and the Consular post brought newspapers up from India, with the latest books and letters. Through it we heard what was going on in the world outside, and now again, thanks to this postal service, I was able to get in touch with friends and correspondents in India and Europe.

In Kashgar I met some Sart traders and merchants whom I had known in Tashkend ; like me, they had fled here to escape from the Socialist paradise established by the Bolsheviks. They were delighted to see me safe and sound.

To make me forget what I had gone through, all members of the European colony vied with each other in showering kindness on me. They simply lionised me, inviting me to teas and dinners and picnics, and making a great fuss of me. It was a delightful life of freedom among decent surroundings and educated people, and the old feeling of depression and persecution was gradually ironed away and the demoralisation due to two years' existence dragged out in the " freest country in the world."

It was particularly nice to see this circle of compatriots living here the old Russian life, untouched by the storms and tempests of the revolution, the even tenor of their life scarcely affected. Here in this distant corner of the vast deserts of Central Asia, this oasis of Russian life, feeling and thought still lingered on.

But, of course, I could hardly expect that the Bolsheviks would have failed to try to instil some of their poison even here. Kashgar was necessary to the Bolsheviks as a land of abundance compared with the Russia they had ruined ; it was, too, a place where the White Bands of Imperialism, as they called them, could collect and threaten the communistic fatherland.

In the Russian colony I was introduced to a young woman

known as Miss O. Her past was a little murky, but according to her own account she had served in the famous woman's Battalion of Death invented by that strangest of commanders-in-chief, the lawyer Kerensky, as a desperate attempt to save the military might of the Russian Empire which he had done so much to ruin when the armies in the field were disintegrated by German agents with the blessing of his precious Provisional Government. To my astonishment I recognised in her a woman I had known well enough in Tashkend, where she had been the 'friend' of a foreign engineer in the service of the same department during the war where I was a director. He was a clever young man who spoke excellent Russian as well as English and French and German almost like a native. When I was arrested and thrown into prison by the Bolsheviks and the participators in the anti-Soviet organisation were obliged to hide in the mountains, a British officer, sent by the British General Staff to Turkestan, was compelled to conceal himself too; incidentally, his remarkable adventures, through which his resourceful boldness brought him safely, form one of the most romantic pages in the history of the struggle with Bolshevism in Turkestan. The inquisitive engineer, Miss O.'s friend, managed to get hold of the rooms where this Englishman had been staying and made full use of the things he had left behind him and then succeeded in getting out of the country and turned up in his native Belgium, while his 'lady friend' made her way through to Kashgar.

Here she was received with open arms by the Russians, who gave her an excellent post in the Consulate, and arranged for her to give Russian lessons to Chinese officials. Not long after, however, she was caught in the act of stealing some important documents out of the Consular archives and handing them over to the Chinese authorities, and some White officers who were here at the time revealed the fact that she was in touch with the Bolsheviks. Of course, she was at once dismissed from the Consulate, and then depended solely on her Chinese pupils.

Of course, I took care not to let her see that I knew whom I was dealing with, and Miss O. kept on questioning me about my friends who had remained in Tashkend, what the ' old generals ' were going to do, what the Whites could still do and so on.

" Take care with Miss O.," a Russian friend whispered to me ; " we've good reason to believe she is a Bolshevik spy."

" Don't you worry," I replied, " I can tell a bird by its flight."

In my various conversations with the lady in question, I made no bones about my feelings towards the Soviet authorities and the Bolsheviks and Communists in general, and their accomplice A. F. Kerensky, of whom, to my surprise, she appeared to be a great admirer. I told her that I knew the creature when he was a schoolboy, with all his boasted claims, a hysterical windbag, a mere super, and I said that we old Tashkenders ought to blush for our beloved Turkestan for giving such base metal to our poor Russia, but for the fact that at the same time she had given her the hero of the White movement, General Korniloff. In fact, I did not mince my words, but let fly my pent-up wrath, loathing and contempt for the Bolsheviks and their miserable herald who prepared the way for them, and I revelled in it, delighted when I saw the spark of hatred flashing in the eyes of the adventuress.

But my sufferings were not over even yet, for it was not

very long after my arrival that I had an accident which almost cost me my life.

With a few friends, including Colonel Etherton, I was riding along one fine morning out for a picnic organised by our friends of the Swedish Mission. I was riding rather fast and a good way ahead on a Karashar loper or trippler ; this breed of horses, as I learnt afterwards, is notorious for the weakness of the forelegs. We were barely clear of the town and were riding down a narrow dusty lane when suddenly I felt her peck and come down. I tried to hold her up, but it was no good, so I made an effort to throw myself from the saddle to prevent being crushed, as I had more than once done in the past, but was too late. In a moment I was down and my left leg pinned by the horse's flanks. It all happened in a flash, and I felt the whole weight of her body roll over my back.

Cries of horror rang out. I stood up with the greatest difficulty ; I felt as though my back was crushed to a pulp ; it hurt terribly to breathe, and I could hardly stir.

Six long weeks I lay in bed, under the devoted attention of the Russian doctor, loaded with kindness by the whole colony. I was compelled to lie motionless, as the slightest attempt to move a leg or even an arm brought on an unendurable spasm of agony. The muscles of the back were crushed, but, by a great stroke of luck, no bones were broken.

It was a time of the greatest physical and mental suffering. My position seemed absolutely hopeless ; all day and all night long I kept thinking of my family and friends, while for the future I could see only the miserable prospect of the life of a helpless cripple. Was it for this that I had endured such risks, privations and labour, and exposed my friends to danger too, to reach the object of all my efforts and strivings, only to drag out a miserable existence, a broken man, in a strange land, in a remote corner of Central Asia, without means or resources, or even the ability to work ?

When I was in this condition of extreme mental depression and melancholy, yet another unexpected blow fell upon me. The Russian Consulate received urgent notice from the Tao Yin to the effect that I was to quit Chinese territory forthwith and return to Soviet Russia, with the threat that, if I refused to go, the order of expulsion would be executed by force.

Sick, broken both physically and morally, crippled and in constant pain, I was now expelled from the land where I thought I had at last found a refuge from persecution, and condemned to be delivered into the hands of my mortal enemies.

.   .   .   .

" What is the cause of this change in the attitude of the Chinese authorities ? " I asked the person who brought me the bad news.

" For this you are indebted entirely to Miss O.," was the reply, with a bitter smile ; " this is the result of her intrigues with the Chinese authorities, and she hopes to get jolly well paid for this by the Bolsheviks."

I had scarcely recovered from the shock of this disaster when the Consulate doctor came, a mournful expression on his face, with some further evil tidings. By a special decree of the President of the Chinese Republic, all Russian diplomatic institutions in China were annulled. Thus crumbled to the earth my last hope of benefiting by the privilege of the extra-territoriality of our old Russian Consulate.

It is easier to imagine than to describe the tragedy of my

situation at that moment and the state of my mind. I
knew very well that the Chinese are capable of anything.

What would happen to me next ? Where could I go ?

The doctor tried to comfort me and persuade me not to
lose heart even now.

" Very powerful forces and influential persons are at work
on your behalf, and they will not give you up," he said.

And this was true. The order for my expulsion was
withdrawn, and I was able to get well, slowly but in peace.
Miss O. left Kashgar soon after for the Far East, to the
delight of everybody. The Chinese authorities completely
forgot that I had become a resident in Kashgar by unlawful
means, and I lived four years in this ancient city as a full-
fledged citizen of that strange young republic, where I
learnt to feel perfectly at home. I met with nothing but
kindness and hospitality on the part of the Chinese officials.

After four years' residence in Chinese Turkestan my circumstances had so much improved that in August 1924 I
was able to leave for Europe through the highest passes in
the world, the mountain deserts of the Karakorum, Kuen
Lung, Western Tibet, the Himalayas, the charming valley
of Kashmir and the burning plains of the Punjab.

EPILOGUE

by Peter Hopkirk

PAUL NAZAROFF was to spend the next four years—from 1920 to 1924—in Kashgar, gradually losing any remaining hopes he might have had that the Bolsheviks would be overthrown and that he would be able to return to his wife and properties in Russia. At first, penniless and knowing no one, he had to take on the humblest of jobs, like so many Russian refugees at that time, even repairing the shoes of passers-by under the city walls. But as word got round he was quickly befriended by members of the small Russian community, anti-Bolshevik to a man, as well as by the British consul-general, Colonel Percy Etherton, and his successor, Clarmont Skrine. The latter two knew of his connections with Colonel Bailey, their colleague in the Indian political service, and of his leading role in the abortive Tashkent plot. They also greatly valued his knowledge of Russian Turkestan, on which they were endeavouring to keep a close watch from this Great Game listening-post of earlier times.

It was from Kashgar that Nazaroff wrote to Colonel Bailey, on 9 November 1920, congratulating him on his escape from the clutches of the Bolsheviks, and telling him of his own flight. 'I lost all my property,' he told Bailey, 'my mines, my library, my collections of minerals and ores, my papers, horses, dogs, furniture, clothes, etc. All are confiscated by the Bolsheviks.' He makes no mention of his wife, and one wonders whether he was somehow planning to get her out of Russia. If so, it appears, he did not succeed, and nothing more is known of her fate.

By the spring of 1924 it became very clear that the Chinese authorities were about to formally recognize the new Soviet regime in Moscow, and that shortly, Bolshevik diplomats would take over the Russian consulate-general in Kashgar, then still occupied by their White Russian predecessors. Lenin's men, knowing very well who Nazaroff was, would not rest until they had settled their score with him, either forcibly returning him to the Soviet Union to face trial and execution there, or arranging his liquidation on the spot. When he spotted a Cheka agent he recognized

317

from Tashkent, he knew that it was time to move on. Hiring a small caravan of ponies and pack animals with money he had earned from geological work, he set off southwards across the Karakorams to Leh, in Ladakh, suffering considerable hardship from mountain-sickness and cold during his two-month journey. From there he rode westwards to Srinagar, in Kashmir, where at last he felt beyond the immediate reach of the Bolshevik hit men. There, too, he encountered his old friends the Skrines, who doubtless smoothed the way for the next stage of his exile, this time to London, where he spent the next three years trying to find work as a geologist.

Finally his luck turned and he secured employment in the wilds of equatorial Africa, where he thought the Bolsheviks would never find him. It was there that he met Malcolm Burr, a fellow geologist, with whom he worked closely for two years, and who persuaded him to write his remarkable story, in Russian, which Burr then translated. It received excellent reviews. 'Few men still living can have been so often near to sudden and violent death', declared *The Sunday Times*. 'An extraordinarily interesting book.' A *Punch* reviewer called it 'one of the most completely fascinating travel stories ever penned'. Greatly encouraged, Nazaroff wrote a second book in which he described his time in Kashgar and his harrowing journey through the Karakorams. Called *Moved On!*, like *Hunted Through Central Asia* it is a brilliant mixture of adventure and observations on birds, plants, rock formations, and other things that caught his highly professional eye. It, too, was translated by Malcolm Burr.

By now, on the strength of his skills as a geologist, Nazaroff had at last begun to prosper, while his books made him sought after socially. I note that my copy of *Moved On!* bears a presentation inscription from him to Lady Lydia Deterding, the wife of an oil baron, 'whom I feel honoured to call my friend'. Later he was to take on South African citizenship, and it was there that he died in the early 1940s. I only learned of this by chance, for in his copy of *Hunted* Colonel Bailey had stuck a brief cutting from *The Times* of 25 September 1942. Writing from Istanbul, where by this time he had become Professor of English at the university, Malcolm Burr reported hearing of Nazaroff's death in Johannesburg 'some time ago . . . after a long life of unusual suffering'. At least, or so it appears, he had escaped the long arm of Bolshevik vengeance.

But that was not the end of the story, for in 1980 it took an unexpected new twist. That year I was puzzled to see that an apparently new book by Nazaroff had been published called *Kapchigai Defile: The Journal of Paul Nazaroff*. Essentially, though shorter and told in somewhat different words, this covered precisely the same ground as *Hunted Through Central Asia*, beginning with his imprisonment in Tashkent and ending with his arrival in Kashgar. I rang the publishers—Athenaeum, who today no longer exist—to ask how they had come by the manuscript, and whether they knew that another version had been published nearly fifty years earlier under a different title. Obviously startled by this discovery, they told me that the typescript had been brought to them by an elderly Englishwoman who had known Nazaroff during his time in London. She had lost contact with him in 1926, around the time he left for Africa, and assuming, rightly, that he must be dead she felt that his story should be told.

What she did not realize, and nor did the publisher, was that Malcolm Burr had persuaded Nazaroff to begin again with a more detailed and finished version of his adventures. At first I wondered whether the posthumously published book was not simply a cut-down version of the earlier one foisted on to an unsuspecting publisher. As the woman who brought it to the publisher is now dead, an element of uncertainty must always remain. But my own instinct, after carefully comparing the texts, is that Nazaroff did produce an earlier draft, possibly when he was living in Kashgar, of which he very likely kept a copy. According to the woman's story, shortly before his disappearance from London, and from her life, he told her that he believed he was being shadowed by Cheka agents. If so, this might explain why he did not disclose to her, or to anyone else, where he was going, lest the Bolsheviks somehow discover and follow him to Africa. All he told her, she recalled, was that he had 'accepted a commission from a foreign government to conduct a geological survey in remote jungle country, since this offered refuge from the relentless Cheka'. Malcolm Burr, it will be noticed, does not reveal Nazaroff's whereabouts in the 1932 introduction to this book, merely saying that they had worked together for two years 'in the bush in equatorial Africa'. Only after Nazaroff's death, ten years later, did he feel free to disclose that his friend had been living in Johannesburg.

Like me, many readers must wonder what became of Nazaroff's wife. It is conceivable that the answer lies in some dusty file in the KGB archives in Tashkent, or in the now dim memory of a Russian family whose parents or grandparents were lucky enough to escape from there at the time. If anyone can help to solve this last sad mystery, I would be most grateful to hear from them.

INDEX.

321

INDEX